Microsoft®
WINDOWS 8

COMPLETE

Microsoft® WINDOWS 8

COMPLETE

Steven M. Freund

Raymond E. Enger

Corinne L. Hoisington

COURSE TECHNOLOGY
CENGAGE Learning™

SHELLY
CASHMAN
SERIES®

Australia • Brazil • Japan • Korea • Mexico • Singapore • Spain • United Kingdom • United States

COURSE TECHNOLOGY
CENGAGE Learning™

Microsoft© Windows® 8
Complete
Steven M. Freund
Raymond E. Enger
Corinne L. Hoisington

Editor-in-Chief: Marie Lee

Executive Editor: Kathleen McMahon

Senior Product Manager: Emma Newsom

Associate Product Manager: Crystal Parenteau

Editorial Assistant: Sarah Ryan

Print Buyer: Julio Esperas

Director of Production: Patty Stephan

Content Project Manager: Jennifer Feltri-George

Development Editor: Lyn Markowicz

Senior Brand Manager: Elinor Gregory

Market Development Manager: Kristie Clark

Market Development Manager: Gretchen Swann

Marketing Coordinator: Amy McGregor

QA Manuscript Reviewers: John Freitas,
    Serge Palladino

Art Director: GEX Publishing Services, Inc.

Cover Designer: Lisa Kuhn, Curio Press, LLC

Cover Photo: Tom Kates Photography

Compositor: Jenna Gray, PreMediaGlobal

Copyeditor: Karen Annett

Proofreader: Andrea Schein

Indexer: Alexandra Nickerson

For product information and technology assistance, contact us at
Cengage Learning Customer & Sales Support, 1-800-354-9706
For permission to use material from this text or product, submit all requests online at **cengage.com/permissions**
Further permissions questions can be emailed to
permissionrequest@cengage.com

Library of Congress Control Number: 2012953440

ISBN-13: 978-1-285-16312-3

ISBN-10: 1-285-16312-5

Course Technology
20 Channel Center Street
Boston, MA 02210
USA

Cengage Learning is a leading provider of customized learning solutions with office locations around the globe, including Singapore, the United Kingdom, Australia, Mexico, Brazil, and Japan. Locate your local office at: **international.cengage.com/region**

Cengage Learning products are represented in Canada by Nelson Education, Ltd.

Visit our website **www.cengage.com/ct/shellycashman** to share and gain ideas on our textbooks!

To learn more about Course Technology, visit **www.cengage.com/ coursetechnology**

Purchase any of our products at your local college store or at our preferred online store **www.cengagebrain.com**

Printed in the United States of America
1 2 3 4 5 6 18 17 16 15 14 13

Microsoft® WINDOWS 8
COMPLETE

Contents

Preface   viii

CHAPTER ONE
Getting Started with Windows 8
Objectives	WIN 1
What is Windows 8?	WIN 2
Overview	WIN 3
Multiple Editions of Windows 8	WIN 3
Navigating Using Touch or a Mouse	WIN 4
Using a Touch Screen	WIN 4
Using an On-Screen Keyboard	WIN 5
Using a Mouse	WIN 6
Scrolling	WIN 6
Using Keyboard Shortcuts	WIN 7
Starting Windows 8	WIN 7
To Sign In to an Account	WIN 8
Exploring the Start Screen	WIN 10
Working with Apps	WIN 11
To Run an App Using the Start Screen	WIN 11
To Navigate within an App	WIN 12
Using Charms	WIN 15
To Return to the Start Screen	WIN 15
Working with Apps	WIN 16
To Switch between Apps	WIN 16
Understanding How to Exit Apps	WIN 17
To Display the Windows Desktop	WIN 17
The Windows 8 Desktop	WIN 18
To Run the File Explorer	WIN 19
To Return to the Start Screen	WIN 19
To Move a Tile	WIN 20
To Resize a Tile	WIN 21
To Run an App Using the Search Box	WIN 23
To Search the Internet Using a Charm	WIN 25
To Search an App Using a Charm	WIN 28
Share Using a Charm	WIN 30
To View Sharing Options Using a Charm	WIN 30
Free and Paid Apps	WIN 31
To Install an App	WIN 31
Using Windows Help and Support	WIN 33
To Start Windows Help and Support	WIN 33
To Browse Help	WIN 36

Shutting Down Windows	WIN 37
To Sign Out of an Account	WIN 37
To Shut Down the Computer	WIN 39
Chapter Summary	WIN 40
Apply Your Knowledge	WIN 41
Extend Your Knowledge	WIN 42
In the Lab	WIN 43
Cases and Places	WIN 47

CHAPTER TWO
File and Folder Management
Objectives	WIN 49
Introduction	WIN 50
Overview	WIN 50
The Computer Folder Window	WIN 50
To Open and Maximize the Computer Folder Window	WIN 51
To Display Properties for the Local Disk (C:) Drive in the Details Pane	WIN 52
To Display the Local Disk (C:) Properties Dialog Box	WIN 53
To Close the Local Disk (C:) Properties Dialog Box	WIN 54
To Switch Folders Using the Address Bar	WIN 55
To View the Contents of a Drive	WIN 56
To Preview the Properties of a Folder	WIN 57
To Display Properties for the Windows Folder in the Details Pane	WIN 57
To Display All of the Properties of the Windows Folder	WIN 58
To View the Contents of a Folder	WIN 59
Searching for Files and Folders	WIN 59
To Search for a File and Folder in a Folder Window	WIN 60
To Clear the Search Box	WIN 61
To Use Shake to Minimize and Restore All Windows	WIN 62
To Use Snap to Maximize Windows	WIN 63
To Restore a Window	WIN 64
The Pictures Library	WIN 65
Item Check Boxes	WIN 66

To Search for Pictures WIN 66
To Copy Files to the Pictures Library WIN 67
To Create a Folder in the Pictures Library WIN 69
To Move Multiple Files into a Folder WIN 71
To Refresh the Image on a Folder WIN 72
To View and Change the Properties of a
    Picture WIN 72
To View a Picture in the Photos App WIN 75
To View Your Pictures as a Slide Show WIN 76
To End a Slide Show WIN 77
Zipping Files and Folders **WIN 78**
To Zip a Folder WIN 78
To View the Contents of a Zipped Folder WIN 79
Chapter Summary **WIN 80**
Apply Your Knowledge **WIN 81**
Extend Your Knowledge **WIN 82**
In the Lab **WIN 84**
Cases and Places **WIN 88**

CHAPTER THREE
Personalizing Windows
Objectives **WIN 89**
Introduction **WIN 90**
Overview WIN 90
User Account **WIN 90**
What Is a Local Account? **WIN 91**
What Is a Microsoft Account? **WIN 91**
To Create a Microsoft Account WIN 92
What Is Cloud Computing? WIN 94
Setting up User Accounts **WIN 94**
To Add a Local Account WIN 94
To Add a Microsoft Account WIN 98
Personalizing the Lock and Start Screens **WIN 100**
To Personalize the Lock Screen WIN 100
To Change the Start Screen Color Scheme WIN 102
To Change the Start Screen
    Background Pattern WIN 103
Adding a Picture Password **WIN 104**
To Create a Picture Password WIN 104
Is a Picture Password Secure? WIN 108
Customizing the Start Screen **WIN 108**
To Display All Apps WIN 109
To Run an App from the Apps List WIN 110
To Pin an App to the Start Screen WIN 110
To Unpin an App from the Start Screen WIN 113
To Turn Off a Live Tile WIN 114
Managing Tile Layout **WIN 115**
To Zoom to View Tile Groups WIN 115
To Create a New Tile Group WIN 117
To Move a Tile to a Different Tile Group WIN 118
To Reorder Tile Groups WIN 118
To Name a Tile Group WIN 119
To Sign Out of an Account and Shut Down
    the Computer WIN 122
Chapter Summary **WIN 122**
Apply Your Knowledge **WIN 123**
Extend Your Knowledge **WIN 124**
In the Lab **WIN 125**
Cases and Places **WIN 128**

CHAPTER FOUR
Connecting to the Internet
Objectives **WIN 129**
Introduction **WIN 130**
Overview WIN 130
Wi-Fi and Broadband Connectivity **WIN 130**
Mobility and Connectivity **WIN 130**
Connecting to a Wireless Network **WIN 131**
Running Internet Explorer **WIN 131**
To Run the Internet Explorer App WIN 131
Browsing and Searching the Web **WIN 132**
To Display a Webpage WIN 132
To Search Using the Address Bar WIN 133
To Add a Tab in the Browser Window WIN 134
To Add an InPrivate Tab in the Browser Window WIN 135
To Switch between Tabs WIN 137
To Close a Tab WIN 138
To Find Information on a Webpage WIN 139
To Pin a Website to the Start Screen WIN 140
To Add a Website to Favorites WIN 142
Running Internet Explorer in the Desktop **WIN 143**
To Display a Webpage on the Desktop WIN 143
To Display a New Tab in Internet Explorer
    on the Desktop WIN 144
To Search Using Keywords in the Address Bar WIN 145
To Add a Website to Favorites from the Desktop WIN 146
To Add a Website to the Favorites Bar WIN 148
To Display a Webpage in a New Tab WIN 149
Using Internet Explorer to Subscribe to RSS Feeds **WIN 150**
To Subscribe to an RSS Feed WIN 150
To Modify Feed Properties WIN 152
To Delete an RSS Feed WIN 153
To Delete an Item from the Favorites Bar WIN 154
Chapter Summary **WIN 155**
Apply Your Knowledge **WIN 155**
Extend Your Knowledge **WIN 156**
In the Lab **WIN 157**
Cases and Places **WIN 160**

CHAPTER FIVE
Working with the Windows Desktop
Objectives **WIN 161**
Introduction **WIN 162**
Overview WIN 162
Windows Desktop **WIN 162**
Creating a Document in WordPad **WIN 163**
To Create a Document in WordPad WIN 163
Saving Documents **WIN 165**
To Save a Document in the Documents Library WIN 165
To Print a Document WIN 167
To Edit a Document WIN 168
To Save and Close a Document WIN 169
Creating a Document in the Documents Library **WIN 169**
To Open the Documents Library WIN 170
To Move a Window by Dragging WIN 170
To Create a Blank Document in the Documents
    Library WIN 171
To Assign a File Name to a Document in
    the Documents Library WIN 172

To Open a Document in WordPad   WIN 173
To Add Text to a Blank Document   WIN 174
To Save a Text Document as a Rich Text
    Format (RTF) File   WIN 175
Working with the Documents Library   **WIN 176**
To Change the View to Small Icons   WIN 176
To Arrange Items in Groups by File Type   WIN 177
To Create and Name a Folder in the
    Documents Library   WIN 178
To Move a Document into a Folder   WIN 178
To Change Location Using the Address Bar   WIN 179
To Display and Use the Preview Pane   WIN 180
To View the File Name Extensions   WIN 182
To Change Location Using the Back Button
    on the Address Bar   WIN 183
Creating Folder Shortcuts   **WIN 183**
To Paste a Shortcut on the Desktop   WIN 184
To Open a Folder Using a Shortcut   WIN 185
To Move a File to the Recycle Bin   WIN 186
To Open and Modify a Document in a Folder   WIN 186
To Open and Modify Multiple Documents   WIN 187
To Display an Inactive Window   WIN 188
To Close Multiple Open Windows and
    Save Documents   WIN 189
Copying a Folder on a USB Flash Drive   **WIN 191**
To Copy a Folder on a USB Flash Drive   WIN 191
To Safely Remove a USB Flash Drive   WIN 192
The Recycle Bin   **WIN 192**
To Restore an Item from the Recycle Bin   WIN 193
Chapter Summary   **WIN 194**
Apply Your Knowledge   **WIN 195**
Extend Your Knowledge   **WIN 196**
In the Lab   **WIN 197**
Cases and Places   **WIN 200**

Appendices

APPENDIX A
Creating a Microsoft Account
Introduction   **APP 1**
To Create a Microsoft Account   APP 1

APPENDIX B
Windows 8 Security
Introduction   **APP 9**
To Display the Windows Action Center   APP 9
Understanding the Action Center   APP 13
Managing Windows Firewall   **APP 13**
To Open the Windows Firewall Window   APP 14
To Allow a Feature through the Firewall   APP 14
To Disallow a Feature through the Firewall   APP 17

Windows Update   **APP 19**
To Install Updates Automatically   APP 19
**Protecting against Computer Viruses
    and Malware**   **APP 21**
To Scan Using Windows Defender   APP 21
To View the Windows Defender Settings for
    Automatic Scanning   APP 24
Summary   **APP 24**

APPENDIX C
Introduction to Networking
Introduction   **APP 25**
Setting up a Network   **APP 25**
Understanding Wireless Networks   APP 26
Understanding Wired Networks   APP 27
Putting It All Together   APP 28
Wireless Security Issues   **APP 29**
Setting up Wireless Security   APP 29
Using the Network and Sharing Center   **APP 29**
To Connect to a Wireless Network   APP 30
To Open the Network and Sharing Center   APP 32
To View the Status of a Connection   APP 34
To Troubleshoot a Networking Problem   APP 34
To Disable a Network Connection   APP 37
To Disconnect a Computer from a Network   APP 38

APPENDIX D
Maintaining Your Computer
Introduction   **APP 41**
Backing up and Restoring Files   **APP 41**
File History Backup   APP 41
To Back up a File History to a Storage Device   APP 42
To Restore Files from File History   APP 43
Creating a Restore Point   APP 45
To Manually Set a Restore Point   APP 46
To Perform a System Restore   APP 48
Refreshing Your Computer   APP 48
To Refresh the Computer   APP 49
Performance Information and Tools   **APP 50**
To Open the Performance Information and
    Tools Window   APP 50
To Run Disk Cleanup   APP 51
To View the Performance Monitor   APP 53
To Use the Resource Monitor   APP 54
To Run the Disk Defragmenter   APP 55
To Generate a System Health Report   APP 56
Summary   **APP 56**

Index   **IND 1**

Preface

The Shelly Cashman Series® offers the finest textbooks in computer education. We are proud of the fact that our Microsoft Windows 3.1, Microsoft Windows 95, Microsoft Windows 98, Microsoft Windows 2000, Microsoft Windows XP, and Microsoft Windows Vista and Windows 7 books have been so well received by students and instructors. With each new edition of our Windows books, we have made significant improvements based on the software and comments made by instructors and students.

Windows 8 introduces a brand new way of interacting with computers and mobile devices such as tablets and smart phones. The new Windows 8 interface, which includes tiles, charms, and apps, will completely revolutionize how people work. This Windows 8 text not only teaches this new interface and approach in a way that is easiest for students to learn, but it also incorporates many important concepts such as file management and

Objectives of This Textbook

Microsoft® Windows® 8: Complete is intended for a six to nine week course that offers an introduction to Windows 8. No experience with a computer is assumed, and no mathematics beyond the high school freshman level is required.

The objectives of this book are:

- To offer a comprehensive presentation of Microsoft Windows 8
- To expose students to practical examples of the computer as a useful tool
- To acquaint students with the proper procedures to manage and organize document storage options for coursework, professional purposes, and personal use
- To help students discover the underlying functionality and customization options of Windows 8 so that they can become more productive
- To develop an exercise-oriented approach that allows learning by doing

critical thinking in greater detail. Recognizing that the new features and functionality of Microsoft Windows 8 would impact the way that students are taught skills, the Shelly Cashman Series development team carefully reviewed our pedagogy and analyzed its effectiveness in teaching today's student. An extensive customer survey produced results confirming what the series is best known for: its step-by-step, screen-by-screen instructions, its project-oriented approach, and the quality of its content.

We learned, though, that students entering computer courses today are different than students taking these classes just a few years ago. Students today read less, but need to retain more. They need not only to be able to perform skills, but to retain those skills and know how to apply them to different settings. Today's students need to be continually engaged and challenged to retain what they're learning.

As a result, we've renewed our commitment to focusing on the user and how they learn best. This commitment is reflected in every change we've made to our Windows 8 books.

Distinguishing Features

A Proven Pedagogy with an Emphasis on Project Planning
The project orientation is strengthened by the use of Plan Ahead boxes that encourage critical thinking about how to proceed at the beginning of each chapter. Step-by-step instructions with supporting screens guide students through the steps. Instructional steps are supported by the Q&A, Experiment Step, and BTW features.

A Visually Engaging Book that Maintains Student Interest
The step-by-step tasks, with supporting figures, provide a rich visual experience for the student. Call-outs on the screens that present both explanatory and navigational information provide students with information they need when they need to know it.

Supporting Reference Materials (Appendices)
The appendices provide additional information about Windows 8, such as the security features and networking.

Integration of the World Wide Web
The World Wide Web is integrated into the Windows 8 learning experience through step-by-step instruction on Internet Explorer, as well as the several additional features.

End-of-Chapter Student Activities
Extensive end of chapter activities provide a variety of reinforcement opportunities for students where they can apply and expand their skills through individual and group work.

Instructor Resources

The Instructor Resources include both teaching and testing aids. These resources are posted to the instructor's resource page found on www.cengage.com

Instructor's Manual Includes lecture notes summarizing the chapter sections, figures and boxed elements found in every chapter, teacher tips, classroom activities, lab activities, and quick quizzes in Microsoft Word files.

Syllabus Easily customizable sample syllabi that cover policies, assignments, exams, and other course information.

Figure Files Illustrations for every figure in the textbook in electronic form.

Powerpoint Presentations A multimedia lecture presentation system that provides slides for each chapter. Presentations are based on chapter objectives.

Solutions to Exercises Includes solutions for all end-of-chapter and chapter reinforcement exercises.

Test Bank Test Banks include 112 questions for every chapter, featuring objective-based and critical thinking question types, and including page number references and figure references, when appropriate.

Data Files for Students Includes all the files that are required by students to complete the exercises.

Additional Activities for Students Consists of Chapter Reinforcement Exercises, which are true/false, multiple-choice, and short answer questions that help students gain confidence in the material learned.

CourseNotes

Course Technology's CourseNotes are six-panel quick reference cards that reinforce the most important concepts and features of a software application in a visual and user-friendly format. CourseNotes serve as a great reference tool during and after the student completes the course. CourseNotes are available for software applications, such as Adobe, Microsoft Office, and Windows 8. There are also topic-based CourseNotes available for Best Practices in Social Networking, Hot Topics in Technology, and Web 2.0. Visit www.cengage.com/ct/coursenotes to learn more!

SAM: Skills Assessment Manager

SAM is designed to help bring students from the classroom to the real world. It allows students to train and test on important computer skills in an active, hands-on environment.

SAM's easy-to-use system includes powerful interactive exams, training and projects on the most commonly used Microsoft® Office applications. SAM simulates the Office 2013 application environment, allowing students to demonstrate their knowledge and think through the skills by performing real-world tasks such as bolding word text or setting up slide transitions. Add in live-in-the-application projects and students are on their way to truly learning and applying skills to business-centric document.

Designed to be used with the Shelly Cashman Series, SAM includes handy page references, so students can print helpful study guides that match the Shelly Cashman Series textbooks used in class. For instructors, SAM also includes robust scheduling and reporting features.

Textbook Walk-Through

Windows Chapter 1

1
• Tap, slide, or click the lock screen (Figure 1–5) to display a sign-in screen.

lock screen

11:05
Monday, October 1

Figure 1–5

2
• Tap or click the user icon (for SC Series, in this case) on the sign-in screen, which depending on settings, either will display a second sign-in screen that contains a password text box (Figure 1–6) or will display the Windows Start screen.

Q&A
Why do I not see a user icon?
Your computer may require you to type a user name instead of tapping or clicking an icon.

What is a text box?
A text box is a rectangular box in which you type text.

Why does my screen not show a password text box?
Your account does not require a password.

sign-in screen

selected user account

SC Series

user account icon

Password

Submit button

password text box

Figure 1–6

Textbook Walk-Through

Q&A boxes offer questions students may have when working through the steps and provide additional information about what they are doing right where they need it.

3 • If Windows 8 displays a password text box, type your password in the text box and then tap or click the Submit button to sign in your account and display the Windows 8 Start screen (Figure 1–7).

Q&A

Why does my Start screen look different from the one shown in Figure 1–7?

The Windows 8 Start screen is customizable, and your school or employer may have modified the screen to meet its needs. Also, your screen resolution, which affects the size of the elements on the screen, may differ from the screen resolution used in this book. Later in this chapter, you will learn how to change screen resolution.

How do I type if my tablet has no keyboard?

You can use your fingers to press keys on a keyboard that appears on the screen, called an on-screen keyboard, or you can purchase a separate physical keyboard that attaches to or wirelessly communicates with the tablet.

Figure 1–7

Exploring the Start Screen

The Windows 8 Start screen provides a scrollable space for you to access apps that have been pinned to the Start screen (shown in Figure 1–7). Pinned apps appear as tiles on the Start screen. In addition to running apps, you can perform tasks such as pinning apps (placing tiles) on the Start screen, moving the tiles around the Start screen, and unpinning apps (removing tiles) from the Start screen.

A tile is shown as a rectangle or square on the Start screen. Tapping or clicking a tile will run the app associated with the tile. **Live tiles** are tiles that when configured, update the tile with information while the Start screen is displayed. For example, if you configure the Weather app to your location, the tile will update with current weather conditions in your city.

Other Ways boxes that follow many of the step sequences explain the other ways to complete the task presented.

Extend Your Knowledge projects at the end of each chapter allow students to extend and expand on the skills learned within the chapter. Students use critical thinking to experiment with new skills to complete each project.

2
- Tap or click the Allow button to allow the Weather app to use the current location (Figure 1–9).
- If your location cannot be detected, type your current city in the Enter Location text box, and then click your city in the drop-down list that appears.

Figure 1–9

Other Ways

1. Tap or click Search charm on Charms bar, type app name in Search box, tap or click app name in results list

To Navigate within an App

To navigate within an app, you can use gestures or the scroll bar to see more of the app, or you can display the Navigation bar for an app. In the Weather app, the Navigation bar lets you move from the Home screen to other places, and even displays world weather. ***Why?*** *You may intend to travel or you may be interested in seeing the weather in a different location.*

The following steps display the current world weather information.

STUDENT ASSIGNMENTS

Extend Your Knowledge

Extend the skills you learned in this chapter and experiment with new skills. You will use Help to complete the assignment.

Using Help

Instructions: Use Windows Help and Support to perform the following tasks.
1. Find Help about Windows shortcuts by typing `shortcuts` in the Search text box and then clicking the Search button (Figure 1–58). Tap or click the result titled 'Copy or move files and folders' and then answer the following questions:
   a. What keyboard shortcut is used to copy a file?
   b. What keyboard shortcut is used to paste a file?
   c. How do you display a shortcut menu?

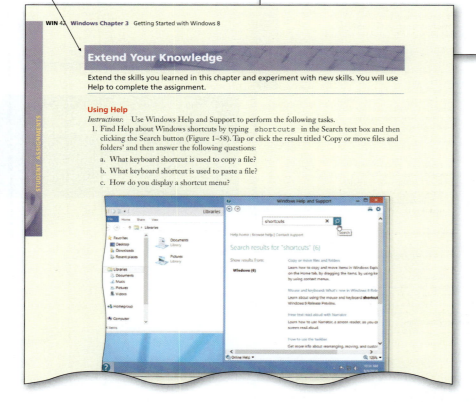

Textbook Walk-Through

The in-depth **In the Lab** assignments require students to utilize the chapter concepts and techniques to solve problems.

Chapter Summary **WIN** 43

2. Use Windows Help and Support to answer the following questions:
   a. What is Windows Defender?
   b. What is Windows Firewall?
   c. What settings can you control in Family Safety?
   d. What are five ways to protect your computer from viruses and other threats?
   e. What is a user account?
   f. What is the difference between a local account and a Microsoft account?
3. Use the Search text box in Windows Help and Support to answer the following questions:
   a. How do you turn on Windows Firewall?
   b. How do you pin a program to the taskbar?
   c. How do you set up a home network in Windows?
   d. How do you add a printer?
4. The tools to solve a problem while using Windows 8 are called troubleshooters. Use Windows Help and Support to find information about troubleshooters, and answer the following questions:
   a. What problems does the Printer troubleshooter allow you to resolve?
   b. List two additional Windows 8 troubleshooters.
5. Close the Windows Help and Support window.

In the Lab

Use the guidelines, concepts, and skills presented in this chapter to increase your knowledge of Windows 8. Labs are listed in order of increasing difficulty.

Lab 1: Using Windows Help and Support

Problem: You have a few questions about using Windows and would like to answer these questions
... to perform the following tasks.

Chapter Summary **WIN** 47

... ing questions:
... ormance?
... ation?
... de?
Help and Support to answer the following questions:
... Windows Media Player?
... hotos?
... xing problems with your computer?

Cases and Places

Apply your creative thinking and problem-solving skills to design and implement a solution.

1: Assessing Windows 8 Compatibility

Academic

You work part-time as a lab technician in your school's computer lab. Your boss wants to upgrade several computers in the lab and has asked you to investigate. You know that the Windows 8 operating system can be installed only on computers found in the Windows 8 Hardware Compatibility List. Locate three older personal computers. Look for them in your school's computer lab, at a local business, or in your house. Use the Windows website on the Internet to locate the Windows 8 Compatibility Center. Check each computer against the list and write a brief report summarizing your results.

2: Sharing Your Pictures

Personal

You recently attended your high school reunion, and your friend has asked for your help. She wants to send photos to several classmates via email messages, and is not sure how best to proceed. Using Windows Help and Support and the keywords, digital pictures, locate the "How to use Windows Photo Viewer" article. In a brief report, summarize the steps required to send a photo in an email message as well as the different ways to get photos from your camera. Next, research Windows Live Essentials and include a description of how to organize and find your pictures.

3: Researching Multiple Operating Systems

Professional

You are working as an information technology intern at a large insurance agency's headquarters. Because the company is thinking about upgrading all its computers, your boss has tasked you with researching different operating systems. Using the Internet, a library, or other research facility, write a brief report on the Windows, Mac OS, and Linux operating systems. Describe the systems, pointing out their similarities and differences. Discuss the advantages and disadvantages of each. Finally, tell which operating system you would purchase and explain why.

Found within the Cases & Places exercises, the **Make It Personal** exercise calls on students to create an open-ended project that relates to their personal lives.

LEARN ONLINE

Reinforce what you learned in this chapter with games, exercises, training, and many other online activities and resources.

Student Companion Site: Reinforce chapter terms and concepts using review questions, flash cards, practice tests, and interactive learning games, such as a crossword puzzle. These and other online activities and resources are available at no additional cost on www.cengagebrain.com <http://www.cengagebrain.com> . Visit www.cengage.com/ct/studentdownload <http://www.cengage.com/ct/studentdownload> for detailed instructions about accessing the resources available at the Student Companion Site.

STUDENT ASSIGNMENTS

Microsoft®
WINDOWS 8

COMPLETE

1 | Getting Started with Windows 8

Objectives

You will have mastered the material in this chapter when you can:

- Describe Windows 8

- Explain the following terms: operating system, server, workstation, and user interface

- Differentiate among the various editions of Windows 8

- Use a touch screen and perform basic mouse operations

- Start Windows 8 and sign in to an account

- Identify the objects on the Windows 8 Start screen

- Run an app

- Navigate within an app

- Display the Charms bar

- Switch between apps

- Move and resize a tile

- Search for an app or a file

- Install an app

- Use Windows Help

- Sign out of an account and shut down the computer

1 | Getting Started with Windows 8

What Is Windows 8?

An **operating system** is a computer program (set of instructions) that coordinates all the activities of computer hardware, such as memory, storage devices, and printers, and provides the capability for you to communicate with the computer.

Windows 8 is the newest version of Microsoft Windows, which is a popular and widely used operating system. The Windows operating system simplifies the process of working with documents and apps by organizing the manner in which you interact with the computer. Windows is used to run apps. An **app** (short for application) consists of programs that are designed to make users more productive and/or assist them with personal tasks, such as word processing or browsing the web.

The new Windows 8 interface begins with the **Start screen**, which shows tiles (shown in Figure 1–3 on page WIN 7). A **tile** is a shortcut to an app or other content. The tiles on the Start screen include installed apps that you use regularly. From the Start screen, you can choose which apps to run using a touch screen, mouse, or other input device.

Windows commonly is used on desktops, laptops, and workstations. A **workstation** is a computer connected to a server. A **server** is a computer that controls access to the hardware and software on a network and provides a centralized storage area for programs, data, and information. Figure 1–1 illustrates a simple computer network consisting of a server, three workstations, and a printer connected to the server.

Windows is easy to use and can be customized to fit individual needs. The operating system simplifies working with documents and programs, transferring data between documents, interacting with the different components of the computer, and using the computer to access information on the Internet or an intranet. The **Internet** is a worldwide group of connected computer networks that allows public access to information about thousands of subjects and gives users the ability to use this information, send messages, and obtain products and services. An **intranet** is an internal network that uses Internet technologies.

Windows 8 has improved memory management so that it runs faster and more efficiently than Windows 7, the previous version of the Windows operating system. The user interface also has been enhanced to create a more user-friendly and customizable experience. Several other improvements over previous versions of Windows make Windows 8 a suitable choice for all users.

This book demonstrates how to use Windows 8 to control the computer and communicate with other computers, both on a network and the Internet. In Chapter 1, you will learn about Windows and how to use some of its basic features.

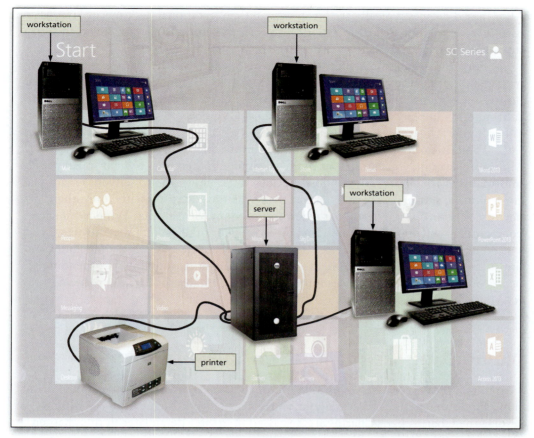

Figure 1–1

Overview

As you read this chapter, you will learn how to use the Windows by performing these general tasks:

- Start Windows and sign in to an account
- Work with the Start screen
- Use the Charms bar
- Run and switch between apps
- Use the Help system to answer questions
- Sign out of an account and turn off the computer

Multiple Editions of Windows 8

Windows 8 is available in multiple editions. The first, Windows 8, is simplified and designed primarily for home and small office users. The next version is **Windows 8 Pro**, which is designed for businesses and technical professionals. **Windows 8 Enterprise** has the same features as Windows 8 Pro but is designed for large enterprises. Finally, **Windows 8 RT** is designed for devices that support the ARM (Advanced RISC Machine) architecture, such as tablets and other mobile devices.

ARM-based devices typically are less powerful than traditional desktops or laptops and usually have longer battery life. Windows 8 RT can be preinstalled on any device that supports the ARM architecture.

For a PC, minimum system requirements specify that the processor is 1 GHz or faster, random access memory (RAM) is at least 1 GB (for 32-bit systems) or 2 GB (for 64-bit systems), the hard drive has at least 16 GB available space, and the video card supports DirectX 9 graphics with WDDM (Windows Display Driver Model) 1.0 or higher driver.

Windows can be customized using a Microsoft account. When you add a Microsoft account, you can sign in to the account and then sync (synchronize) your information with all of your Windows devices. This allows you to set your email configuration settings, for example, and then sync those settings with your other devices. When you sign in to your Microsoft account with another Windows device, your settings will appear the same as they do on your other Windows 8 devices.

For laptops and other devices dependent on batteries, Windows 8 includes improved power management features to ensure longer battery life by suspending background apps, putting devices into low-powered modes sooner, and reducing RAM usage.

Navigating Using Touch or a Mouse

Windows 8 provides touch support. With touch, you can use your fingers to control how Windows functions. For example, you can swipe your finger from the right to display the Charms bar. (Charms are discussed in greater detail later in this chapter.) Touch also allows Windows 8 to work on devices such as smartphones and tablets.

Using a Touch Screen

Windows users who have computers or devices with touch screen capability can interact with the screen using gestures. A **gesture** is a motion you make on a touch screen with the tip of one or more fingers or your hand. Touch screens are convenient because they do not require a separate device for input. Table 1–1 presents common ways to interact with a touch screen.

Table 1–1 Touch Screen Gestures		
Motion	**Description**	**Common Uses**
Tap	Quickly touch and release one finger one time.	Activate a link. Press a button. Run an app.
Double-tap	Quickly touch and release one finger two times.	Run a program or app. Zoom in (make the screen contents larger) at the location of the double tap.

Press and hold	Press and hold one finger until an action occurs.	Display a shortcut menu (immediate access to allowable actions). Activate a mode enabling you to move an item with one finger to a new location.
Drag	Press and hold one finger on an object and then move the finger to the new location.	Move an item around the screen. Scroll.
Swipe	Press and hold one finger and then move the finger horizontally or vertically on the screen.	Select an object. Swipe from edge to display a bar such as the Charms bar, App bar, and Navigation bar (all discussed later).
Stretch	Move two fingers apart.	Zoom in (make the screen contents larger).
Pinch	Move two fingers together.	Zoom out (make the screen contents smaller).

Using an On-Screen Keyboard

When using touch, you can access an on-screen keyboard that allows you to enter data using your fingers. To display the on-screen keyboard, tap or click the Touch Keyboard button on the taskbar. You tap a key on the keyboard to enter data or manipulate what you see on the screen. Figure 1–2 displays the on-screen keyboard.

on-screen keyboard

Figure 1–2

Using a Mouse

Windows users who do not have touch screen capabilities typically work with a mouse that has at least two buttons. For a right-handed user, the left button usually is the primary mouse button, and the right mouse button is the secondary mouse button. Left-handed people, however, can reverse the function of these buttons.

Table 1–2 explains how to perform a variety of mouse operations. Some apps also use keys in combination with the mouse to perform certain actions. For example, when you hold down the CTRL key while rolling the mouse wheel, text on the screen may become larger or smaller based on the direction you roll the wheel. The function of the mouse buttons and the wheel varies depending on the app.

Table 1–2 Mouse Operations		
Operation	**Mouse Action**	**Example**
Point	Move the mouse until the pointer on the desktop is positioned on the item of choice	Position the pointer on the screen
Click	Press and release the primary mouse button, which usually is the left mouse button	Select or deselect items on the screen or run an app or app feature
Right-click	Press and release the secondary mouse button, which usually is the right mouse button	Display a shortcut menu
Double-click	Quickly press and release the left mouse button two times without moving the mouse	Run an app or app feature
Triple-click	Quickly press and release the left mouse button three times without moving the mouse	Select a paragraph
Drag	Point to an item, hold down the left mouse button, move the item to the desired location on the screen, and then release the left mouse button	Move an object from one location to another or draw pictures
Right-drag	Point to an item, hold down the right mouse button, move the item to the desired location on the screen, and then release the right mouse button	Display a shortcut menu after moving an object from one location to another
Rotate wheel	Roll the wheel forward or backward	Scroll vertically (up and down)
Free-spin wheel	Whirl the wheel forward or backward so that it spins freely on its own	Scroll through many pages in seconds
Press wheel	Press the wheel button while moving the mouse	Scroll continuously
Tilt wheel	Press the wheel toward the right or left	Scroll horizontally (left and right)
Press thumb button	Press the button on the side of the mouse with your thumb	Move forward or backward through webpages and/or control media, games, and so forth

BTW

Minimizing Wrist Injury

Computer users frequently switch between the keyboard and the mouse during a word processing session; such switching strains the wrist. To help prevent wrist injury, minimize switching. For instance, if your fingers already are on the keyboard, use keyboard keys to scroll. If your hand already is on the mouse, use the mouse to scroll. If you are using touch input, minimize switching between touch input and the keyboard or mouse.

Scrolling

A **scroll bar** is a horizontal or vertical bar that appears when the contents of an area may not be visible completely on the screen (Figure 1–3). A scroll bar contains **scroll arrows** and a **scroll box** that enable you to view areas that currently cannot be seen on the screen. Tapping or clicking the up and down scroll arrows moves the screen content up or down one line. You also can tap or click above or below the scroll box to move up or down a section, or drag the scroll box up or down to move to a specific location.

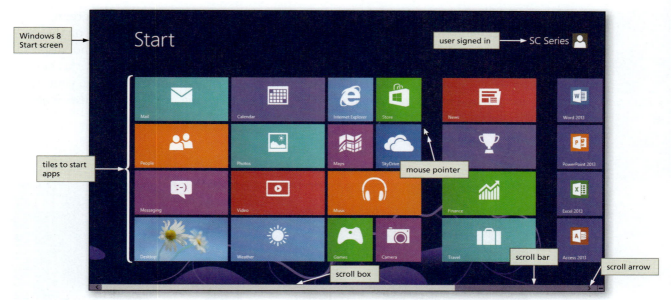

Figure 1–3

Using Keyboard Shortcuts

In many cases, you can use the keyboard instead of the mouse to accomplish a task. To perform tasks using the keyboard, you press one or more keys on the keyboard, sometimes identified as a **keyboard shortcut**. Some keyboard shortcuts consist of a single key, such as the F1 key. For example, to obtain help about Windows, you can press the F1 key while viewing the Desktop. Other keyboard shortcuts consist of multiple keys, in which case a plus sign separates the key names, such as CTRL+ESC. This notation means to press and hold down the first key listed, press one or more additional keys, and then release all keys. For example, to display the Start screen, press CTRL+ESC, that is, hold down the CTRL key, press the ESC key, and then release both keys.

Starting Windows 8

It is not unusual for multiple people to use the same computer in a work, educational, recreational, or home setting. Windows enables each user to establish a **user account**, which identifies to Windows the resources, such as apps and storage locations, a user can access when working with the computer.

Each user account has a user name and may have a password and an icon, as well. A **user name** is a unique combination of letters or numbers that identifies a specific user to Windows. A **password** is a private combination of letters, numbers, and special characters associated with the user name that allows access to a user's account resources. A **picture password** also can be used to control access to a user's account resources. A picture password requires that the user perform mouse or touch gestures on specific areas of the picture to sign in to Windows. An icon is a small image that represents an object; thus, a **user icon** is a picture associated with a user name.

BTW

Scrolling

If you have a mouse with a wheel, you can spin the wheel to scroll left and right on the Start screen.

BTW

Keyboard Layouts

On some keyboards, there may be keys that serve more than one purpose. For example, the F1 key also may adjust the brightness of the screen. It may be necessary to press and hold another key on the keyboard for some keys to serve your intended purpose.

BTW

Strong Passwords

You should consider using a strong password with your Windows user account. A strong password is more secure because it is more difficult to guess. Strong passwords have at least eight characters and contain a combination of uppercase and lowercase letters, numbers, and special characters.

When you turn on a computer, Windows starts and displays **a lock screen** consisting of the time and date. After tapping, sliding, or clicking anywhere on the lock screen, depending on your computer's settings, Windows may or may not display a sign-in screen that shows the user names and user icons for users who have accounts on the computer (Figure 1–4). This **sign-in screen** enables you to sign in to your user account and makes the computer available for use. Tapping or clicking the user icon begins the process of signing in, also called logging on, your user account.

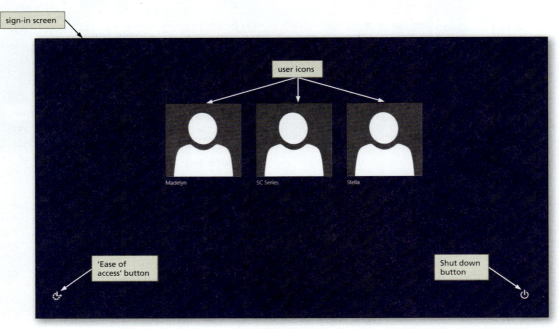

Figure 1–4

BTW

Shut Down Options
If you are walking away from your computer for only a brief period, you should put the computer in Sleep mode instead of turning it off completely. Keeping the computer in Sleep mode for this short period often uses less power than powering on the computer.

At the bottom of the sign-in screen are the 'Ease of access' button and a Shut down button. Tapping or clicking the 'Ease of access' button displays the 'Ease of access' menu, which provides tools to optimize a computer to accommodate the needs of users with mobility, hearing, and vision impairments.

Tapping or clicking the Shut down button displays a menu containing commands related to restarting the computer, putting it in a low-power state, and shutting down the computer. The commands available on your computer may differ.

- The **Sleep command** saves your work, turns off the computer fans and hard disk, and places the computer in a lower-power state. To wake the computer from sleep mode, press the power button or lift a laptop's cover, and sign in to the computer.
- The **Shut down command** closes open apps, shuts down Windows, and then turns off the computer.
- The **Restart command** closes open apps, shuts down Windows, turns off the computer, turns on the computer, and then restarts Windows.

To Sign In to an Account

The following steps, which use SC Series as the user name, sign in to an account based on a typical Windows installation. ***Why?*** *After starting Windows, you might be required to sign in to access the computer's resources.* You may need to ask your instructor how to sign in to your account.

1
- Tap, swipe, or click the lock screen (Figure 1–5) to display a sign-in screen.

lock screen

11:05
Monday, October 1

Figure 1–5

2
- Tap or click the user icon (for SC Series, in this case) on the sign-in screen, which depending on settings, either will display a second sign-in screen that contains a password text box (Figure 1–6) or will display the Windows Start screen.

Q&A

Why do I not see a user icon?

Your computer may require you to type a user name instead of tapping or clicking an icon.

What is a text box?

A text box is a rectangular box in which you type text.

Why does my screen not show a password text box?

Your account does not require a password.

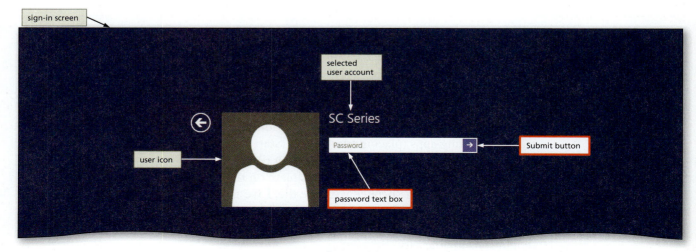

sign-in screen

selected user account

SC Series

user icon

Password

Submit button

password text box

Figure 1–6

3

- If Windows 8 displays a password text box, type your password in the text box and then tap or click the Submit button to sign in to your account and display the Start screen (Figure 1–7).

Q&A

Why does my Start screen look different from the one shown in Figure 1–7?

The Windows 8 Start screen is customizable, and your school or employer may have modified the screen to meet its needs. Also, your screen resolution, which affects the size of the elements on the screen, may differ from the screen resolution used in this book. Later in this chapter, you will learn how to change screen resolution.

How do I type if my tablet has no keyboard?

You can use your fingers to press keys on a keyboard that appears on the screen, called an on-screen keyboard, or you can purchase a separate physical keyboard that attaches to or wirelessly communicates with the tablet.

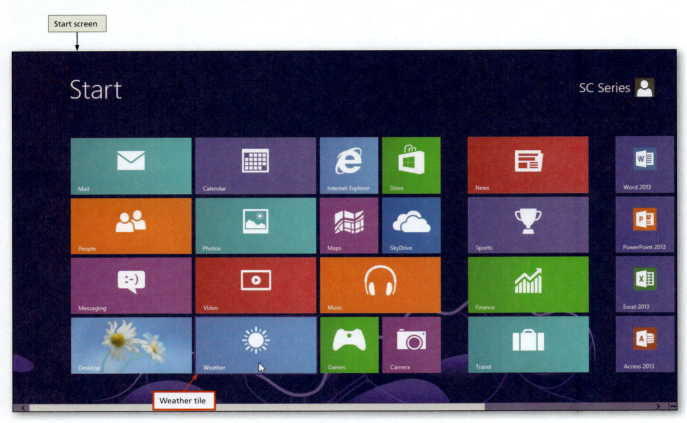

Figure 1–7

Exploring the Start Screen

The **Start screen** is a new addition to the Windows operating system and uses Microsoft's **Modern UI** (user interface) to display tiles that can be used to run apps. The Start screen provides a scrollable space for you to access apps that have been pinned to it (shown in Figure 1–7). In addition to running apps, you can perform tasks such as pinning apps (placing tiles) on the Start screen, moving the tiles around the Start screen, and unpinning apps (removing tiles) from the Start screen.

A tile is shown as a rectangle or square on the Start screen. Tapping or clicking a tile will run the app associated with the tile. **Live tiles** are tiles that when configured, update the tile with information while the Start screen is displayed. For example, if you configure the Weather app to your location, the tile will update with current weather conditions in your city.

Working with Apps

An app uses the entire screen by default. They work smoothly with touch and other input devices. When using the app, the **App bar** provides the primary command interface for the app. Because the app runs full screen, you will experience no distraction from any other app running at the same time and can focus on the current app and performing the task at hand.

To Run an App Using the Start Screen

The Start screen contains tiles that allow you to run apps, some of which may be stored on your computer. *Why? When you install an app, one or more tiles are added to the Start screen so that you easily can run the app.* The following steps, which assume Windows is running, use the Start screen to run the Weather app based on a typical installation. Although the steps illustrate running the Weather app, the steps to run any app are similar.

- If necessary, swipe or scroll to display the Weather tile on the Start screen.

- Tap or click the Weather tile to run the Weather app (Figure 1–8).

Q&A   What happens when you run an app?

Many apps, including the Weather app, appear full screen. Other apps run in the desktop using a window. A **window** is a rectangular area that displays data and information. The top of a window has a **title bar**, which is a horizontal space that contains the window's name.

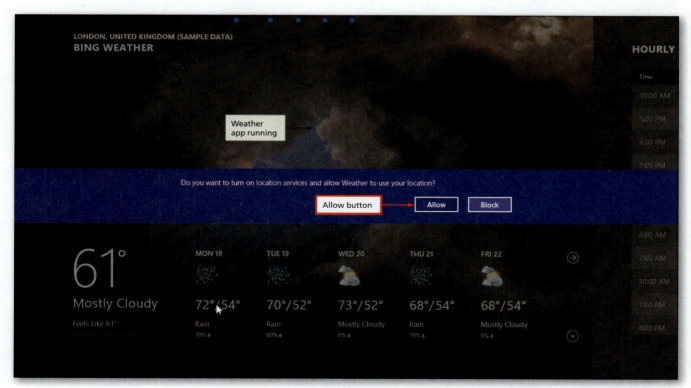

Figure 1–8

2

- Tap or click the Allow button to allow the Weather app to use the current location (Figure 1–9).

- If your location cannot be detected, type your current city in the Enter Location text box, and then tap or click your city in the list that appears.

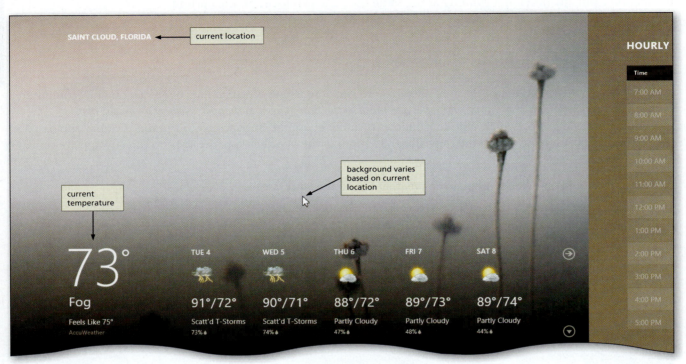

Figure 1–9

Other Ways

1. Tap or click Search charm on Charms bar, type app name in Search box, tap or click app name in results list

To Navigate within an App

To navigate within an app, you can use gestures or the scroll bar to see more of the app, or you can display the Navigation bar for an app. In the Weather app, the Navigation bar lets you move from the Home screen to other places, and even displays world weather. *Why? You may intend to travel or you may be interested in seeing the weather in a different location.*

The following steps display the current world weather information.

1

• Press and hold, and then release, or right-click the screen to display the Navigation bar (Figure 1–10).

Figure 1–10

2

• Tap or click the World weather button to display the current world weather information (Figure 1–11).

Figure 1–11

3
- After viewing the current world weather information, press and hold, and then release, or right-click the screen to display the Navigation bar (Figure 1–12).

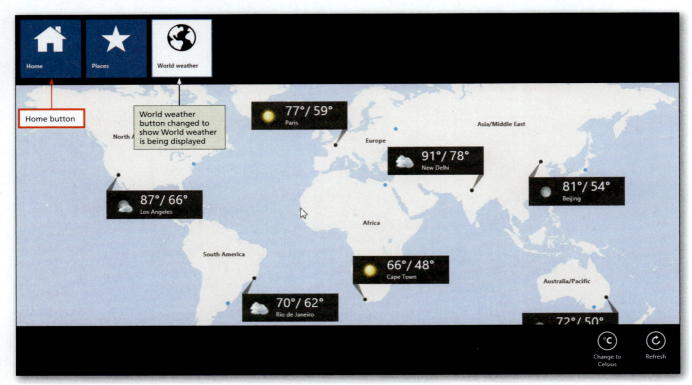

Figure 1–12

4
- Tap or click the Home button to return to the Home screen for the Weather app (Figure 1–13).

Figure 1–13

Using Charms

Windows includes several charms that can be used to find files, share information, display the Start screen, manipulate connected devices, and change settings. No matter where you are or what you are doing in Windows, you always are able to display the Charms bar.

To Return to the Start Screen

When you are finished using an app, returning to the Start screen allows you to perform another action, such as starting another app, in Windows. *Why? When working with Windows, you may decide to return to the Start screen in order to run another app.*

The following steps display the Start screen without exiting the Weather app.

- Swipe from the right or point to the upper-right corner of the screen to display the Charms bar (Figure 1–14).

Figure 1–14

- Tap or click the Start charm on the Charms bar to return to the Start screen (Figure 1–15 on the next page).

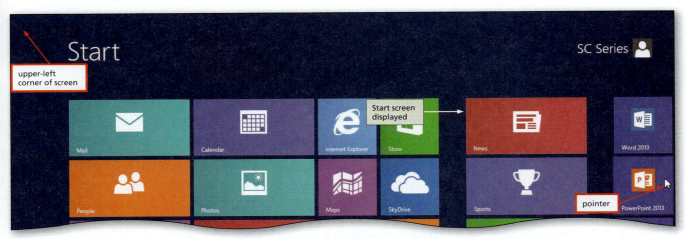

Figure 1–15

Other Ways

1. Press WINDOWS key
2. Click lower-left corner of screen, tap or click Start screen live preview
3. Swipe from left side of screen

Working with Apps

As discussed previously in this chapter, one way you can run an app in Windows is by clicking that app's tile on the Start screen. In addition to running apps, Windows enables you to switch between apps easily so that you can work with multiple apps at one time or exit apps when you have finished using them.

To Switch between Apps

In Windows, you can switch between apps easily. **Why?** *You may have several apps running and want to work with a different app than the one you currently are using.*

The following steps switch from the Start screen to the Weather app.

• Point to the upper-left corner of the screen to display the current apps running (Figure 1–16).

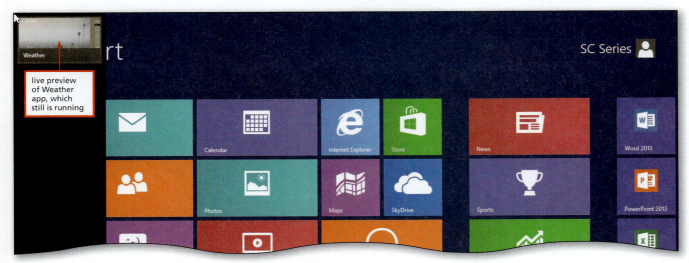

Figure 1–16

2
- Tap or click the Weather app live preview to switch to the Weather app (Figure 1–17).

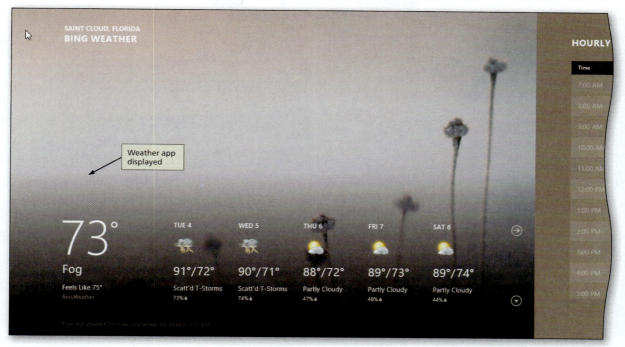

Figure 1–17

Other Ways

1. Swipe from left
   side of screen

Understanding How to Exit Apps

With Windows, apps that you currently are not using run in the background. Windows automatically exits those apps that you have not used for an extended period of time. If you choose to do so, however, you can exit apps rather than allowing Windows to do it for you.

To Display the Windows Desktop

With Windows, you still can run and use traditional apps that require the use of the Windows desktop. *Why? The desktop provides many useful functions, and not all apps use the Modern UI.*

The step on the following page displays the Windows desktop.

1

- Press the WINDOWS key to return to the Start screen.

- Tap or click the Desktop tile to display the desktop (Figure 1–18).

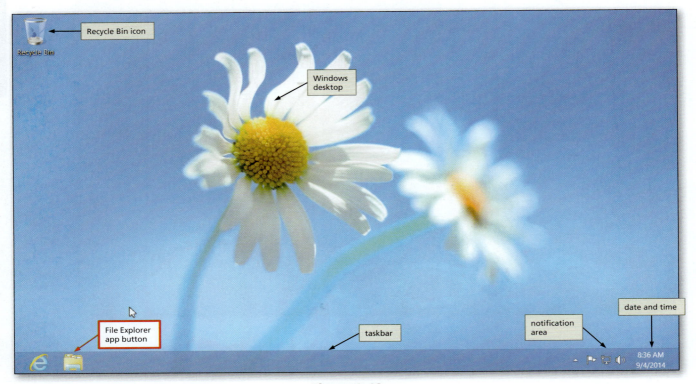

Figure 1–18

The Windows 8 Desktop

Think of the Windows desktop as an electronic version of the top of your desk. You can perform tasks such as placing objects on the desktop, moving the objects around the desktop, and removing items from the desktop.

When you run an app in Windows, it may appear on the desktop. Some icons also may be displayed on the desktop. For instance, the icon for the **Recycle Bin**, the location of files that have been deleted, appears on the desktop by default. You can customize your desktop so that icons representing apps and files you use often appear on your desktop. When you run an app, that app's app button appears on the taskbar. By default, the **taskbar** appears at the bottom of the Windows desktop and displays the Internet Explorer app button, the File Explorer app button, and app buttons representing apps that currently are running. The right side of the taskbar contains the notification area, date, and time. The **notification area** contains icons designed to provide information about the current state of the computer. For example, the notification area can tell you if your virus protection is out of date, how much battery life you have remaining (if you are using a laptop), and whether you are connected to a network.

To Run the File Explorer

In Windows, you can use the File Explorer to view your files and organize them into folders as well as access these files and folders. *Why? If you want to move files and folders around on your hard disk, or copy or move files to or from a removable drive such as a USB flash drive, the File Explorer can help you perform these operations.*

The following step runs the File Explorer.

- Tap or click the File Explorer app button on the taskbar (shown in Figure 1–18) to run the File Explorer (Figure 1–19).

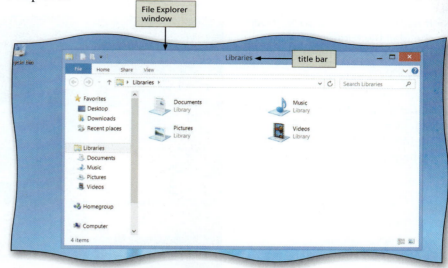

Figure 1–19

To Return to the Start Screen

The following steps display the Start screen.

- Swipe from the right or point to the upper-right corner of the screen to display the Charms bar.

- Tap or click the Start charm to return to the Start screen (Figure 1–20).

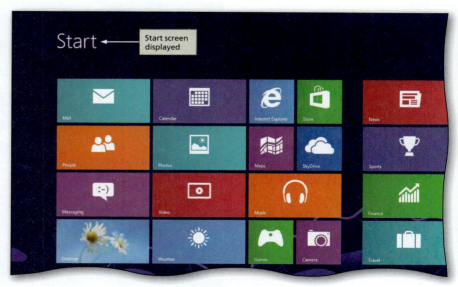

Figure 1–20

Other Ways

1. Press WINDOWS

2. Click upper-left corner of screen, tap or click Start screen live preview

To Move a Tile

After using the Start screen, you may decide to rearrange the tiles. ***Why?*** *You can place the apps that you use most often on the left side of the screen so that you can find them easily without having to scroll.* The following steps move the Mail tile to the lower left of the Start screen.

1
- If necessary, swipe or scroll to see the Mail tile (Figure 1–21).

Q&A What if I do not have the Mail tile on my Start screen?

Your Start screen can be different depending on the setup of your school/work computer. If you have no Mail tile, choose another tile to move.

Figure 1–21

2
- Drag the Mail tile to the lower left of the Start screen tiles to move the tile to that location (Figure 1–22).

Figure 1–22

To Resize a Tile

Windows allows you to change the size of your tiles on the Start screen. ***Why?*** *You can see more or less of a tile's information by resizing the tile.* To resize a tile, you press and hold, and then release, or right-click to display the App bar and then choose Smaller or Larger depending on how you want to resize the tile. You also can choose to unpin the app from the Start screen. The All apps button also is shown, which allows you to see all apps installed on your computer.

The following steps change the size of the Weather tile.

1

• Press and hold, and then release, or right-click the Weather tile to display the App bar (Figure 1–23).

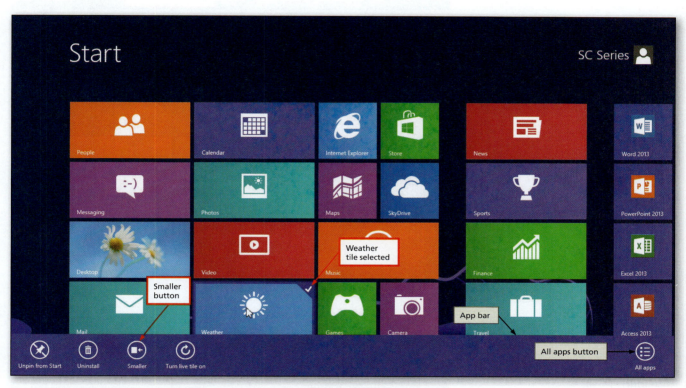

Figure 1–23

2

- Tap or click the Smaller button on the App bar to change the size of the Weather tile to smaller (Figure 1–24).

Figure 1–24

3

- Right-click the Weather tile to display the App bar (Figure 1–25).

Figure 1–25

4

- Tap or click the Larger button on the App bar to change the size of the Weather tile to larger (Figure 1–26).

Figure 1–26

To Run an App Using the Search Box

The following steps use the Search box to run the Maps app based on a typical installation; however, you would follow similar steps to run any app. *Why? Sometimes an app does not appear on the Start screen, so you can find it quickly by searching.* Rather than searching for apps, you can tap or click the Files link to search for only files. You may need to ask your instructor how to run apps for your computer.

- Swipe from the right or point to the upper-right corner of the Start screen to display the Charms bar (Figure 1–27).

Figure 1–27

2
- Tap or click the Search charm on the Charms bar to display the Search menu (Figure 1–28).

Figure 1–28

3
- Type   `Maps`   as the search text in the Search text box, and watch the search results appear in the Apps list (Figure 1–29).

Q&A   Do I need to type the complete app name or use correct capitalization?

No, you need to type just enough characters of the app name for it to appear in the Apps list. For example, you may be able to type M or Map, instead of Maps.

Figure 1–29

4

- Tap or click the app name, Maps in this case, in the search results to run the Maps app (Figure 1–30).

- If necessary, tap or click the Allow button to allow Maps to use your current location.

Figure 1–30

To Search the Internet Using a Charm

You also can use the Search charm to search the Internet. *Why? You need more information on a subject and want to search the Internet.* The following steps use Bing to search the Internet.

1

- Swipe from the right or point to the upper-right corner of the screen to display the Charms bar.

- Tap or click the Search charm on the Charms bar to display the Search menu (Figure 1–31 on the next page).

Figure 1–31

2

- Tap or click the Bing link to display the Bing search area (Figure 1–32).

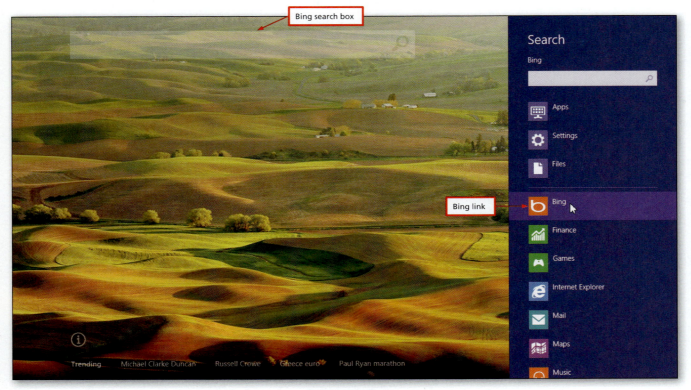

Figure 1–32

3
- Type `Windows 8` in the Search box and then press the ENTER key to search for websites about Windows 8 using the Bing app (Figure 1–33).

Figure 1–33

To Switch between Apps

The following steps switch from the Bing app to the Weather app.

1 Swipe from the right, and then to the left, or point to the upper-left corner of the screen and then move the mouse down to display the apps currently running.

2 Tap or click the Weather app's live preview to switch to the Weather app (Figure 1–34).

Figure 1–34

To Search an App Using a Charm

Using the Search charm, you can search an app when the app is open. *Why? While using the Weather app, you may want to find what the weather is for Las Vegas, as you will be vacationing there.* The following steps find information about the weather in Las Vegas.

1
- Swipe from the right or point to the upper-right corner of the screen to display the Charms bar.
- Tap or click the Search charm on the Charms bar to display the Search menu (Figure 1–35).

Figure 1–35

2
- Type `Las Vegas` in the Search box and then press the ENTER key to search for weather for cities named Las Vegas (Figure 1–36).

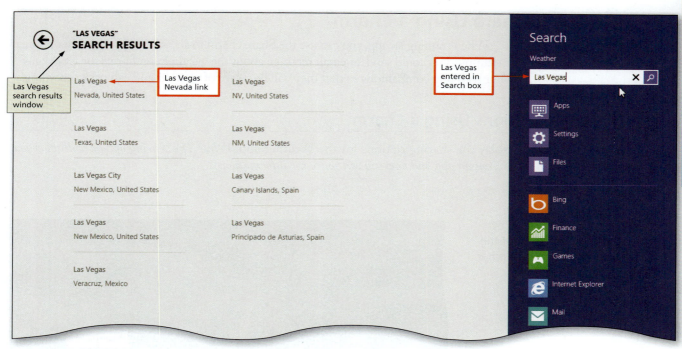

Figure 1–36

❸
• Tap or click the Las Vegas, Nevada, link to show weather for Las Vegas, Nevada (Figure 1–37).

Figure 1–37

Share Using a Charm

When running an app, you can use the Share charm to access the app's sharing options. For example, you could send an email message about the weather conditions for Las Vegas to your traveling companions so that they will be aware of weather and can pack accordingly.

To View Sharing Options Using a Charm

The following steps display the sharing options for the Weather app. *Why? The sharing options will show you what information you can share from an app and how you can share the information.*

- Swipe from the right or point to the upper-right corner of the screen to display the Charms bar (Figure 1–38).

Figure 1–38

2

- Tap or click the Share charm on the Charms bar to display sharing options (Figure 1–39).

Figure 1–39

Other Ways

1. Press WINDOWS+H

Free and Paid Apps

Many apps are available for Windows, which you can find using the Windows Store. Some apps are free, allowing you to download them without making a payment. Other apps require payment, so you will need to pay the fee before you can download them.

To Install an App

When using the Windows Store, you can install apps that are free or paid. ***Why?*** *You find an app that you want to use and download and install it so that it is on your computer.* The following steps download and install the Wikipedia app from the Windows Store. If you are not able to download and install apps on the computer you are using, read these steps without performing them.

1
- Swipe from the right or point to the upper-right corner of the screen to display the Charms bar and then tap or click the Start charm on the Charms bar to return to the Start screen.

2
- Tap or click the Store tile to run the Store app (Figure 1–40).

Figure 1–40

3
- If necessary, scroll to display the Wikipedia app.
- Tap or click the Wikipedia app to display the Wikipedia install options (Figure 1–41 on the next page).

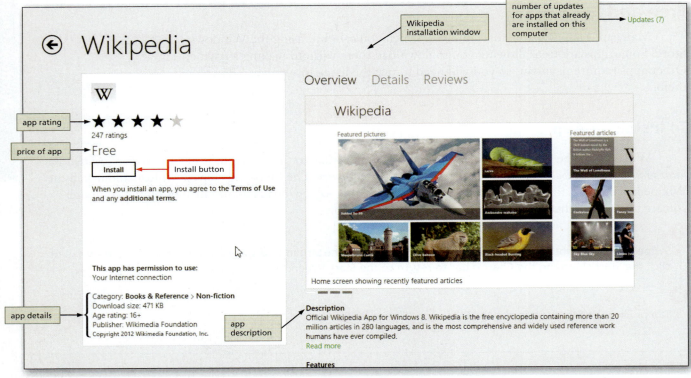

Figure 1–41

4

- Tap or click the Install button to install the Wikipedia app (Figure 1–42).

- If prompted, enter your Microsoft account information to authorize the installation and then tap or click the OK button.

Figure 1–42

5
- Swipe from the right or point to the upper-right corner of the screen to display the Charms bar.

- Tap or click the Start charm on the Charms bar to return to the Start screen.

- Scroll to see the installed Wikipedia app (Figure 1–43).

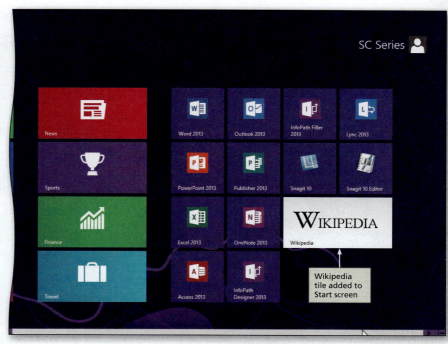

Figure 1–43

Using Windows Help and Support

One of the more powerful Windows features is Windows Help and Support. **Windows Help and Support** is available when using Windows or when using any Microsoft app running under Windows.

Different Help options are offered depending upon whether you are at the Start screen or the Windows desktop. The links displayed in Help will depend on the app or location you currently are using.

To Start Windows Help and Support

The steps on the following pages start Windows Help and Support and open the Windows Help and Support window, which contains links to more information about Windows. *Why? This feature is designed to assist you in using Windows or the various apps.*

1

- Point to the upper-left corner of the screen to display the running apps (Figure 1–44).

Figure 1–44

2

- Tap or click the Desktop's live preview to switch to the desktop (Figure 1–45).

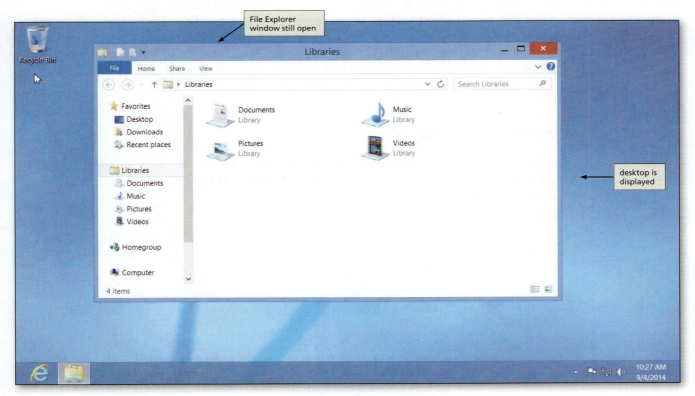

Figure 1–45

3

- Swipe from the right or point to the upper-right corner of the screen to display the Charms bar (Figure 1–46).

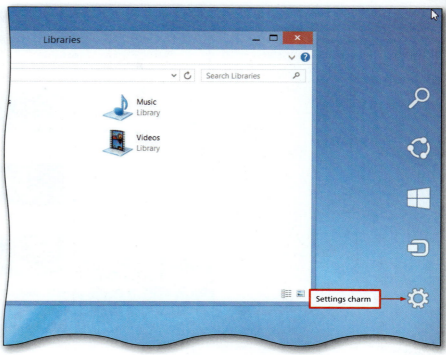

Figure 1–46

4

- Tap or click the Settings charm on the Charms bar to display the Settings menu (Figure 1–47).

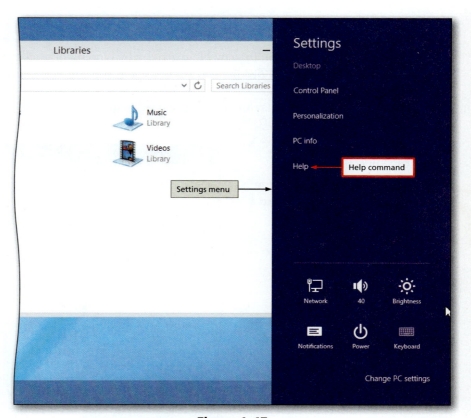

Figure 1–47

5

- Tap or click Help to open the Windows Help and Support window (Figure 1–48).

Figure 1–48

Other Ways

1. In the desktop, press **F1**

To Browse Help

Browsing Help allows you to view Help articles by tapping or clicking predefined links to assist you with finding the help you require. **Why?** *You may not be certain about the topic you want to research, so you browse Help and Support to find the topic you need.*

The following steps display the Getting started help link.

1

- Tap or click the Browse help link to display the Help topics (Figure 1–49).

Q&A

Why does the pointer turn into a hand?

The pointer changes to a hand when it is positioned on a link that you can click.

Why is the content in my Windows Help and Support window different?

Windows Help and Support updates regularly from the Internet. As these updates occur, you may notice content changing in Windows Help and Support.

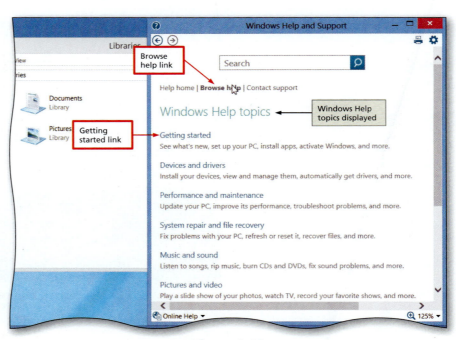

Figure 1–49

2

- Tap or click the Getting started link to display the Help links (Figure 1–50).

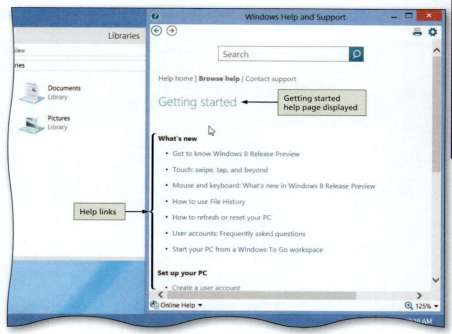

Figure 1–50

Shutting Down Windows

After completing your work with Windows, you should end your session by signing out of your account. In addition to signing out, several options are available for ending your Windows session. You can choose to sign out only, to lock the computer until you come back, to put the computer in sleep mode that saves power, or to shut down the computer as well as sign out of your account.

To Sign Out of an Account

If you are leaving the computer but do not want to turn it off, you can choose to sign out of your account. *Why? You are using a computer in the school lab and are leaving the class. The computer does not need to be shut down because a student in the following class will need to use the computer.*

The following steps sign out of an account.

1

- Swipe from the right or point to the upper-right corner of the screen to display the Charms bar.

- Tap or click the Start charm on the Charms bar to return to the Start screen (Figure 1–51).

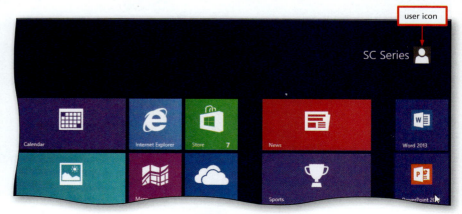

Figure 1–51

2
- Tap or click the user icon to display user options (Figure 1–52).

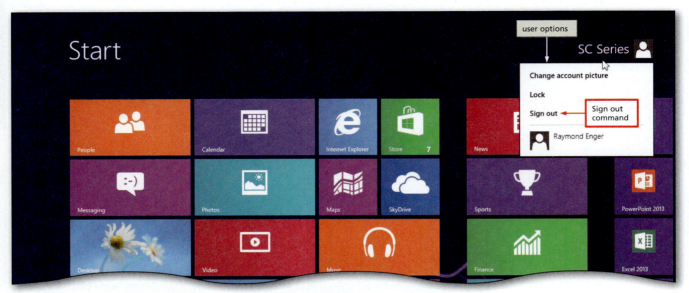

Figure 1–52

3
- Tap or click Sign out to sign out of your account (Figure 1–53).

Figure 1–53

To Shut Down the Computer

When you have finished using the computer, you should shut it down. *Why? You are finished using your computer and want to shut it down to conserve power.*

The following steps shut down the computer.

1
- Tap, swipe, or click the lock screen to display the sign-in screen (Figure 1–54).

Figure 1–54

2
- Tap or click the Shut down button to display the Shut down menu (Figure 1–55).

Figure 1–55

3

- Tap or click Shut down to shut down the computer (Figure 1–56).

4

- If necessary, turn off any other devices you have connected to your computer.

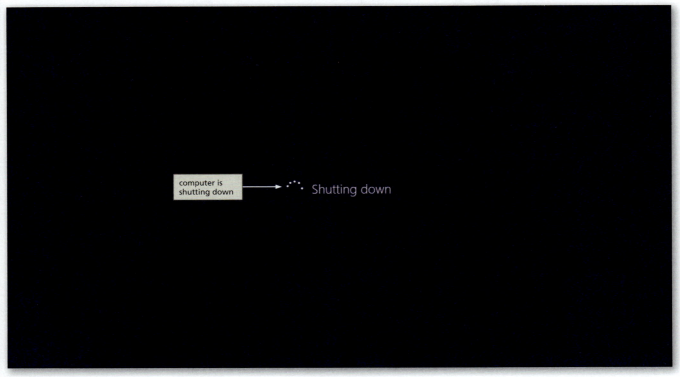

computer is shutting down

Shutting down

Figure 1–56

Chapter Summary

In this chapter, you have learned how to work with the Modern UI using touch and mouse operations. You started Windows, signed to in to an account, learned about the Start screen, and ran apps.

You learned how to switch between apps and use the Search box to find apps. Using Windows Help and Support, you located Help topics to learn more about Microsoft Windows. You learned how to sign out of an account and shut down the computer. The items listed below include the Windows skills you have learned in this chapter.

1. Sign In to an Account (WIN 8)
2. Run an App Using the Start Screen (WIN 11)
3. Navigate within an App (WIN 12)
4. Return to the Start Screen (WIN 15)
5. Switch between Apps (WIN 16)
6. Display the Windows Desktop (WIN 17)
7. Run the File Explorer (WIN 19)
8. Return to the Start Screen (WIN 19)
9. Move a Tile (WIN 20)
10. Resize a Tile (WIN 21)

11. Run an App Using the Search Box (WIN 23)
12. Search the Internet Using a Charm (WIN 25)
13. Search an App Using a Charm (WIN 28)
14. View Sharing Options Using a Charm (WIN 30)
15. Install an App (WIN 31)
16. Start Windows Help and Support (WIN 33)
17. Browse Help (WIN 36)
18. Sign Out of an Account (WIN 37)
19. Shut Down the Computer (WIN 39)

Apply Your Knowledge

What's New in Windows 8?

Instructions: Use Windows Help and Support to perform the following tasks.

Part 1: Starting Windows Help and Support

1. Display the Windows desktop and then tap or click the Settings charm on the Charms bar. On the Settings menu, tap or click Help to open the Windows Help and Support window.

2. Tap or click the Get started link in the Windows Help and Support window.

Part 2: Exploring What's New in Windows 8

1. Tap or click the 'Get to know Windows' link to display information about the new features in Windows 8 (Figure 1–57).

   a. What are four reasons to connect to the cloud?

   b. What does it mean to snap an app?

   c. What is the function of the Devices charm?

Part 3: What's New in Security?

1. Tap or click the Browse help link.

2. If necessary, scroll to display the 'Security, privacy, and accounts' link. Tap or click the 'Security, privacy, and accounts' link to display the Security, privacy, and accounts page.

3. Tap or click the 'Security checklist for Windows' link to display the Security checklist for Windows page.

4. Answer the following questions:

   a. What is the Action Center?

   b. What is User Account Control?

   c. What is Windows Update?

5. Tap or click the Close button in the Windows Help and Support window.

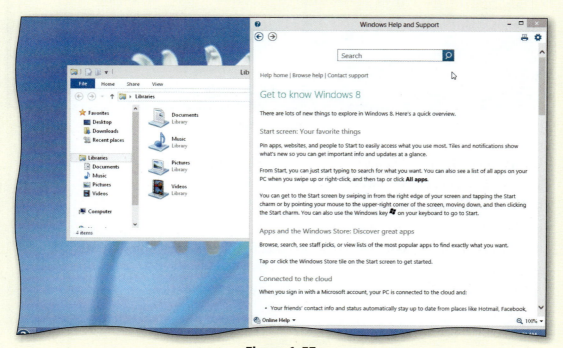

Figure 1–57

Extend Your Knowledge

Extend the skills you learned in this chapter and experiment with new skills. You will use Help to complete the assignment.

Using Help

Instructions: Use Windows Help and Support to perform the following tasks.

1. Open the Windows Help and Support window.

2. Find Help about Windows shortcuts by typing shortcuts in the Search text box and then tapping or clicking the Search button (Figure 1–58). Tap or click the result titled 'Copy or move files and folders' and then answer the following questions:

   a. What keyboard shortcut is used to copy a file?

   b. What keyboard shortcut is used to paste a file?

   c. How do you display a shortcut menu?

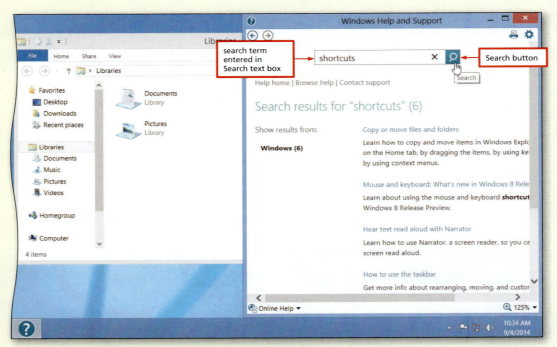

Figure 1–58

3. Use Windows Help and Support to answer the following questions:

   a. What is Windows Defender?

   b. What is Windows Firewall?

   c. What settings can you control in Family Safety?

   d. What are five ways to protect your computer from viruses and other threats?

   e. What is a user account?

   f. What is the difference between a local user account and a Microsoft account?

4. Use the Search text box in Windows Help and Support to answer the following questions:

    a. How do you turn on Windows Firewall?

    b. How do you pin a program to the taskbar?

    c. How do you set up a home network in Windows?

    d. How do you add a printer?

5. The tools to solve a problem while using Windows 8 are called troubleshooters. Use Windows Help and Support to find information about troubleshooters, and answer the following questions:

    a. What problems does the Printer troubleshooter allow you to resolve?

    b. List two additional Windows 8 troubleshooters.

6. Close the Windows Help and Support window.

In the Lab

Use the guidelines, concepts, and skills presented in this chapter to increase your knowledge of Windows 8. Labs are listed in order of increasing difficulty.

Lab 1: Using Windows Help and Support

Problem: You have a few questions about using Windows and would like to answer these questions using Windows Help and Support.

Instructions: Use Windows Help and Support to perform the following tasks.

1. Open the Windows Help and Support window.

2. Use Help and Support to answer the following questions:

    a. What is a way to improve your computer's performance?

    b. How do you view your computer information?

    c. Which power plans does Windows provide?

3. Use the Search Help text box in Windows Help and Support to answer the following questions:

    a. How can you rip music from a CD using Windows Media Player?

    b. How can you play a slide show of your photos?

    c. What tools does Windows provide for fixing problems with your computer?

4. Use Windows Help and Support to obtain information about the Internet and networking (Figure 1–59).

    a. How do you set up a wireless router?

    b. How do you turn on sharing?

    c. What advice does Windows provide about fixing network adapter problems?

5. Close the Windows Help and Support window.

Continued >

In the Lab continued

Figure 1–59

In the Lab

Lab 2: Working with Multiple Apps

Instructions: Perform the following steps to run multiple apps with the desktop and the Search menu and then use different methods to switch among the open windows (Figure 1–60).

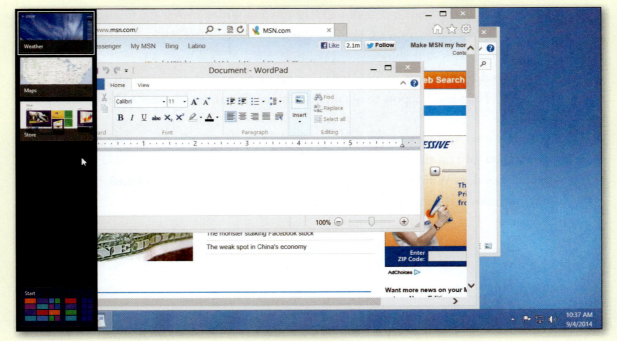

Figure 1–60

Part 1: Running Internet Explorer, the File Explorer, and WordPad

1. Display the Desktop and then tap or click the Internet Explorer app button on the taskbar to run Internet Explorer.

2. Tap or click the File Explorer app button to open the File Explorer window.

3. Display the Search charm and search for WordPad. Tap or click WordPad to run the WordPad app.

Part 2: Switching among the Windows

1. Press ALT+TAB to switch to the next open window.

2. Press CTRL+ALT+TAB to view the programs that are running. Press the TAB key. Tap or click the WordPad live preview to switch to the WordPad app.

3. Press CTRL+WINDOWS+TAB to view the programs that are running. Press the TAB key. Tap or click the Internet Explorer live preview to switch to Internet Explorer.

Part 3: Reporting Your Findings

1. What happens when you press ALT+TAB?

2. What is the difference between pressing ALT+TAB and CTRL+ALT+TAB?

In the Lab

Lab 3: Using Internet Explorer

Instructions: Perform the following steps to run Internet Explorer and explore a selection of websites.

Part 1: Running Internet Explorer

1. If necessary, connect to the Internet.

2. Display the desktop and then run Internet Explorer.

Part 2: Exploring the Cengage Website

1. Tap or click the web address in the address bar to select it.

2. Type cengage.com in the address bar and then press the ENTER key (Figure 1–61 on the next page).

3. Answer the following questions:

   a. What web address is displayed in the address bar?

   b. What window title appears on the title bar?

4. If necessary, swipe or scroll to view the contents of the webpage. List three links shown on this webpage.

5. Tap or click any link on the webpage. Which link did you tap or click?

6. Describe the webpage that was displayed when you tapped or clicked the link.

7. If requested by your instructor, tap or click the Print button to print the webpage.

Continued >

In the Lab continued

Figure 1–61

Part 3: Exploring Universal Studios: Orlando's Website
1. Tap or click the web address in the address bar to select it.
2. Type `universalorlando.com` in the address bar and then press the ENTER key.
3. What title is displayed on the title bar?
4. Swipe or scroll the webpage to view its contents. Do any graphic images display on the webpage?
5. Does the webpage include an image that is a link? (Recall that pointing to an image on a webpage and having the pointer change to a hand indicates the image is a link.) If so, describe the image.
6. Tap or click the image to display another webpage. What window title is displayed on the title bar?
7. If requested by your instructor, tap or click the Print button to print the webpage.

Part 4: Displaying Previously Displayed Webpages
1. Tap or click the Back button. What webpage is displayed?
2. Tap or click the Back button twice. What webpage is displayed?
3. Tap or click the Print button to print the webpage, if requested by your instructor.
4. Tap or click the Close button on the Internet Explorer title bar to exit Internet Explorer.

STUDENT ASSIGNMENTS

Cases and Places

Apply your creative thinking and problem-solving skills to design and implement a solution.

1: Assessing Windows 8 Compatibility

Academic

You work part-time as a lab technician in your school's computer lab. Your boss wants to upgrade several computers in the lab and has asked you to investigate. You know that the Windows 8 operating system can be installed only on computers found in the Windows 8 Hardware Compatibility List. Locate three older personal computers. Look for them in your school's computer lab, at a local business, or in your house. Use the Windows website to locate the Windows 8 Compatibility Center. Check each computer against the list and write a brief report summarizing your results.

2: Sharing Your Pictures

Personal

You recently attended your high school reunion, and your friend has asked for your help. She wants to send photos to several classmates via email messages and is not sure how best to proceed. Using Windows Help and Support and the keywords, digital pictures, locate the 'How to use Windows Photo Viewer' article. In a brief report, summarize the steps required to send a photo in an email message as well as the different ways to get photos from your camera.

3: Researching Multiple Operating Systems

Professional

You are working as an information technology intern at a large insurance agency's headquarters. Because the company is thinking about upgrading all its computers, your boss has tasked you with researching different operating systems. Using the Internet, a library, or other research facility, write a brief report on the Windows, Mac OS, and Linux operating systems. Describe the most recent version of each operating system, pointing out their similarities and differences. Discuss the advantages and disadvantages of each. Finally, tell which operating system you would purchase and explain why.

LEARN ONLINE

Reinforce what you learned in this chapter with games, exercises, training, and many other online activities and resources.

Student Companion Site: Reinforce chapter terms and concepts using review questions, flash cards, practice tests, and interactive learning games, such as a crossword puzzle. These and other online activities and resources are available at no additional cost on www.cengagebrain.com. Visit www.cengage.com/ct/studentdownload for detailed instructions about accessing the resources available at the Student Companion Site.

2 | File and Folder Management

Objectives

You will have mastered the material in this chapter when you can:

- View the contents of a drive and folder using the Computer folder window

- View the properties of files and folders

- Find files and folders from a folder window

- Use Shake and Snap to manipulate windows

- View the contents of the Pictures library

- View and change the properties of a picture

- Run and use the Photos app

- View pictures as a slide show

- Zip a folder and view the contents of a zipped folder

2 | File and Folder Management

Introduction

In Chapter 2, you will use Windows to create documents on the desktop and work with documents and folders in the Documents library. Windows also allows you to examine the files and folders on the computer in a variety of other ways, enabling you to choose the easiest and most accessible manner when working with a computer or mobile device. The Computer folder window and the Documents library provide two ways for you to work with files and folders. In addition, the Pictures library allows you to organize and share picture files, and the Music library allows you to organize and share your music files.

Overview

As you read this chapter, you will learn how to work with the Computer folder window, as well as the Documents, Pictures, and Music libraries, by performing these general tasks:

- Open and use the Computer folder window
- Search for files and folders
- Manage open windows
- Open and use the Pictures library
- Zip folder content
- Use the Photos app
- View pictures as a slide show

The Computer Folder Window

BTW
Managing Windows
Having multiple windows open on the desktop can intimidate some users. Consider working in a maximized window, and when you want to switch to another open window, use the Switch List to switch to that window.

As noted in the previous chapter, the desktop displays the File Explorer app button. Tapping or clicking the File Explorer app button opens the File Explorer window. Using the navigation bar, you can navigate to the Computer folder that contains the storage devices that are installed on the computer. Windows uses folder windows to display the contents of the computer. A **folder window** consists of tabs at the top that display the ribbon with multiple commands, an address bar below the ribbon, a toolbar to the left of the address bar containing buttons to help you navigate your computer's folder structure, a navigation pane on the left below the toolbar, a headings bar and list area on the right below the address bar, and a status bar at the bottom of the window. Depending upon which folder or library you are viewing — Computer, Documents, Pictures, and so on — the folder window will display the toolbar options that are most appropriate for working with the contents.

To Open and Maximize the Computer Folder Window

The list area of the Computer folder window groups objects based upon the different types of devices connected to your computer. The Hard Disk Drives group contains the Local Disk (C:) icon that represents the hard disk on the computer. The **hard disk** is where you can store files and folders. Storing data on a hard disk is more convenient than storing data on a USB flash drive because the hard disk is readily available and generally has more available storage space. A computer always will have at least one hard disk, which normally is designated as drive C. On the computer represented by the Computer folder window in Figure 2–1, the icon consists of an image of a hard disk and a **disk label**, or title, Local Disk, and a drive letter (C:). The disk label can change and may differ depending upon the name assigned to the hard disk. For example, some people label their hard disks based upon usage; therefore, it could be called PRIMARY (C:), where PRIMARY is the label given to the hard disk as it is the drive that houses the operating system and main apps.

The following steps open and maximize the Computer folder window. *Why? This will allow you to view the content in its entirety.*

1

- If necessary, sign in to your Windows account.
- Display the Start screen.
- Display the desktop.

2

- Tap or click the File Explorer app button to run the File Explorer app.

3

- Tap or click Computer in the navigation pane to open the Computer folder window. If necessary, maximize the Computer folder window (Figure 2–1).

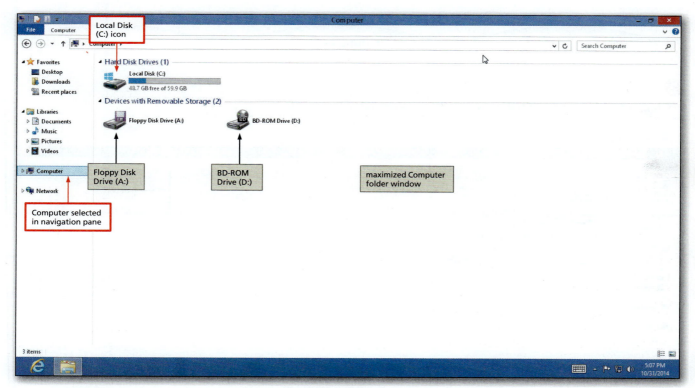

Figure 2–1

To Display Properties for the Local Disk (C:) Drive in the Details Pane

The details pane of a folder window displays the properties of devices, apps, files, and folders, which all are considered to be objects by Windows. Every object in Windows has properties that describe the object. A **property** is a characteristic of an object such as the amount of storage space on a storage device or the number of items in a folder. The properties of each object will differ, and in some cases, you can change the properties of an object. *Why? For example, in the Local Disk (C:) properties, you could check the file system being used on the drive using the File system property. To determine the drive's capacity, you would view the Total size property.* The following steps display the properties for the Local Disk (C:) in the details pane of the Computer folder window.

1
- Tap or click the Local Disk (C:) icon to select the hard disk and select the Local Disk (C:) (Figure 2–2).

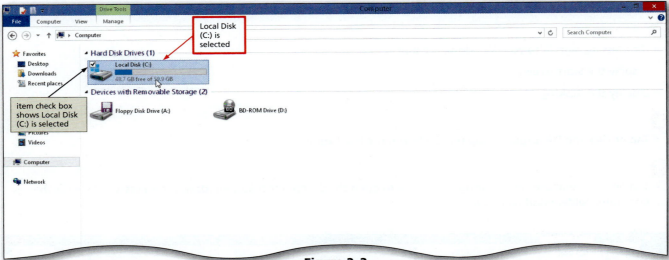

Figure 2–2

2
- Tap or click View on the ribbon to display the View tab (Figure 2–3).

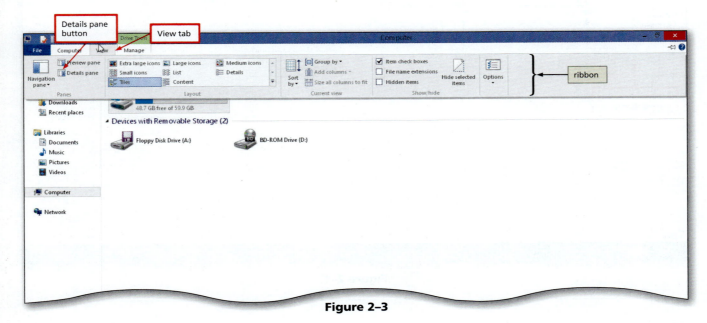

Figure 2–3

3

• Tap or click the Details pane button to display the details pane (Figure 2–4).

Experiment

See what properties are displayed for the other disks and devices shown. Tap or click each one and note what properties appear in the details pane. Return to the Local Disk (C:) when you are done.

Q&A

Why do the properties of my local disk differ from those in the figure?

The size and contents of your disk will be different from the one in the figure. As a result, the properties of the disk also will be different. Depending upon what has been installed on the disk and how it is formatted, the Space used, Space free, Total size, and File system properties will vary.

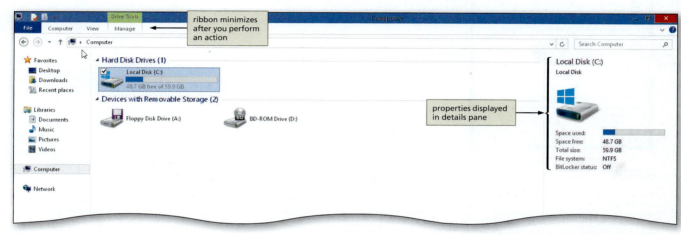

Figure 2–4

Other Ways

1. Tap or click Local Disk (C:) icon, press ALT+SHIFT+P

To Display the Local Disk (C:) Properties Dialog Box

The properties shown in the details pane are just a few of the properties of drive C. In fact, the details pane is used to highlight the most popular properties of a hard disk: how much space is used, how much space is free, the size of the disk, and how the disk is formatted. You can display more detailed information about the hard disk.

Why? *You would like to view information about the hard disk, such as the disk capacity, and perform other actions to help increase the disk's performance.* The Tools sheet, accessible by tapping or clicking the Tools tab, allows you to check for errors on the hard disk, defragment the hard disk, or back up the hard disk. The Hardware sheet allows you to view a list of all disk drives, troubleshoot disk drives that are not working properly, and display the properties for each disk drive. The Sharing sheet allows you to share the contents of a hard disk with other computer users. To protect a computer from unauthorized access, however, sharing the hard disk is not recommended. The Security sheet displays the security settings for the drive, such as user permissions. The Previous Versions sheet allows you to work with copies of your hard disk that are created when using backup utilities or from automatic saves. Finally, the Quota sheet can be used to see how much space is being used by various user accounts. Other tabs might be displayed in the Local Disk (C:) Properties dialog box on your computer.

The following step displays the Properties dialog box for the Local Disk (C:) drive.

- Tap or click the Properties button (Computer tab | Location group) to display the Local Disk (C:) Properties dialog box (Figure 2–5).

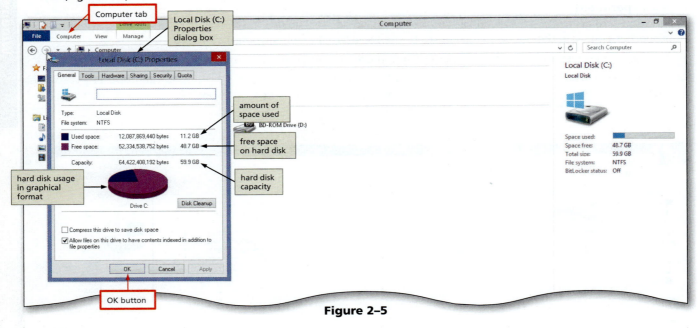

Figure 2–5

Other Ways

1. Press and hold, then release or right-click Local Disk (C:) icon, tap or click Properties on shortcut menu

2. Select drive icon, press ALT+ENTER

To Close the Local Disk (C:) Properties Dialog Box

Now that you have reviewed the Local Disk (C:) Properties dialog box, you should close it. The following step closes the dialog box. *Why? Closing the dialog box lets you continue working in the Computer folder window without the dialog box being displayed.*

- Tap or click the OK button (Local Disk (C:) Properties dialog box) to close it (Figure 2–6).

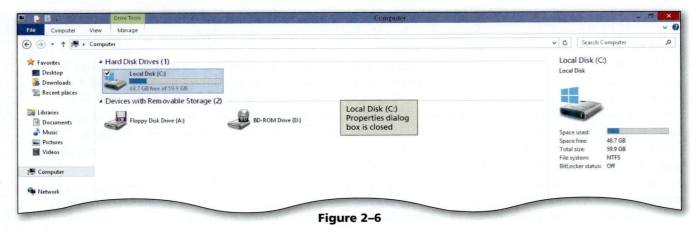

Figure 2–6

Other Ways

1. Tap or click Cancel button
2. Tap or click Close button
3. Press ESC

To Switch Folders Using the Address Bar

Why? *Found in all folder windows, the address bar lets you know which folder you are viewing.* A useful feature of the address bar is its capability to allow you to switch to different folder windows by tapping or clicking the arrows preceding or following the folder names. Tapping or clicking the arrow to the right of the computer icon, for example, displays a menu containing options for showing the desktop in a folder window, switching to the Computer folder, the Recycle Bin, the Control Panel, and other locations and folders that can vary from computer to computer. The following steps change the folder window from displaying the Computer folder to displaying the desktop and then return to the Computer folder.

1

- Tap or click the arrow to the right of the computer icon on the address bar to display a menu that contains folder switching commands (Figure 2–7). Depending upon your computer's configuration, the list of commands might differ.

Figure 2–7

2

- Tap or click Desktop on the menu to switch to viewing the contents of the desktop in the folder window (Figure 2–8).

Q&A Why do icons appear in this folder window that are not displayed on the desktop?

Although these icons are not displayed on the desktop, Microsoft provides you with convenient access to Libraries, the Control Panel, and the Network folder window (if applicable) by placing these icons in the Desktop folder window.

Figure 2–8

- Tap or click the 'Back to Computer' button to return to the Computer folder (Figure 2–9 on the next page).

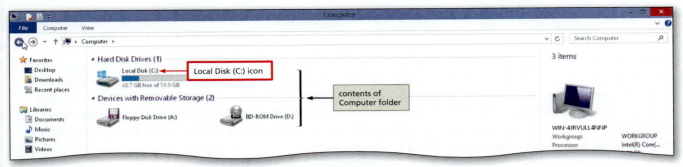

Figure 2–9

To View the Contents of a Drive

In addition to viewing the contents of the Computer folder, you can view the contents of drives and folders. In fact, the contents of any folder or drive on the computer will be displayed in a folder window. By default, Windows uses the active window to display the contents of a newly opened drive or folder. The following step displays the contents of drive C in the active window. *Why? You should know the contents of the drive so that you can see where your information is stored.*

1
- Double-tap or double-click the Local Disk (C:) icon in the Computer folder window to display the contents of the Local Disk (C:) drive (Figure 2–10).

Q&A Why do I see different folders?

The contents of the Local Disk (C:) window that appear on your computer can differ from the contents shown in Figure 2–10 because each computer has its own folders, apps, and documents.

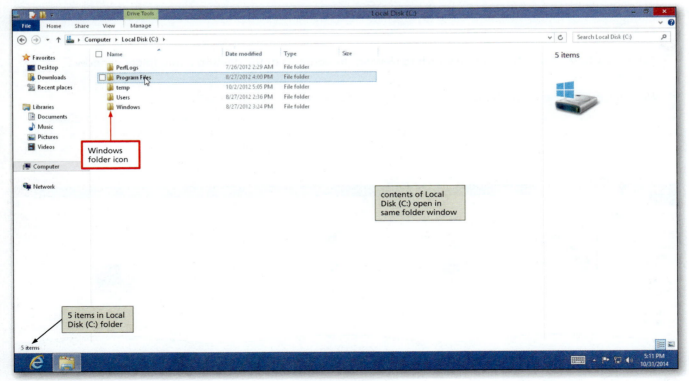

Figure 2–10

Other Ways

1. Press and hold, then release or right-click Local Disk (C:), tap or click Open on shortcut menu

2. Tap or click Local Disk (C:), press ENTER

To Preview the Properties of a Folder

Why? When you move the pointer over a folder icon, a preview of the folder properties will display in a ScreenTip. A **ScreenTip** is a brief description that appears when you position the pointer over an object on the screen. ScreenTips do not appear for every object, but when they do, they provide useful information. The properties typically consist of the date and time created, the folder size, and the name of the folder. The Windows folder in the Local Disk (C:) window contains apps and files necessary for the operation of the Windows operating system. As such, you should exercise caution when working with the contents of the Windows folder, because changing the contents of the folder might cause the operating system to stop working correctly.

The following step shows a ScreenTip displaying the properties of the Windows folder.

1
- Point to the Windows folder icon to display a ScreenTip displaying the properties of the Windows folder (Figure 2–11).

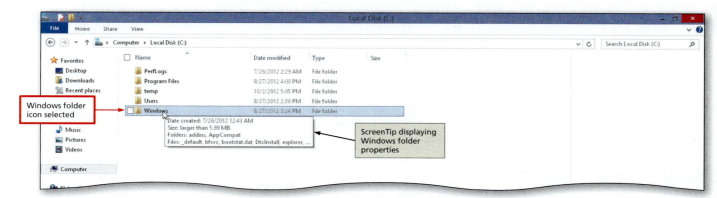

Figure 2–11

To Display Properties for the Windows Folder in the Details Pane

Just like with drives, some properties of folders can be displayed in the details pane. The following step displays the properties for the Windows folder in the details pane of the Computer folder window.

1
- Tap or click the Windows folder icon to display the properties in the details pane (Figure 2–12).

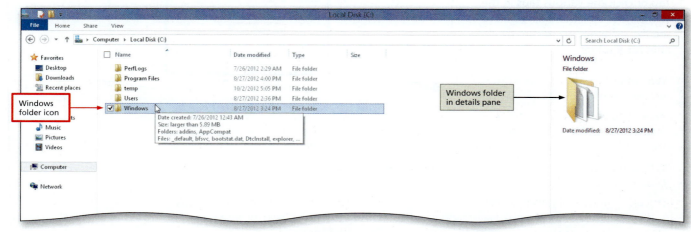

Figure 2–12

To Display All of the Properties of the Windows Folder

Why? If you want to see all of the properties for the Windows folder, you will need to display the Properties dialog box. The following steps display the Properties dialog box for the Windows folder.

1

• Press and hold, then release, or right-click the Windows folder icon to display a shortcut menu (Figure 2–13). (The commands on your shortcut menu might differ.)

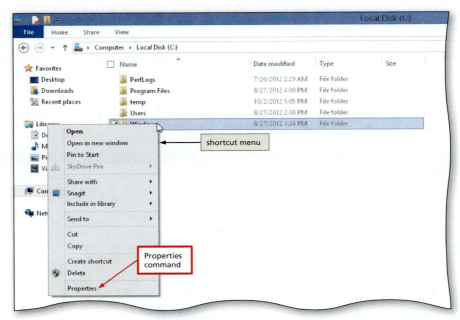

Figure 2–13

2

• Tap or click Properties on the shortcut menu to display the Windows Properties dialog box (Figure 2–14).

3

• Tap or click the OK button (Windows Properties dialog box) to close it.

Experiment

Tap or click the various tabs in the Windows Properties dialog box to see the different properties available for a folder.

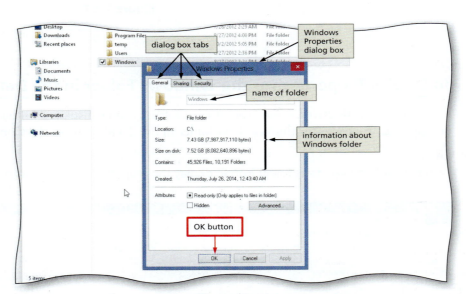

Figure 2–14

Q&A

Why might I want to look at the properties of a folder?

When you are working with folders, you might need to look at folders' properties to make changes, such as configuring a folder for sharing over a network or hiding folders from users who do not need access to them.

Why are the tabs of the Windows folder properties different from the Local Disk (C:) properties?

Drives, folders, and files have different properties and, therefore, need different tabs. A folder's Properties dialog box typically shows the General, Sharing, Security, and Previous Versions tabs; however, depending upon your Windows 8 edition and installed apps, the tabs may differ. The Properties dialog box always will have the General tab, although what it displays also may differ.

To View the Contents of a Folder

The following step opens the Windows folder so that you can view its contents. *Why? You will be able see what sort of files your operating system installed.*

- Double-tap or double-click the Windows folder icon to display the contents of the Windows folder (Figure 2–15).

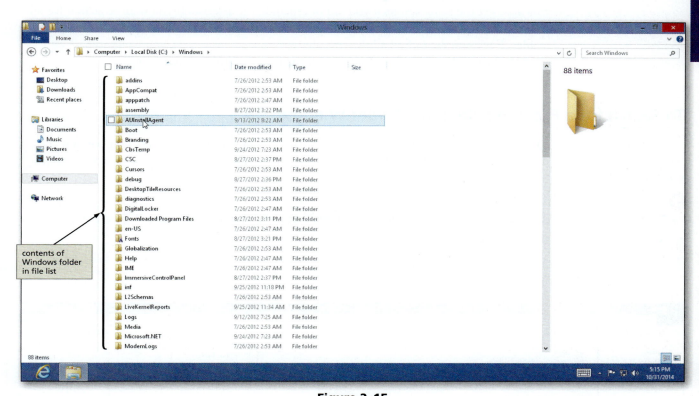

Figure 2–15

Other Ways

1. Press and hold, then release, or right-click Windows folder, tap or click Open on shortcut menu

2. Tap or click Windows folder, press ENTER

Searching for Files and Folders

The majority of objects displayed in the Windows folder, as shown in Figure 2–15, are folder icons. Folder icons always are displayed in alphabetical order at the top of the file list in a folder window, before the icons for apps or files.

Folders such as the Windows folder can contain many files and folders. When you want to find a particular file or folder but do not know where it is located, you can use the **Search box** to find the file or folder quickly. When you are in a folder, the Search box displays the word, Search, plus the folder name. For example, in the Windows folder, the Search box contains the text, Search Windows. As soon as you start typing, the window updates to show search results that match what you are typing. As Windows is searching for files or folders that match your search criteria, you will see a searching message displayed in the list area, an animated circle attached to the pointer, and an animated progress bar on the address bar, which provides

BTW

Hidden Files and Folders

Hidden files and folders usually are placed on your computer's hard disk by software vendors such as Microsoft and often are critical to the operation of their apps. Rarely will you need to designate a file or folder as hidden. You should not delete a hidden file or folder, as doing so might interrupt how or whether an app works. By default, hidden files and folders are not displayed in a file listing.

live feedback as to how much of the search has been completed. When searching is complete, you will see a list of all the items that match your search criteria.

If you know only a portion of a file's name and can specify where the known portion of the name should appear, you can use an asterisk in the name to represent the unknown characters. For example, if you know a file starts with the letters MSP, you can type `msp*` in the Search box. All files that begin with the letters, msp, regardless of what characters follow, will be displayed. With Windows 8's powerful search capabilities, however, you would get the same results if you did not include the asterisk. If you want to search for all files with a particular extension, you can use the asterisk to substitute for the name of the files. For example, to find all the text files with the extension .rtf, you would type `*.rtf` in the Search box. Windows will find all the files with the .rtf extension.

To Search for a File and Folder in a Folder Window

The following step uses the Search box to search the Windows folder for all the objects that contain the letters, aero, in the file name. *Why? Sometimes you may forget where a file is stored. Knowing how to search can help you find files faster.*

1

• Type `aero` in the Search box to search for all files and folders that match the search criteria (Figure 2–16).

Q&A How can I stop a search while it is running?

If you decide to stop a search before it is finished running, tap or click the Stop button (the small x) that appears next to the Search box.

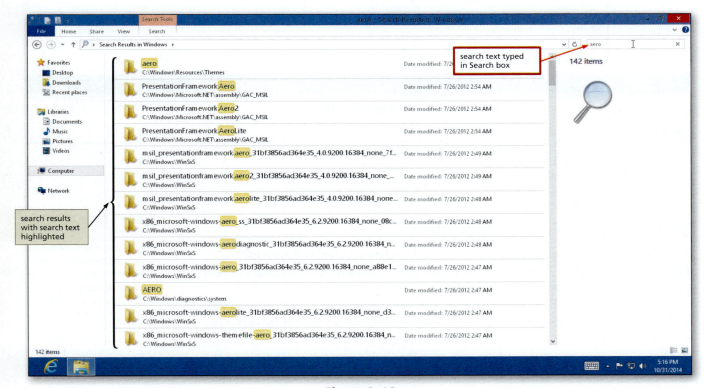

Figure 2–16

To Clear the Search Box

When you finish searching, you can end the search by clearing the Search box. The following step clears the Search box. **Why?** *You clear the Search box so that you can resume normal navigation of the folder you are viewing.*

- Tap or click the Stop button (denoted with an x in the Search box) to clear the Search box and redisplay all files and folders in the Windows folder (Figure 2–17).

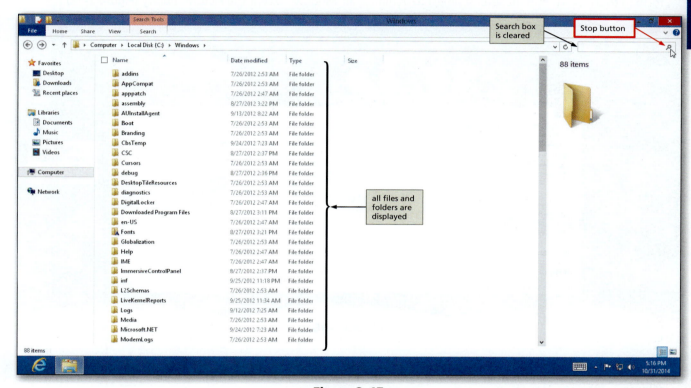

Figure 2–17

To Open Windows

In this chapter, you have been working with one window open. Windows allows you to open many more windows depending upon the amount of RAM that is installed on the computer. Too many open windows on the desktop, however, can become difficult to use and manage. Windows provides several tools for managing open windows. You already have used one tool, maximizing a window. When you maximize a window, it occupies the entire screen and cannot be confused with other open windows.

Sometimes, it is important to have multiple windows appear on the desktop simultaneously. Windows offers simple commands that allow you to arrange multiple windows in specific ways. The following sections describe the ways that you can manage multiple open windowsv. The following steps open another File Explorer window.

1 Press and hold, then release or right-click the File Explorer app button.

2 Tap or click File Explorer on the shortcut menu to open another File Explorer window.

3 Tap or click the Pictures folder to display its contents.

To Use Shake to Minimize and Restore All Windows

Shake lets you minimize all windows except the active window and then restore all those windows by shaking the title bar of the active window. The following steps use Shake to minimize all windows except the Music library and then restore those windows.

1
- Tap or click the title bar of the Pictures library window, and then shake the title bar (drag the title bar back and forth in short, swift motions several times) to minimize all windows except the Pictures library (Figure 2–18).

Figure 2–18

2
- Tap or click the title bar of the Pictures library window, and then shake the title bar to restore all the windows (Figure 2–19).

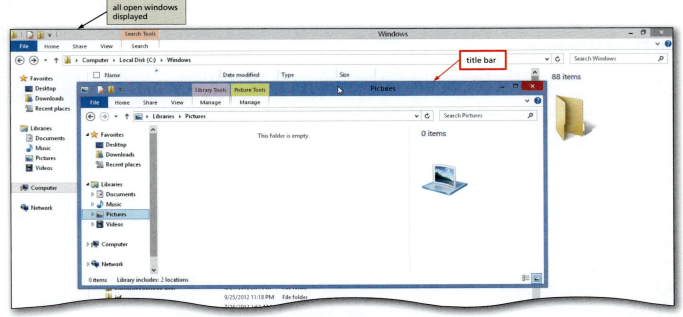

Figure 2–19

To Use Snap to Maximize Windows

Why? *Sometimes you want to see a larger portion of a window.* Snap allows you to maximize a window by dragging its title bar to the top of the screen. The following steps maximize the Pictures library window.

1
- Press and hold or click the title bar of the Pictures library window.

2
- Drag the Pictures library window to the top of the screen to maximize the Pictures library window (Figure 2–20).

Q&A
Can only Snap be used to maximize windows?

No. If you drag a window's title bar to the right side of the screen, the window will resize to fill the right half of the screen. If you drag the title bar to the left side of the screen, the window will resize to fill only the left half of the screen.

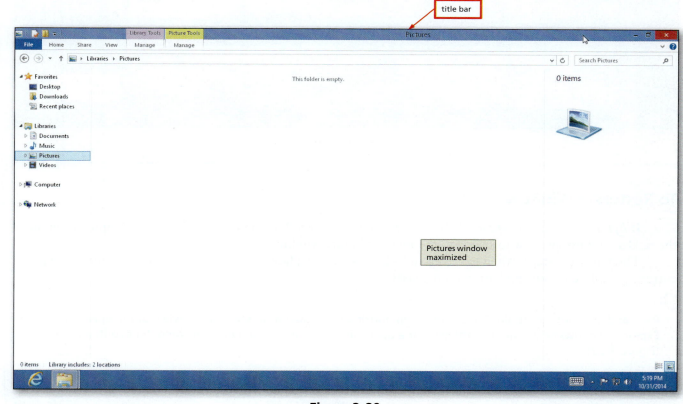

Figure 2–20

To Use the Show Desktop Button to Minimize All Windows

Why? *You need to access an app or file that is on the desktop, so you minimize all open windows so that you can access it.* The following step minimizes all windows to show the desktop.

1
- Tap or click the Show Desktop button on the taskbar to minimize all windows (Figure 2–21 on the next page).

Figure 2–21

To Restore a Window

Why? *To work with one of the windows, you first must restore it.* You can use the File Explorer app button on the taskbar and live preview to switch to the Pictures library window.

The following steps switch to the Pictures library window; however, the steps are the same for any app currently displayed as an app button on the taskbar.

1

- Press and hold or point to the File Explorer app button on the taskbar to see a live preview of the open File Explorer windows or the window title(s) of the open window(s), depending on your computer's configuration (Figure 2–22).

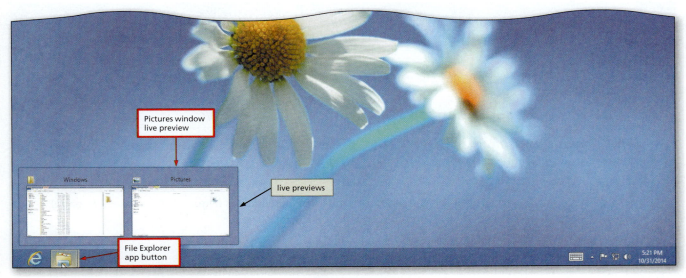

Figure 2–22

2
- Tap or click the live preview of the Pictures library window to restore the window (Figure 2–23).

Q&A

What happens if I tap or click the wrong window?

Tap or click the remaining windows until the Pictures window is displayed in the foreground.

Figure 2–23

Other Ways

1. Press ALT+TAB until Pictures folder window is selected, release ALT key

The Pictures Library

You can organize your pictures and share them with others using the Pictures library. By putting all your pictures in the Pictures library, you always will know where to find them. When you save pictures from a digital camera, scanner, or the Internet, they are saved to the Pictures library by default. More specifically, they are saved to the My Pictures folder. The My Pictures folder is part of the Pictures library and is set as the default save location to be used when working with the library. Each library has a default save location; the default save location for the Documents library is the My Documents folder.

Windows 8 also includes the Photos app. The **Photos app** is used when you download pictures from your digital camera. Unlike the Pictures library, files saved in the Photos app are stored in the app and not the My Pictures folder. You can use the Photos app to work with your pictures even if they are stored in the Pictures library.

Using the Pictures library allows you to organize pictures, preview pictures, share your pictures with others, display your pictures as a slide show, print your pictures, attach your pictures to email messages, or save your pictures on an optical disc. You will work with a few of the options now, and the rest will be covered in a later chapter when multimedia files are covered in greater depth.

Many different formats are available for picture files. Some pictures have an extension of .bmp to indicate that they are bitmap files. Other pictures may have the .gif extension, which indicates that they are saved in the Graphics Interchange Format. Too many file types exist to mention them all; however, some common types include .bmp, .jpg, .gif, .png, and .tif.

When working with pictures, you should be aware that most pictures that you did not create yourself, including other multimedia files, are copyrighted. A **copyright** means that a picture belongs to the person who created it. The pictures that come with Windows are part of Windows, and you are allowed to use them; however, they are not yours. You can use them only according to the rights given to you by Microsoft. Pictures that you take using your digital camera are yours because you created them. Before using pictures and other multimedia files, you should be aware of any copyrights associated with them, and you should know whether you are allowed to use them for your intended purpose.

Item Check Boxes

As you saw in the Local Disk (C:) folder window (Figure 2–12 on page WIN 57), when an item is selected, you clearly can see the item check box for that item. By tapping or clicking the item check box for several items, you can select them for your use. For example, you can copy files or folders from one location to another.

To Search for Pictures

***Why?** You want to copy three files (img0, img2, and img4) from the Windows folder to the Pictures library, but you have to find these files first.* Because the three files all have the .jpg extension, you can search for them using an asterisk (*) in place of the number in the name, as discussed earlier in this chapter. The following steps open the Windows folder window and display the icons for the files you want to copy.

1
- Restore the Windows folder window, and, if necessary, maximize it.

2
- Type `img*.jpg` in the Search box and then press the ENTER key to search for all files that begin with img and have a .jpg file extension.

3
- If necessary, scroll down the middle pane of the Windows folder window until the icons for the img0, img2, and img4 files are visible (Figure 2–24). If one or more of these files are not available, select any of the other picture files.

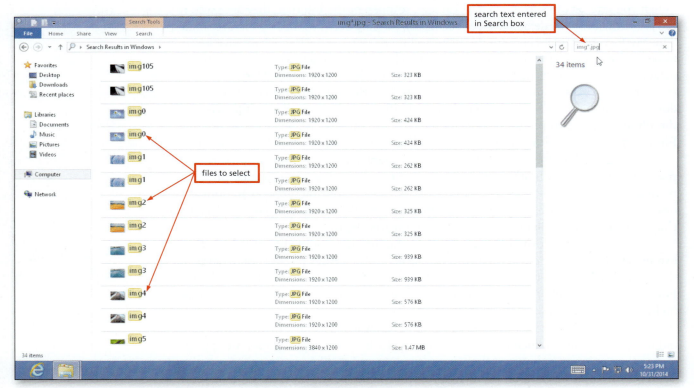

Figure 2–24

To Copy Files to the Pictures Library

A method you can use to copy a file or folder is the **copy and paste** method. When you **copy** a file, you place a copy of the file in a temporary storage area of the computer called the **Clipboard**. When you **paste** the file, Windows copies it from the Clipboard to the location you specify, giving you two copies of the same file.

Why? *Because the search results include the pictures you were looking for, you now can select the files and then copy them to the Pictures library.* Once the three files have been copied to the Pictures library, the files will be stored in both the My Pictures folder (the default save location) and Windows folder on drive C. Copying and moving files are common tasks when working with Windows. If you want to move a file instead of copy a file, you use the Cut button on the ribbon to move the file to the Clipboard and the Paste command to copy the file from the Clipboard to the new location. When the paste is complete, the files are moved into the new folder and no longer are stored in the original folder.

The following steps copy the img0, img2, and img4 files from the Windows folder to the Pictures library.

1

- Tap or click the item check boxes for the img0, img2, and img4 pictures to select the files (Figure 2–25). If you do not see the item check boxes to the left of the image names, tap or click the 'Item check boxes' check box (View tab | Show/hide group).

Q&A Are copying and moving the same?

No. When you copy a file, it is located in both the place to which it was copied and in the place from which it was copied. When you move a file, it is located only in the location to which it was moved.

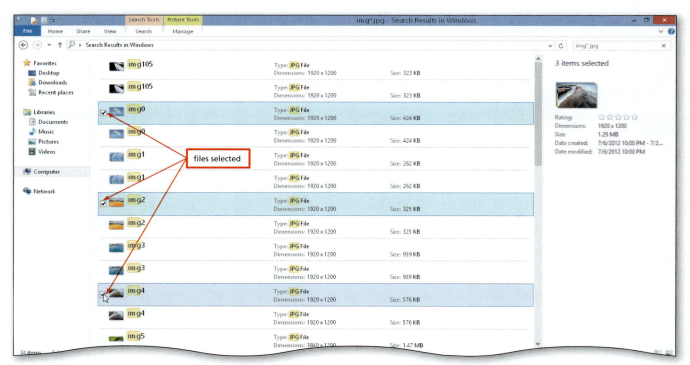

Figure 2–25

2

- Tap or click Home on the ribbon to display the Home tab.
- Tap or click the Copy button (Home tab | Clipboard group) to copy the files to the Clipboard (Figure 2–26).

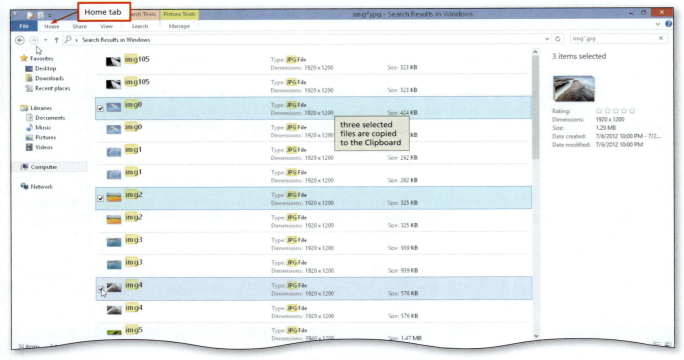

Figure 2–26

3

- Make the Pictures library the active window (Figure 2–27).

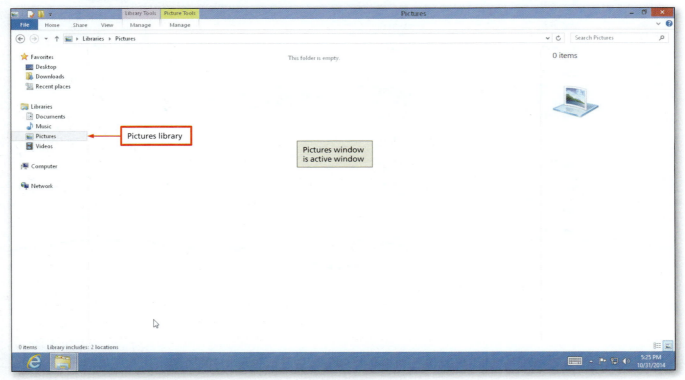

Figure 2–27

- Tap or click Home on the ribbon to display the Home tab.
- Tap or click the Paste button (Home tab | Clipboard group) to paste the files in the Pictures library (Figure 2–28).

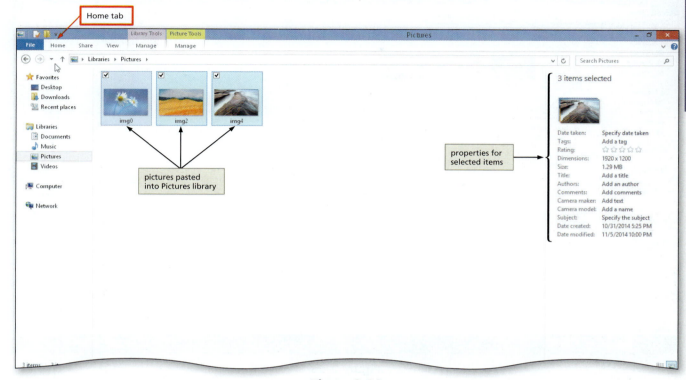

Figure 2–28

Other Ways

1. Select file icons, press and hold, then release, or right-click, tap or click Copy on shortcut menu; display window where you want to store files, press and hold, then release, or right-click, tap or click Paste on shortcut menu

2. Select file icons, press CTRL+C, display window where you want to store files, press CTRL+V

To Close the Search Results Window

You no longer need the Search Results window open, so you can close it. Whenever you are not using a window, it is a good idea to close it so as not to clutter your desktop. The following steps close the Search Results window.

1 Display the Search Results window.

2 Close the Search Results window.

To Create a Folder in the Pictures Library

Why? *When you have several related files stored in a folder with a number of unrelated files, you might want to create a folder to contain the related files so that you can find and reference them easily.* To reduce clutter and improve the organization of files in the Pictures library, you will create a new folder in the Pictures library and then move the pictures you copied into the new folder. The following steps create the Backgrounds folder in the Pictures library.

1

- Tap or click the New folder button on the Quick Access Toolbar to create a new folder (Figure 2–29).

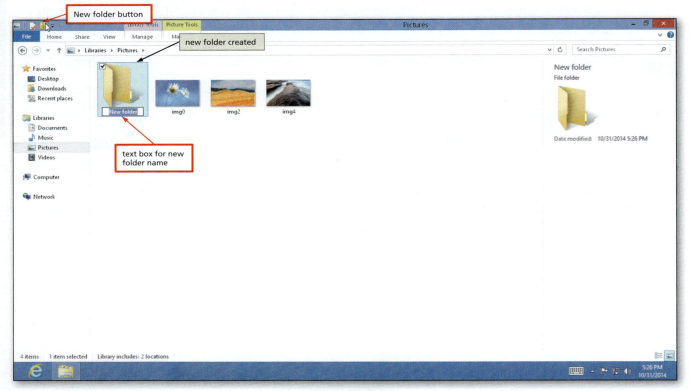

Figure 2–29

2

- Type Backgrounds in the new folder's text box and then press the ENTER key to assign the name to the new folder (Figure 2–30).

Figure 2–30

Other Ways

1. Right-click, point to New, tap or click Folder on shortcut menu   2. Tap or click New folder button (Home tab | New group)

To Move Multiple Files into a Folder

Why? *After you create the Backgrounds folder in the Pictures library, the next step is to move the three picture files into the folder.* The following steps move the img0, img2, and img4 files into the Backgrounds folder.

1
- Tap or click the check box for the Backgrounds folder to deselect the folder.
- Tap or click the item check boxes for the img0, img2, and img4 pictures to select the files (Figure 2–31).

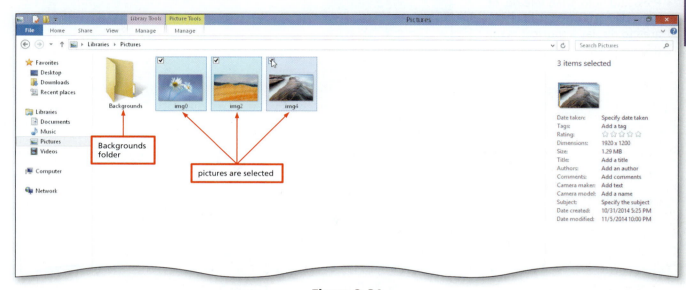

Figure 2–31

2
- Drag the selected icons to the Backgrounds folder and then release to move the files to the Backgrounds folder (Figure 2–32).

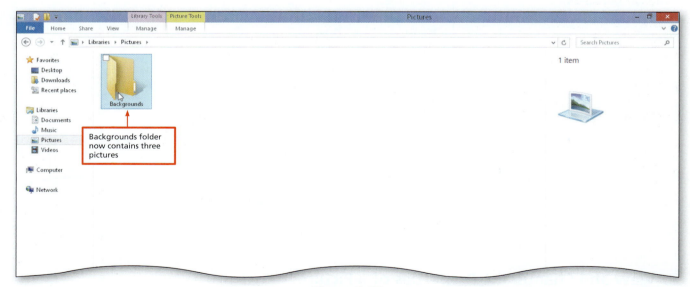

Figure 2–32

Other Ways

1. Drag icons individually to folder icon

2. Press and hold, then release, or right-click icon, tap or click Cut on shortcut menu; press and hold, then release, or right-click folder icon, tap or click Paste on shortcut menu

To Refresh the Image on a Folder

Why? *After moving the three files into the Backgrounds folder, it still appears as an empty open folder icon.* To replace the empty folder icon with a live preview of the three files stored in the Backgrounds folder (img0, img2, and img4), the Pictures library must be refreshed. The following steps refresh the Pictures library to display the live preview for the Backgrounds folder.

- Press and hold, then release, or right-click any open part of the list area to display a shortcut menu (Figure 2–33).

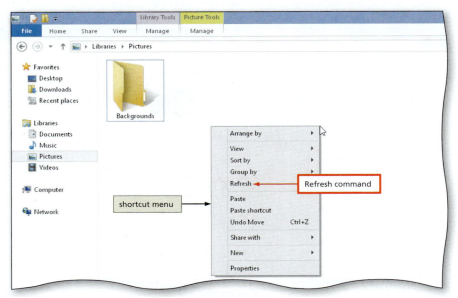

Figure 2–33

- Tap or click Refresh on the shortcut menu to refresh the list area (Figure 2–34).

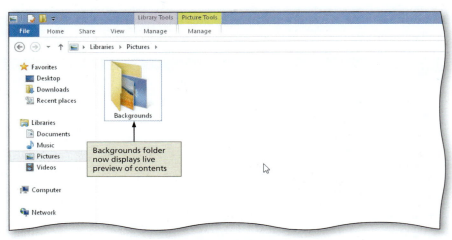

Figure 2–34

To View and Change the Properties of a Picture

As mentioned earlier in the chapter, in Windows, all objects have properties. You already have explored the properties of a drive, and now you will review the properties of a picture. Picture properties include the Size, Title, Authors, State, Date taken, Tags, Rating, and Dimensions. State refers to whether or not the picture is shared with other users on the computer. Date taken refers to the date the person created the picture.

Why? *Tags are keywords you associate with a picture file to aid in its classification. For example, you could tag a family photo with the names of the people in the photo.* When you create a tag, it should be meaningful. For example, if you have pictures from a family vacation at the beach and you add the title, vacation, you later will be able to find the file using the tag, vacation, in a search. Be aware that you can search only for tags that you already have created. If your family vacation photo was saved as photo1.jpg and tagged with the tag, vacation, you will not find it by searching for the word, beach, as it is not part of the name or tag. Rating refers to the ranking, in stars, that you assign to a picture. You can rate a picture from zero to five stars. Date taken, Tags, and Rating all can be changed using the details pane. Because you do not know when the Background pictures were created, you will change only the Tags and Rating properties. The following steps display and change the Tags and Rating properties of the Monet image in the Backgrounds folder.

1
- Display the contents of the Backgrounds folder.
- Tap or click the img4 icon to select it (Figure 2–35).

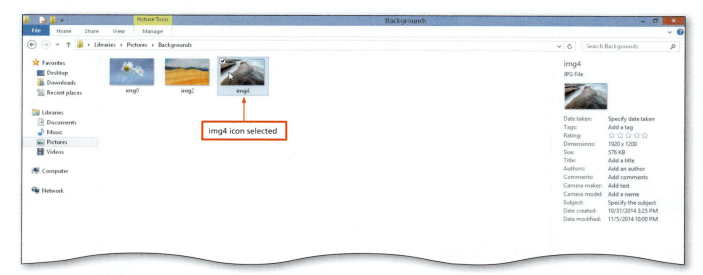

Figure 2–35

2
- Tap or click the 'Add a tag' text box in the details pane to activate it (Figure 2–36).

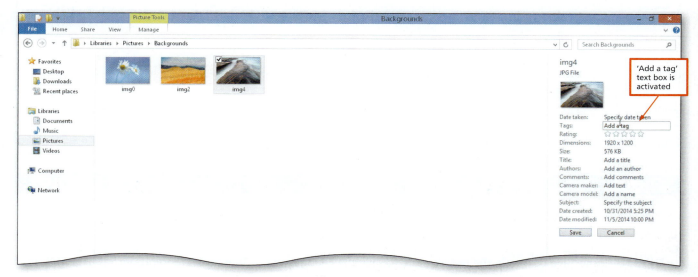

Figure 2–36

3

• Type `Majestic Scene` in the text box to create a tag for the picture (Figure 2–37).

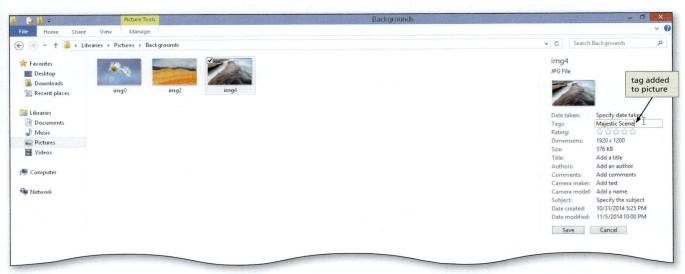

Figure 2–37

4

• Tap or click the third star next to the Rating heading in the details pane to assign a three-star rating to the picture (Figure 2–38).

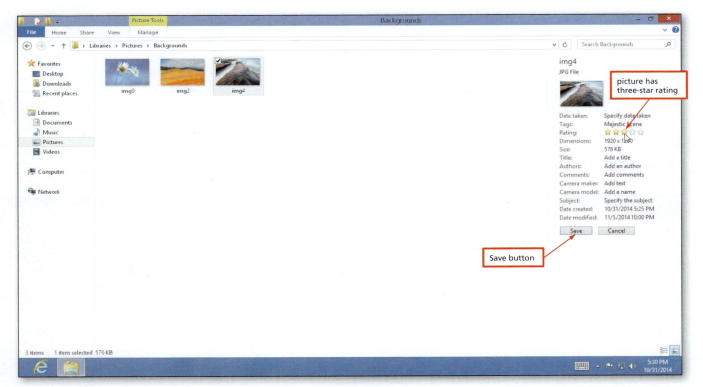

Figure 2–38

5

• Tap or click the Save button in the details pane to save the changes to the Tags and Rating properties (Figure 2–39).

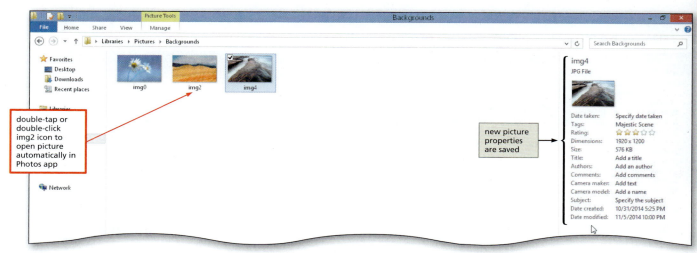

double-tap or double-click img2 icon to open picture automatically in Photos app

new picture properties are saved

Figure 2–39

Other Ways

1. Press and hold, then release, or right-click icon, tap or click Properties, tap or click Details tab, tap or click third star next to Rating, enter text next to Tags, tap or click OK button

To View a Picture in the Photos App

Why? *You can view the images in a folder in the Photos app or as a slide show.* The **Photos app** allows you to view, print, burn, send via email, and open the pictures in your Pictures library. You can view pictures individually or as part of a slide show.

The following steps display the img2 picture in the Backgrounds folder in the Photos app.

1
- Select the img2 picture.
- Double-tap or double-click the icon to display the picture in the Photos app (Figure 2–40).

img2 opened in Photos app

Figure 2–40

2

- After viewing the picture, display the desktop (Figure 2–41).

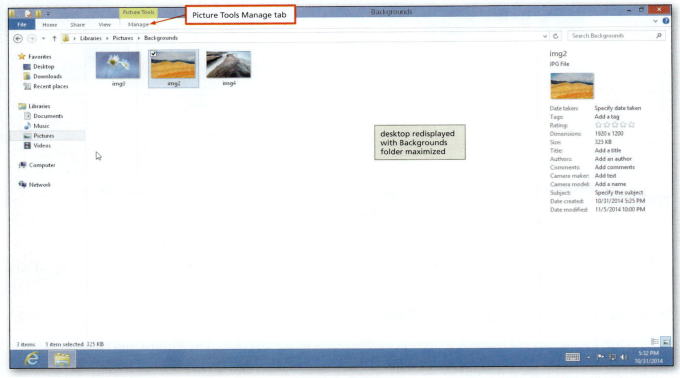

Figure 2–41

To View Your Pictures as a Slide Show

In Windows, you can view your pictures as a **slide show**, which displays each image in the folder in a presentation format on the computer screen. The slide show automatically will display one picture at a time while everything else on the desktop is hidden from sight. The slide show allows you to select whether the pictures will loop in order or will be shuffled to appear in random order. You also can select the speed at which the pictures are displayed, pause the slide show, and exit the slide show. The following steps view the images in the Backgrounds folder as a slide show.

1

- Tap or click the Slide show button (Picture Tools Manage tab | View group) to view the selected files as a slide show (Figure 2–42).

2

- Watch the show for a few seconds while the pictures change.

Q&A Can I change the slide show speed?

Yes, you can press and hold, then release, or right-click and then select speeds of Slow, Medium, and Fast on the shortcut menu.

Figure 2–42

To End a Slide Show

When you are done viewing the slide show, the next step is to end it. The following step ends the slide show.

1
- Press the ESC key to end the slide show (Figure 2–43).

Figure 2–43

Zipping Files and Folders

Sometimes when working with files, you may need to send them via email, post them online, or even transfer them to another computer. If the files are large or numerous, you can make it easier to manage by zipping the files. Zipping a file creates a **zipped file** that will contain compressed copies of the files. You also can zip folders so that your zipped file has a copy of your folder in it.

To Zip a Folder

Why? *You want to send the pictures to a friend via an email message, but you want to attach only one file, not three separate ones.* The following step zips the Backgrounds folder.

1

• Navigate to the Pictures library.

• If necessary, select the Backgrounds folder.

• Click Share on the ribbon to display the Share tab.

• Tap or click the Zip button (Share tab | Send group) to create a zipped file (Figure 2–44). Press the ENTER key to accept the file name Windows gave to the file.

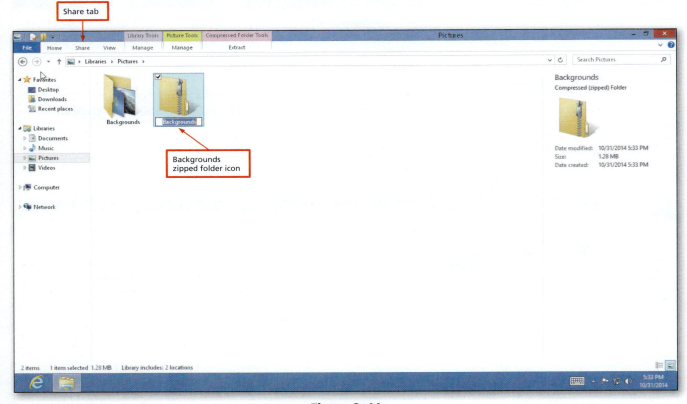

Figure 2–44

To View the Contents of a Zipped Folder

Why? *You want to verify that the files are in the zipped folder before you share it.* You can open a zipped folder and then view the contents as if you were browsing a regular folder. The following steps display the contents of the Backgrounds zipped folder.

- Double-tap or double-click the Backgrounds zipped folder icon to display the contents of the zipped folder (Figure 2–45).

Figure 2–45

2

- Double-tap or double-click the Backgrounds folder to display the contents of the folder (Figure 2–46).

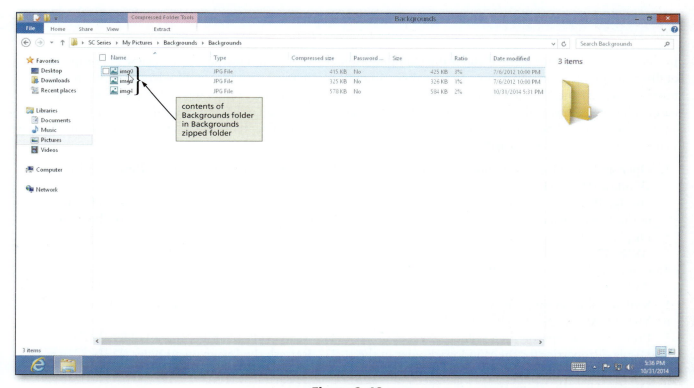

Figure 2–46

Other Ways

1. Right-click or press and hold folder, tap or point to Send on shortcut menu, tap or click Compressed (zipped) folder command

To Delete a Folder from the Pictures Library

To return the Pictures library to its original state, you will delete the Backgrounds folder and the Backgrounds zipped folder. The following steps delete the Backgrounds folder and the Backgrounds zipped folder.

1 Navigate to the Pictures library.

2 Select the Backgrounds folder, display the Home tab, and then tap or click the Delete button (Home tab | Organize group) to delete the Backgrounds folder.

3 Select the Backgrounds zipped folder, display the Home tab, and then tap or click the Delete button (Home tab | Organize group) to delete the Backgrounds zipped folder.

4 Close the Pictures library window.

To Sign Out of Your Account and Turn Off the Computer

After completing your work with Windows, you should follow these steps to end your session by signing out of your account and then turning off the computer.

1 Display the Charms bar.

2 Tap or click the Settings charm.

3 Tap or click the Power button to display the Power menu.

4 Tap or click the Shut down button to sign out of your account and shut down the computer.

Chapter Summary

In this chapter, you have learned about the Computer folder window. You learned how to view the properties of drives and folders, as well as how to view their content. You worked with files and folders in the Pictures library, reviewed and changed their properties, and viewed images in the Photos app and as a slide show. As part of this process, you also learned how to copy and move files as well as how to create folders. Finally, you gained knowledge of how to zip folders so that you can share them. The items listed below include all of the new Windows skills you have learned in this chapter.

1. Open and Maximize the Computer Folder Window (WIN 51)
2. Display Properties for the Local Disk (C:) Drive in the Details Pane (WIN 52)
3. Display the Local Disk (C:) Properties Dialog Box (WIN 53)
4. Close the Local Disk (C:) Properties Dialog Box (WIN 54)
5. Switch Folders Using the Address Bar (WIN 55)
6. View the Contents of a Drive (WIN 56)
7. Preview the Properties of a Folder (WIN 57)
8. Display Properties for the Windows Folder in the Details Pane (WIN 57)
9. Display All of the Properties of the Windows Folder (WIN 58)
10. View the Contents of a Folder (WIN 59)
11. Search for a File and Folder in a Folder Window (WIN 60)
12. Clear the Search Box (WIN 61)
13. Use Shake to Minimize and Restore All Windows (WIN 62)
14. Use Snap to Maximize Windows (WIN 63)
15. Use the Show Desktop Button to Minimize All Windows (WIN 63)
16. Restore a Window (WIN 64)
17. Search for Pictures (WIN 66)
18. Copy Files to the Pictures Library (WIN 67)
19. Create a Folder in the Pictures Library (WIN 69)
20. Move Multiple Files into a Folder (WIN 71)
21. Refresh the Image on a Folder (WIN 72)
22. View and Change the Properties of a Picture (WIN 72)
23. View a Picture in the Photos App (WIN 75)
24. View Pictures as a Slide Show (WIN 76)
25. End a Slide Show (WIN 77)
26. Zip a Folder (WIN 78)
27. View the Contents of a Zipped Folder (WIN 79)

Apply Your Knowledge

Use Windows 8 and its apps to perform the following tasks.

File and App Properties

Instructions: You want to demonstrate to a friend how to display the properties of an image, display the image using the Paint app instead of the Windows Photo Viewer app, and print the image. You also want to demonstrate how to display the properties of an app.

Part 1: Displaying File Properties

1. Display the desktop and then tap or click the File Explorer app button to open the File Explorer window.
2. Tap or click the Computer icon in the navigation pane to display its contents.
3. Double-tap or double-click the Local Disk (C:) icon.
4. Double-tap or double-click the Windows folder.
5. Search for the img3 picture file. If the img3 file is not available on your computer, find another image file.
6. Press and hold, then release, or right-click the img3 icon. Tap or click Properties on the shortcut menu. Answer the following questions about the img3 file:
   a. What type of file is img3?
   b. What app is used to open the img3 image?
   c. What is the path for the location of the img3 file?
   d. What is the size (in bytes) of the img3 file?
   e. When was the file created?
   f. When was the file last modified?
   g. When was the file last accessed?

Part 2: Using the Paint App to Display an Image

1. Tap or click the Change button in the img3 Properties dialog box. Answer the following question:
   a. Which app(s) can you use to open the file?
2. Tap or click the Paint icon in the dialog box.
3. Tap or click the OK button in the img3 Properties dialog box.
4. Double-tap or double-click the img3 icon to run the Paint app and open the img3 file in the img3 – Paint window (Figure 2–47 on the next page).
5. Print the image by tapping or clicking the File tab on the ribbon, tapping or clicking the Print command, and then tapping or clicking the Print button (Print dialog box).
6. Close the Paint window. Do not save any changes.

Part 3: Resetting the App Selection

1. Press and hold, then release, or right-click the img3 icon. Tap or click Properties on the shortcut menu.
2. Tap or click the Change button (img3 Properties dialog box).
3. If necessary, tap or click the Windows Photo Viewer icon in the dialog box to select the icon.
4. Tap or click the OK button.

Continued >

Apply Your Knowledge *continued*

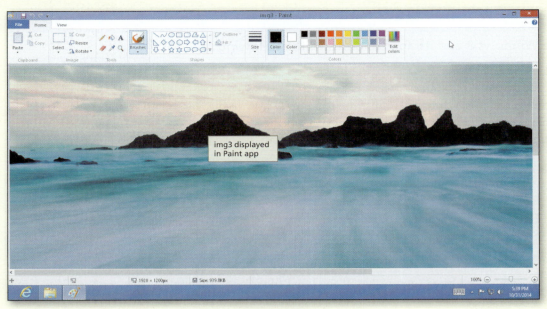

Figure 2–47

Part 4: Displaying App Properties

1. Return to the search results in the Windows folder and clear the Search box.

2. Scroll through the file list until the HelpPane icon appears. If the HelpPane icon does not appear, scroll to display another file.

3. Press and hold, then release, or right-click the icon. Tap or click Properties on the shortcut menu. Answer the following questions:

   a. What type of file is selected?

   b. What is the file's description?

   c. What is the path of the file?

   d. What size is the file when stored on disk?

4. Tap or click the Cancel button (HelpPane.exe Properties dialog box).

5. Close the Windows window.

Extend Your Knowledge

Extend the skills you learned in this chapter and experiment with new skills. You might need to use Help to complete the assignment.

Creating a Picture

Instructions: You want to use Paint to design a get well soon greeting for a friend and then print the message. Because you do not know the location of the Paint app, you first will search to find it.

Part 1: Searching for the Paint App

1. Display the Charms bar and then tap or click the Search charm.

2. Type paint in the Search box.

3. Tap or click Paint to run the Paint app (Figure 2–48).

Part 2: Creating a Bitmap Image

1. Use the Pencil button shown in Figure 2–48 to write the message, Get Well Soon! *Hint:* Hold down the left mouse button to write and release the left mouse button to stop writing. If you make a mistake and want to start over, tap or click the Undo button on the Quick Access Toolbar.

2. Tap or click the File tab on the ribbon and then tap or click Save as. When the Save As dialog box is displayed, type `Get Well Soon` in the File name text box, if necessary tap or click the Pictures library in the navigation pane, and then tap or click the Save button (Save As dialog box) to save the file in the Pictures library.

3. Exit Paint.

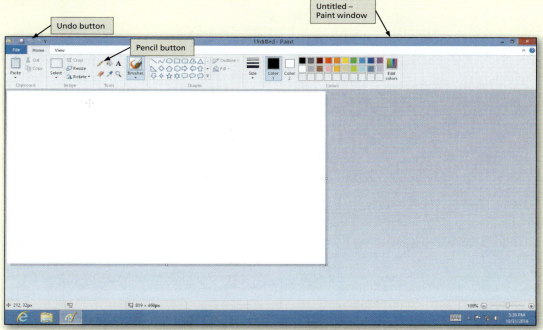

Figure 2–48

Part 3: Viewing and Printing the Get Well Soon Image

1. Open the Pictures library folder.

2. Double-tap or double-click the Get Well Soon icon in the Pictures window to open the picture in the Photos app.

3. After viewing the image in the Photos app, display the desktop.

4. Display the Share tab, and then tap or click Print (Share tab | Send group) to display the Print Pictures dialog box.

5. Tap or click the Print button (Print Pictures dialog box) to print the image.

6. Close the Print Pictures dialog box.

Part 4: Deleting the Get Well Soon Image

1. Tap or click the Get Well Soon icon to select the file.

2. Tap or click the Delete button (Home tab | Organize group).

3. Close the Pictures library window.

STUDENT ASSIGNMENTS

In the Lab

Use the guidelines, concepts, and skills presented in this chapter to increase your knowledge of Windows 8. Labs are listed in order of increasing difficulty.

Lab 1: Using Search to Find Picture Files

Instructions: You know that searching is an important feature of Windows. You decide to use the Search box to find the images on the hard disk. You will store the files in a folder in the Pictures library and then print the images.

Part 1: Searching for Files in the Search Results Window

1. If necessary, start Windows and sign in to your account.
2. Display the desktop.
3. Tap or click the File Explorer app button. Navigate to the Computer folder. Maximize the Computer folder window.
4. Double-tap or double-click Local Disk (C:), and then double-tap or double-click the Windows folder to open it.
5. In the Search box, type bears as the entry.
6. Copy the image to the Pictures library using the navigation pane.

Part 2: Searching for Groups of Files

1. Navigate to the Computer folder. Maximize the Computer folder window.
2. Double-tap or double-click Local Disk (C:) and then double-tap or double-click the Windows folder to open it.
3. In the Search box of the Windows folder, type img1* as the search text (Figure 2–49).
4. Answer the following question:
   a. How many files were found?
5. Tap or click the img101 icon to select the icon. If the img101 icon does not appear, select another icon.
6. Copy the image to the Pictures library.

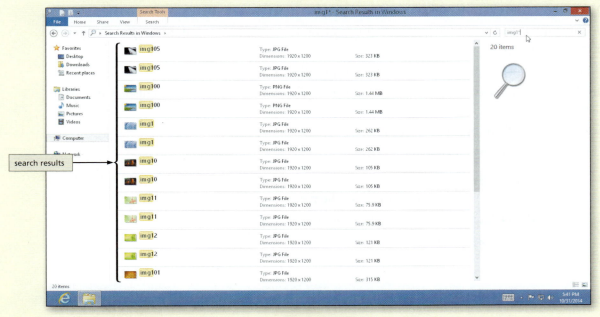

Figure 2–49

Part 3: Creating the More Backgrounds Folder in the Pictures Library

1. If necessary, navigate to the Pictures library. Tap or click the New folder button on the Quick Access Toolbar, type `More Backgrounds` in the new folder's text box, and then press the ENTER key.

2. Select the icons of the images you copied to the Pictures library and then move the images to the More Backgrounds folder.

3. Press and hold, then release, or right-click an open area of the window and refresh the image on the More Backgrounds folder.

Part 4: Printing the Images

1. Open the More Backgrounds folder.

2. Select the pictures.

3. Display the Share tab, tap or click the Print button (Share tab | Send group) and then tap or click the Print button (Print Pictures dialog box) to print the photos.

4. Delete the Backgrounds folder from the Pictures library.

5. Close the Pictures library window.

In the Lab

Lab 2: Finding Pictures Online

Instructions: A friend informs you that the Internet is a great source of photos, pictures, and images. You decide to run Internet Explorer, search for well-known company logos on the Internet, and then save them in a folder. A **logo** is an image that identifies businesses, government agencies, products, and other entities. In addition, you want to print the logos.

Part 1: Running the Internet Explorer App Using the File Explorer

1. Display the desktop and then double-click the File Explorer app button.

2. In the navigation pane, if necessary, click the white arrow next to Computer to display its contents.

3. Tap or click the white arrow next to Local Disk (C:) to display its contents.

4. Tap or click the white arrow next to the Program Files folder to display its contents.

5. Display the contents of the Internet Explorer folder.

6. Double-tap or double-click the iexplore icon to run Internet Explorer and open the Internet Explorer window.

Part 2: Finding and Saving Logo Images

1. Type `www.google.com` in the address bar in the Internet Explorer window, and then tap or click the Go button.

2. Locate the Google logo icon. Press and hold, then release, or right-click the icon, tap or click 'Save picture as' on the shortcut menu, name the file Google logo, and then tap or click the Save button (Save As dialog box) to save the logo in the Pictures library. If you are unable to save this image, contact your instructor for an alternate image to save for this step.

3. Type `www.microsoft.com` in the address bar and then tap or click the Go button. Locate the Microsoft picture that matches the one in Figure 2–50 and use the file name, Microsoft logo, to save the Microsoft logo in the Pictures library.

4. Close the Internet Explorer window.

Continued >

In the Lab *continued*

5. Make the File Explorer window the active window and navigate to the Pictures library. The Google logo and Microsoft image appear in the Pictures window (Figure 2–50). The logos in the Pictures library window on your computer might be different from the logos shown in Figure 2–50 if the businesses have changed their logos.

Part 3: Displaying File Properties

1. Press and hold, then release, or right-click each logo file in the Pictures library, tap or click Properties on the shortcut menu, answer the following questions about the logos, and then close the Properties dialog box.

  a. What type of file is the Google logo file?

  b. What type of file is the Microsoft logo file?

2. Tap or click an open area of the Pictures library to deselect the logo file.

Part 4: Creating the Logos Folder in the Pictures Library

1. Create a new folder in the Pictures library, type Logos in the new folder's text box, and then press the ENTER key.

2. Tap or click the item check boxes for each logo to select the files.

3. Drag the icons to the Logos folder.

4. Refresh the image on the Logos folder.

Part 5: Printing the Logo Images

1. Open the Logos folder.

2. Select both of the logos.

3. Display the Share tab, tap or click the Print button (Share tab | Send group), and then tap or click the Print button (Print Pictures dialog box) to print the pictures.

4. Delete the Logos folder from the Pictures library.

5. Close the Pictures window.

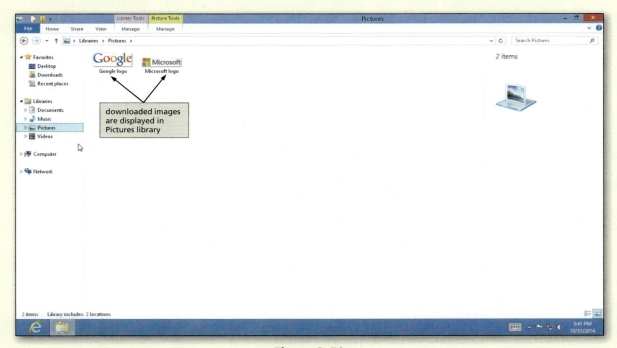

Figure 2–50

In the Lab

Lab 3: Managing Your Music

Instructions: You want to investigate the different ways you can organize the music stored on your computer. Once you determine which method of organizing your music you prefer, you decide that you want to add to your music collection. First you will learn about the copyright laws that pertain to digital music and then you will research a few websites that allow you to download music files.

Part 1: Researching Copyright Laws Regarding Digital Music Files

1. Tap or click the Internet Explorer app button on the taskbar. Type `www.copyright.gov` in the address bar and then press the ENTER key. Tap or click the link to display the Frequently Asked Questions, and then answer the following questions:

    a. Can you copyright a domain name?

    b. Can a minor claim a copyright?

    c. What does a copyright protect?

Part 2: Finding Music Online

1. Type `www.globalmusicproject.org` in the address bar, press the ENTER key, and then answer the following questions:

    a. What types of music can be downloaded from this website?

    b. What is the Global Music Project?

    c. Would you use this service?

2. Type `rhapsody.com` in the address bar, press the ENTER key (Figure 2–51), and then answer the following questions:

    a. What does Rhapsody provide?

    b. On what types of devices can you use Rhapsody to listen to music?

    c. Is there a fee for using this service?

    d. Would you use this service?

Figure 2–51

Continued >

STUDENT ASSIGNMENTS

In the Lab continued

3. Type www.apple.com/itunes in the address bar, press the ENTER key, and then answer the following questions:

    a. What is the latest version of iTunes?

    b. What is the iTunes Player?

    c. What is the top song right now on the iTunes Charts?

    d. Would you use this service?

Cases and Places

Apply your creative thinking and problem-solving skills to design and implement a solution.

1: Finding Apps

Academic

You are interested in identifying which apps are installed on your school computer. To find all the apps, you decide to search the Program Files folder on the computer. Using techniques you learned in this chapter, open the Program Files folder on drive C. Search for *.exe files. Summarize your findings in a brief report. Be sure to indicate the number of apps you found.

2: Researching Photo Printing Sites

Personal

Now that you know how to work with the Pictures library, you want to find websites where you can upload and print your photos. Using the Internet, search for three photo printing websites. Find the prices per 4 × 6 photo and which file formats are required, and explore any other photo products that you would be interested in purchasing. Write a brief report that compares the three websites and indicate which one you would use.

3: Researching Data Security

Professional

Data stored on disk is one of a company's most valuable assets. If that data were to be stolen, lost, or compromised so that it could not be accessed, the company could go out of business. Therefore, companies go to great lengths to protect their data. Working with classmates, research how the companies where you each work handle their backups. Find out how each one protects its data against malware, unauthorized access, and even against natural disasters such as fire and floods. Prepare a brief report that describes the companies' procedures. In your report, point out any areas where you find a company has not protected its data adequately.

LEARN ONLINE

Reinforce what you learned in this chapter with games, exercises, training, and many other online activities and resources.

Student Companion Site: Reinforce chapter terms and concepts using review questions, flash cards, practice tests, and interactive learning games, such as a crossword puzzle. These and other online activities and resources are available at no additional cost on www.cengagebrain.com. Visit www.cengage.com/ct/studentdownload for detailed instructions about accessing the resources available at the Student Companion Site.

3 Personalizing Windows

Objectives

You will have mastered the material in this chapter when you can:

- Differentiate among the various types of user accounts
- Create user accounts
- Understand cloud computing
- Personalize the lock screen
- Customize the Start screen
- Create a picture password
- Turn off a live tile
- Create a tile group on the Start screen
- Name a tile group

3 | Personalizing Windows

Introduction

One of the best ways to improve productivity while using a computer is to personalize your work environment. For example, you can rearrange the tiles on the Start screen so that the tiles you use most often are first or remove tiles for apps you do not use frequently. Similarly, users often personalize their computers by adding unique touches. This includes changing their lock screen and Start screen to display the apps and colors relevant to them. By personalizing the work environment, users feel more in tune with their computers, which can put them more at ease and lead to improved productivity.

Overview

As you read this chapter, you will learn how to personalize your Windows 8 environment by performing these general tasks:

- Add an account
- Customize the lock screen
- Personalize the Start screen
- Manipulate tiles
- Create and name a tile group

User Account

A **user account** is a collection of information that Windows requires about a computer user. When you sign in to an account, the Start screen shows the user account that is signed in at the upper-right corner of the screen. Information is saved for each user account, including the user name, password, picture, and rights and permissions the user has for accessing a computer or network resources. User accounts make it possible for each user to perform tasks, such as sign in to the computer, keep information confidential and computer settings protected, customize Windows, store files in unique folders, and maintain a personal list of favorite websites.

Normally, user accounts operate in standard user mode, which allows you to use most of the capabilities of the computer. A standard user cannot install software that affects other users or change system settings that affect security. An administrator account has full control of the computer and operating system and can change user permissions, install software that affects all users, and change all system settings. When a task requires administrator access, depending on how Windows is configured, the User Account Control feature might prompt you to authorize the task. By default, you are asked for permission only when programs attempt to make a change to the computer. Once authorized, the user has temporary administrator privileges. After the task is finished, the user returns to standard user mode. User Account Control is designed to prevent malicious software from being installed inadvertently, even by administrators. For standard user accounts, the user needs to know an administrator account user name and the password to authorize User Account Control. Only administrators are prompted to continue without requiring a user name and password. Table 3–1 provides a list of the different privileges for the account types.

Table 3–1 User Accounts and Privileges

User Account Type	Privileges
Administrator	• Create, change, and delete user accounts and groups • Install programs • Set folder sharing • Set permissions • Access all files • Take ownership of files • Grant rights to other user accounts and to themselves • Install or remove hardware devices • Sign in using safe mode
Standard	• Change the password and picture for their own user accounts • Use programs that have been installed on the computer • View permissions • Create, change, and delete files in their libraries • View files in shared document folders
Guest	• Same as standard account, but cannot create a password • Is turned off by default, and must be turned on before it can be used

What Is a Local Account?

Windows supports Microsoft accounts and local accounts. A **local account** is an account that works on only one computer. A local account can be either an administrative or a standard account. A local account does not integrate automatically with the cloud, which enables features such as saving files on SkyDrive. **SkyDrive** is a cloud storage location used for storing files on the Internet and for sharing files with other users.

What Is a Microsoft Account?

If you create a Microsoft account on Microsoft's website, you can have access to email, SkyDrive, and Microsoft Office web apps. When you are signed in with a Microsoft account, you can access the services provided on the web for Microsoft account holders. Apps that support Microsoft accounts will allow you to use the associated services that a local account may not be able to use, such as SkyDrive. When you add a Microsoft account to your computer, like a local account, it can be an administrative or a standard account.

When using a Microsoft account, your sign-in settings can be saved on the Internet. When you sign in to Windows on another computer, your settings will be used from your Microsoft account. You can sync your account to the web, which allows you to carry your settings from computer to computer without needing a local account. In some lab settings, you may not be able to use your Microsoft account if the lab does not allow you to sign in without a local account. Your instructor can tell you if you can sign in using your Microsoft account.

To Create a Microsoft Account

The following steps create a Microsoft account. *Why? You might want to have a Microsoft account so that you can save files on SkyDrive and synchronize your user settings.*

1

• Click the Desktop tile to display the desktop (Figure 3–1).

desktop
displayed

Figure 3–1

2

• Tap or click the Internet Explorer app button on the taskbar to run Internet Explorer (Figure 3–2).

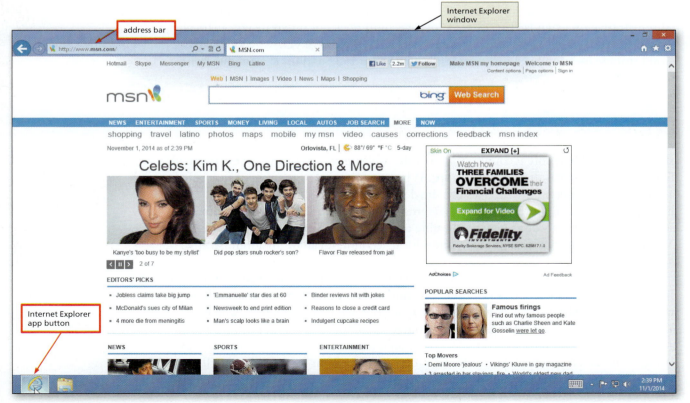

Internet Explorer
window

address bar

Internet Explorer
app button

Figure 3–2

3

- Type `windows.live.com` in the address bar to display the windows.live.com webpage (Figure 3–3).

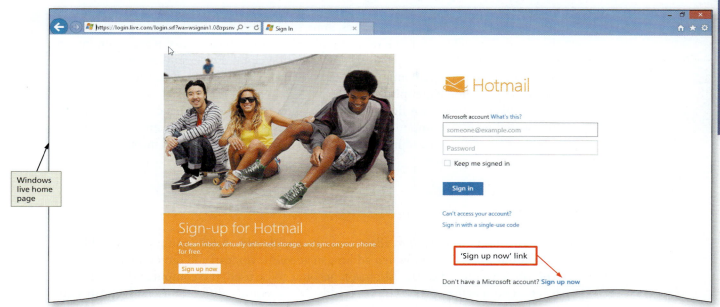

Windows live home page

'Sign up now' link

Figure 3–3

4

- Tap or click the 'Sign up now' link to display the Sign up - Microsoft account webpage (Figure 3–4).
- Complete the Microsoft Account form to create your account.
- Tap or click the I accept button at the bottom of the form.
- Tap or click the Close button to exit Internet Explorer.

Sign up - Microsoft account webpage

Close button

Microsoft account   Sign in

If you use **Hotmail**, **SkyDrive**, **Xbox LIVE**, or have a Windows Phone, you already have a Microsoft account. Sign in

Who are you?

Name

| First | Last |

Birth date

| Month ∨ | Day ∨ | Year ∨ |

Gender

| Select one ∨ |

How would you like to sign in?

Microsoft account name

| | @ | hotmail.com ∨ | form to enter new account information

Create a password

| |

8-character minimum; case sensitive

Reenter password

| |

If you lose your password, how can we help you reset it?

2:39 PM
11/1/2014

Figure 3–4

What Is Cloud Computing?

Cloud computing is the use of computing resources (hardware and software) that are delivered as a service over the Internet or any other network to which you may be connected. Primarily, services, apps, settings, and so forth would be stored on the cloud. This allows for greater portability because you can move from computer to computer and use the files you have stored on the cloud. For example, you can save your files from a school computer on the cloud and then go home and access the same files from your home computer.

This provides great flexibility because you do not need to have your account or files stored on each computer you use. Instead, you can work online and store your work online, without needing to use external storage devices to pass information from computer to computer.

Setting Up User Accounts

Windows users who want to allow multiple people use of their computer can add an account for each user. When adding an account, you can add either a local or Microsoft account. For the Microsoft account to be used, the computer should have an Internet connection. Once you have added the accounts, different users then can sign in to their account by selecting it on the sign-in screen.

To add an account, you must change your PC settings. The 'Change PC settings' command can be used to customize your Windows environment. Adding accounts is one of the ways to personalize your computer.

To Add a Local Account

The following steps add a local account for SC Student. *Why? You have decided to let another person use your computer.*

- Display the Charms bar.
- Tap or click the Settings charm to display the Settings menu (Figure 3–5).

Figure 3–5

2

• Tap or click 'Change PC settings' to display the PC settings pane (Figure 3–6).

PC settings pane

Figure 3–6

3

• Tap or click Users in the PC settings pane to display the Users settings in the right pane (Figure 3–7).

Q&A Why does my account information look different from the one shown in Figure 3–7?

The information that is displayed depends on your account settings. The account that displays on your computer may be configured differently.

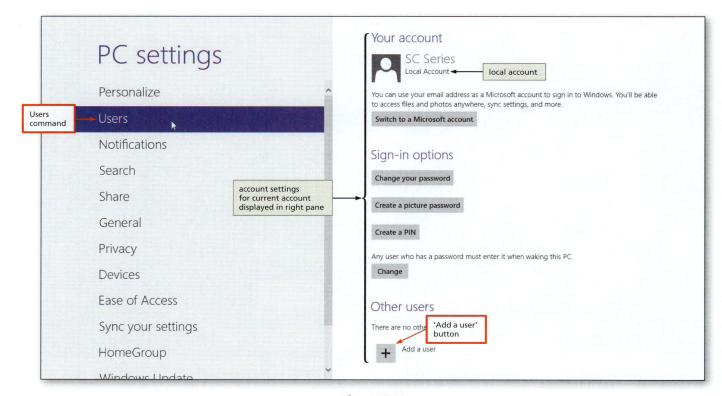

Figure 3–7

4

• Tap or click the 'Add a user' button in the right pane to display the Add a user screen (Figure 3–8).

Figure 3–8

5

• Tap or click the 'Sign in without a Microsoft account' link to display account options (Figure 3–9).

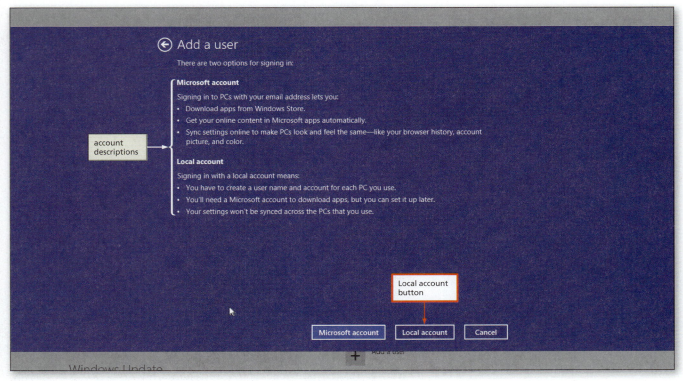

Figure 3–9

6

- Tap or click the Local account button to display the local account form (Figure 3–10).

Figure 3–10

7

- Enter the information for the new account.

- Tap or click the Next button to continue (Figure 3–11).

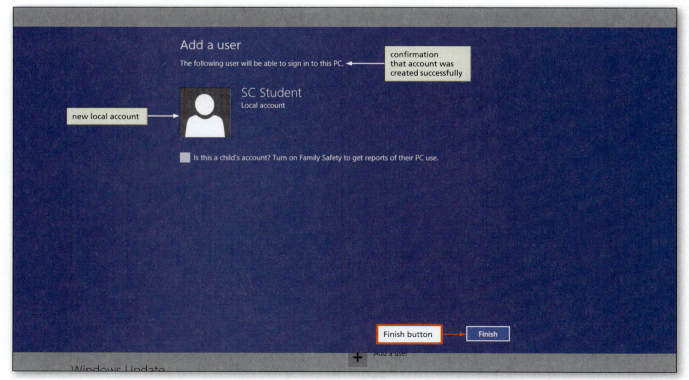

Figure 3–11

8
- Tap or click the Finish button to add the account.
- Scroll down to display the accounts available on your computer (Figure 3–12).

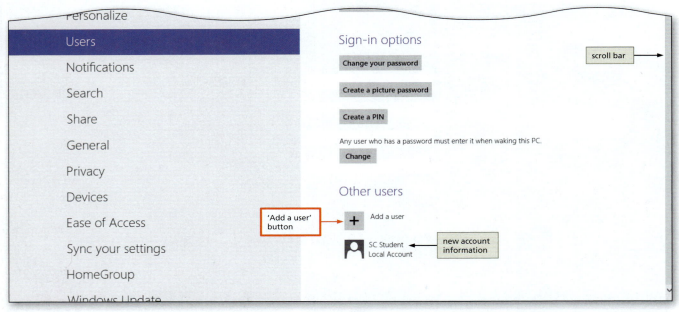

Figure 3–12

To Add a Microsoft Account

The following steps add a Microsoft account. *Why? You recently created a Microsoft account and would like to add it so that you can use the cloud storage options associated with a Microsoft account.*

- Tap or click the 'Add a user' button in the right pane (shown in Figure 3–12) to display the Add a user screen (Figure 3–13).

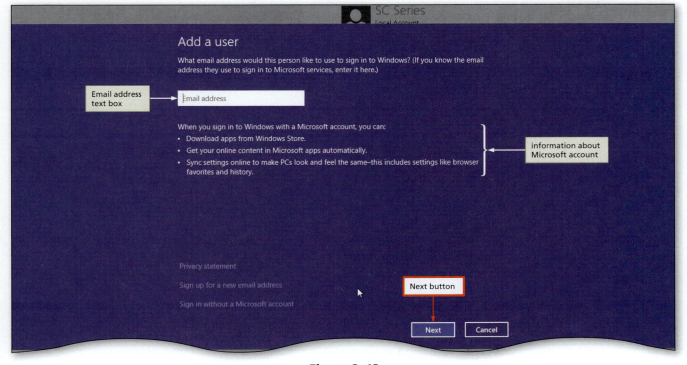

Figure 3–13

2

- Type your Microsoft account email address into the Email address text box.
- Tap or click the Next button to continue creating the account (Figure 3–14).
- Tap or click the Finish button to add the account.

Q&A Why is the email address on my screen different from Figure 3–14?

You used your own Microsoft account. The one in the figure is not your email address.

Figure 3–14

To Sign In to a Microsoft Account

To sign in to a different account, you will first need to sign out of the current account. After you have signed out, you will be able to sign in to the newly created Microsoft account.

1 Display the Charms bar.

2 Tap or click the Start charm on the Charms bar to return to the Start screen.

3 Tap or click the user icon to display user options.

4 Tap or click Sign out to sign out of your account.

5 Swipe or click the lock screen to display the sign-in screen.

6 Tap or click the user icon for your Microsoft account (for SC Series Microsoft, in this case) on the sign-in screen, which depending on settings, either will display a second sign-in screen that contains a password text box or will display the Windows Start screen.

7 If Windows displays a password text box, type your password in the text box and then tap or click the Submit button to sign in to your account and display the Start screen.

Personalizing the Lock and Start Screens

One way to personalize your Windows settings is to change the appearance of the lock screen and the Start screen. For the lock screen, you can change the apps that are displayed to the apps that you want or use most frequently. They will run in the background and be available whenever the lock screen is displayed. You can change the background pattern, as well as the color scheme, displayed on the Start screen.

You personalize the lock screen and Start screen using the PC settings pane.

To Personalize the Lock Screen

The following steps add the Weather app to the lock screen. ***Why?*** *You want to be able to check the weather quickly without having to return to the Start screen each time.*

- Display the Charms bar.
- Tap or click the Settings charm to display the Settings menu (Figure 3–15).
- Tap or click 'Change PC settings' to display the PC settings pane.

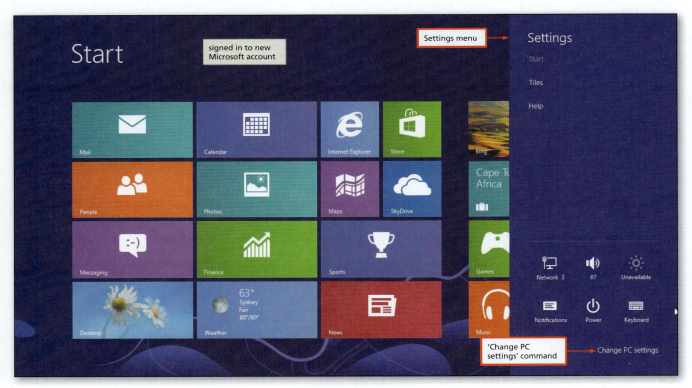

Figure 3–15

2
- Scroll down in the right pane to display the Lock screen apps area (Figure 3–16).

Figure 3–16

3
- Tap or click the first plus sign icon to display the Choose an app menu (Figure 3–17).

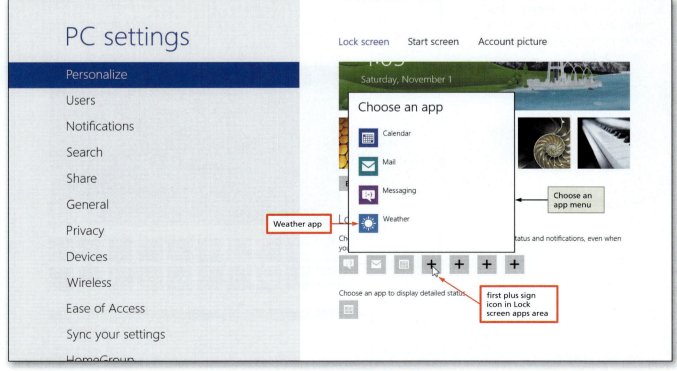

Figure 3–17

4

- Tap or click the Weather app to add it to the lock screen apps (Figure 3–18).

Figure 3–18

To Change the Start Screen Color Scheme

Why? You want to change the color scheme of the Start screen to light blue. The following steps change the Start screen color scheme.

1

- Tap or click Start screen in the right pane to display the Start screen personalization options (Figure 3–19).

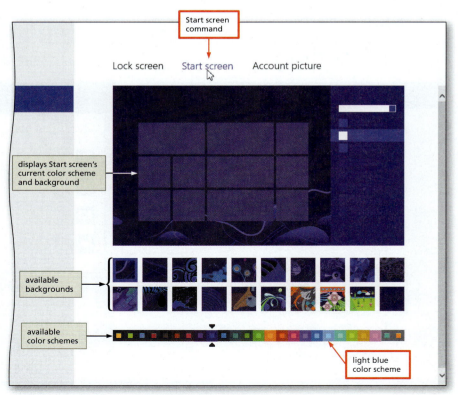

Figure 3–19

- Tap or click the light blue color scheme to change the color scheme to light blue (Figure 3–20).

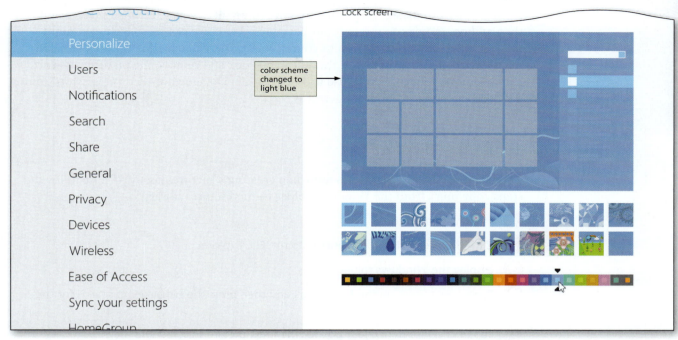

Figure 3–20

To Change the Start Screen Background Pattern

Why? *You want a pattern that makes the light blue color stand out.* The following step changes the Start screen background pattern.

- Tap or click the fourth background pattern in the first row to change the background pattern (Figure 3–21).

Figure 3–21

Adding a Picture Password

Instead of using a password that you have to type in, Windows allows you to use a picture password instead. A **picture password** involves you selecting a picture and then adding gestures to use for your password. A gesture can be a circle, a straight line, or a tap. When you sign in to your account, you will use those gestures to sign in, rather than a password. You always can go back and remove the picture password should you no longer want to use it. Also, you can change your picture password to use a different picture or different gestures.

To Copy a Picture

You will need a picture to use when creating a picture password. The following steps copy img1 from the Windows folder to the Pictures library.

1. Display the desktop.

2. Click the File Explorer app button to run File Explorer.

3. Display the Windows folder.

4. Type `img1.jpg` in the Search box and then press the ENTER key to search for the img1 picture.

5. Tap or click the item check box for the img1 picture to select the file.

6. Tap or click the Copy button (Home tab | Clipboard group) to copy the files to the Clipboard.

7. Tap or click the Pictures folder in the navigation pane to display the Pictures library.

8. Tap or click the Paste button (Home tab | Clipboard group) to paste the file in the Pictures library.

9. Display the PC settings pane.

To Create a Picture Password

Why? *You want to use a picture password so that it is easier to enter on a touch-enabled device.* Once you create the gestures, you will have to repeat them to make sure you are using the same exact gestures. If you recognize that you have made a mistake, you can tap or click the Start over button to begin again. Should you fail to enter them correctly the second time, you will be prompted to try again. The following steps create a picture password.

1
• Tap or click Users in the PC settings pane to display user account information in the right pane (Figure 3–22).

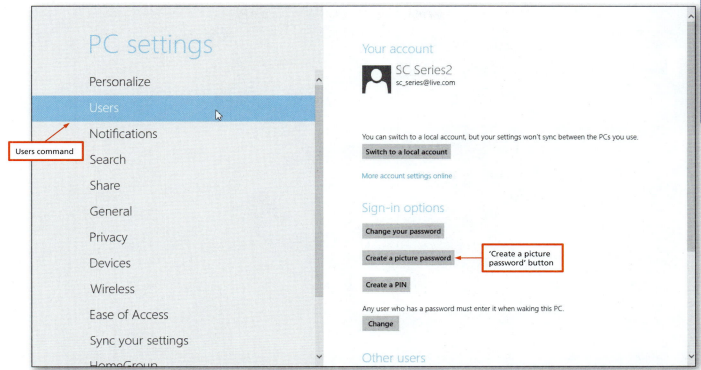

Figure 3–22

2
• Tap or click the 'Create a picture password' button to display the Create a picture password screen (Figure 3–23).

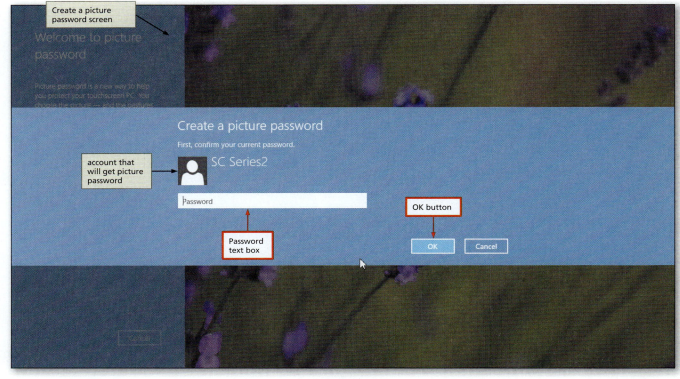

Figure 3–23

- Type your password in the Password text box and then tap or click the OK button to display the picture password instructions (Figure 3–24).

Figure 3–24

- Tap or click the Choose picture button to display a list of pictures.
- Tap or click the img1 file to select the picture (Figure 3–25).

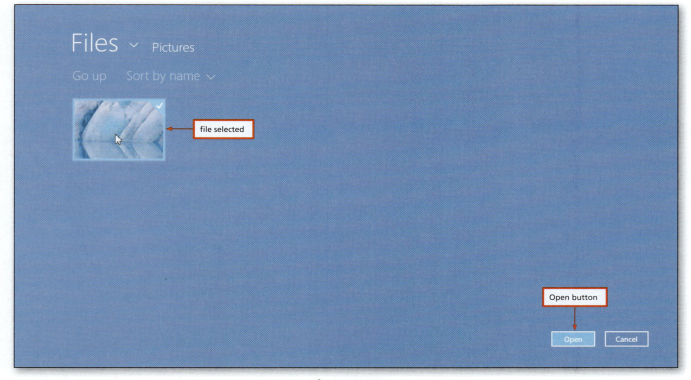

Figure 3–25

5

• Tap or click the Open button to open the picture (Figure 3–26).

Figure 3–26

6

• Tap or click the 'Use this picture' button to use the picture (Figure 3–27).

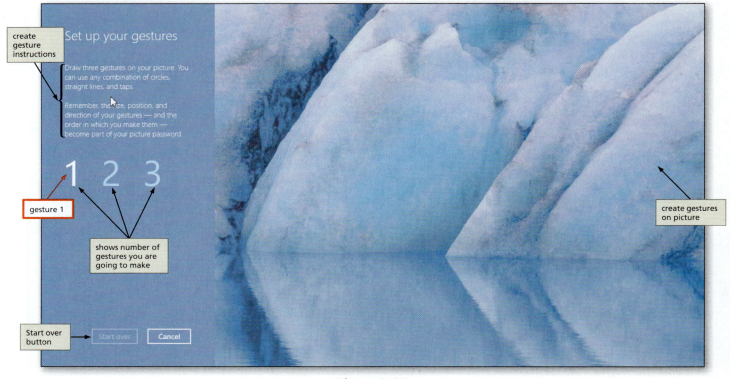

Figure 3–27

7

- Perform three gestures to add gestures to the picture password.
- Perform the three gestures again to confirm the picture password.
- Click the Finish button to return to the PC settings pane (Figure 3–28).

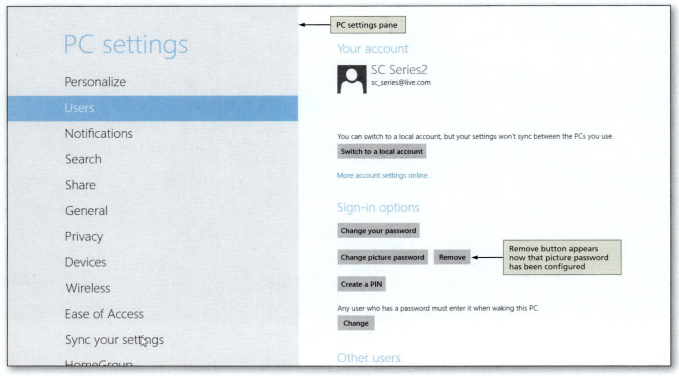

Figure 3–28

Is a Picture Password Secure?

Because picture passwords use gestures that you have made, they are just as secure as regular passwords. In fact, some would say they are more secure because they use touch gestures and not letters, numbers, and so on. Someone would have to guess which gestures you used, in what order, and where on the picture you made them to guess your password.

Customizing the Start Screen

In Chapter 1, you moved and resized tiles on the Start screen. Using the App bar, you also can display all apps, unpin apps from the Start screen, and turn live tiles off and on. Unpinning an app does not uninstall it; rather, it just removes the tile from the Start screen.

You also can change the tile layout on the Start screen. Changing the layout allows you to organize your tiles in the order that works best for you. You can create new tile groups to help in the organization. A **tile group** is a collection of tiles in one section of the Start screen.

After you have created the tile group, you can move other tiles by dragging the tiles to that group. After you have created your tile groups, you can use **Semantic Zoom**, which is a button on the Start screen that allows you to zoom out to view your tiles. You also can zoom with touch gestures or your mouse. Once zoomed out, you can give a name to the new tile group. Once named, the tile group name will be displayed on the Start screen.

To Display All Apps

Using the App bar, you can display all the apps on your computer. The following steps display all apps. *Why? You want to see which apps are installed on your computer.*

- Press the WINDOWS key to return to the Start screen.

- Swipe from the bottom of the Start screen or right-click an open space on the Start screen to display the App bar (Figure 3–29).

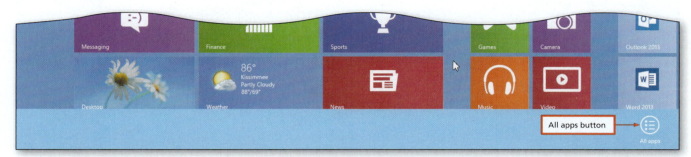

Figure 3–29

2

- Tap or click the All apps button to display the list of the installed apps (Figure 3–30).

Figure 3–30

To Run an App from the Apps List

The following steps display the Weather app. **Why?** *You want to see if clicking an app in the Apps list runs the app the same way it does when run from the Start screen.*

1
- Tap or click the Weather app to run the Weather app (Figure 3–31).

2
- Display the Charms bar.
- Tap or click the Start charm to return to the Start screen.

Weather app

Figure 3–31

To Pin an App to the Start Screen

When an app that you regularly use is not on the Start screen, you can pin it to place it there. **Why?** *The app then can be easily accessed on the Start screen, eliminating the need to search for it.* The following steps pin the Reader app to the Start screen.

1

- Swipe from the bottom of the Start screen or right-click an open space on the Start screen to display the App bar (Figure 3–32).

Figure 3–32

2

- Tap or click the All apps button to display the Apps list (Figure 3–33).

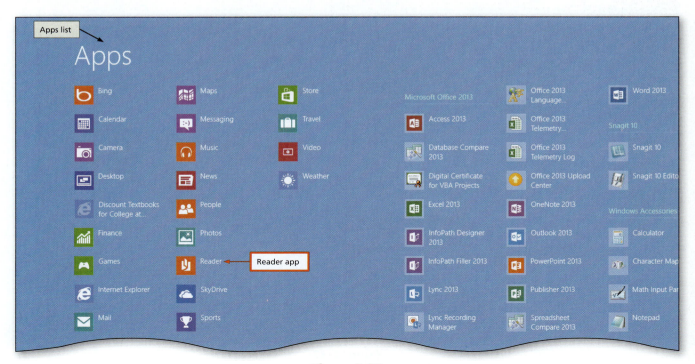

Figure 3–33

3

• Press and hold or right-click the Reader app to select it and display the App bar (Figure 3–34).

Figure 3–34

4

• Tap or click the 'Pin to Start' button to pin the app to the Start screen.

• Display the Start screen.

• Scroll to the right to display the newly pinned Reader app (Figure 3–35).

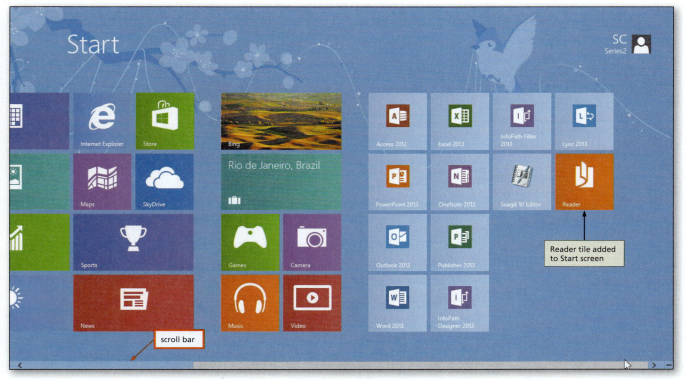

Figure 3–35

To Unpin an App from the Start Screen

Why? *You discovered that you no longer use an app very often and want to remove it from the Start screen to save* *space.* When you no longer want an app to appear on the Start screen, you can unpin the app. The following steps unpin the Sports app from the Start screen.

- Scroll to the left to display the Sports tile (Figure 3–36).

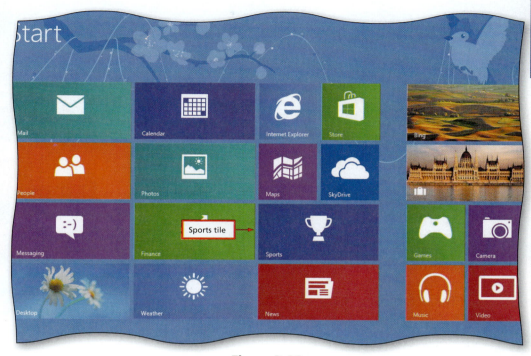

Figure 3–36

- Press and hold or right-click the tile to select it and display the App bar (Figure 3–37).

Figure 3–37

3

- Click the 'Unpin from Start' button to unpin the tile from the Start screen (Figure 3–38).

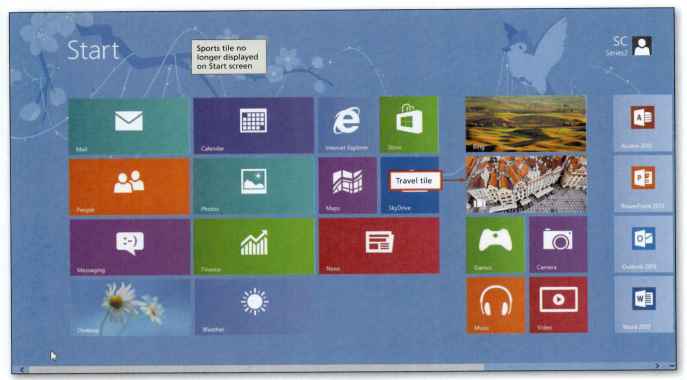

Figure 3–38

To Turn Off a Live Tile

In Chapter 1, you learned that some tiles are live tiles that actively display content. If you would rather not have them display the live content, you can turn off the live tile. **Why?** *You may decide that you want the tile to show a logo instead of active content.*

The following steps turn off the Travel live tile.

1

- Press and hold or right-click the Travel tile to select it and display the App bar (Figure 3–39).

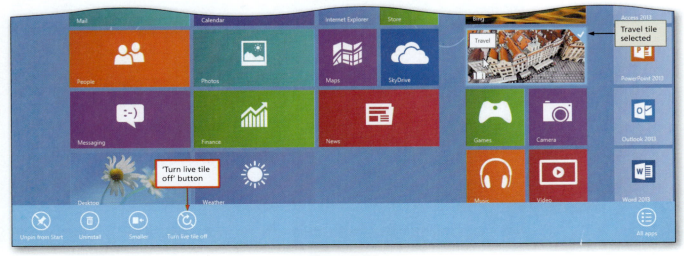

Figure 3–39

2

- Tap or click the 'Turn live tile off' button to turn off the live tile (Figure 3–40).

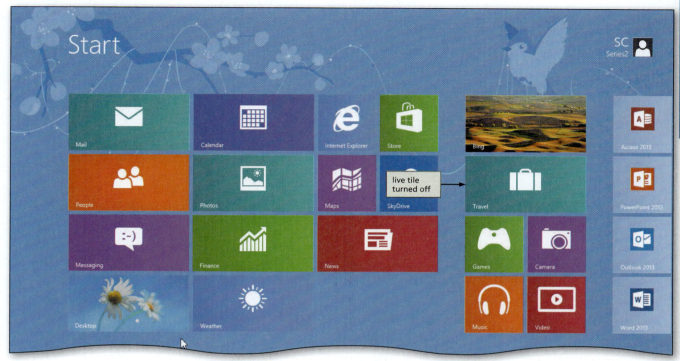

Figure 3–40

Managing Tile Layout

Along with the other personalization you have done, you can manipulate the tile layout on the Start screen. In Chapter 1, you learned how to move a tile. Now you will learn how to create tile groups, name tile groups, and place tiles into groups. As discussed earlier, a tile group is a collection of tiles. The Start screen already contains several groups. For example, the Desktop tile is in the first tile group.

Creating a new tile group is accomplished by dragging a tile to the right or left until the new group is created. Once created, you can zoom out or in so that you can reorder and name your tile groups. This allows you to place the tile group you use most often on the left side of the Start screen to reduce scrolling. By naming a tile group, you can identify what the tiles are used for in that tile group.

To Zoom to View Tile Groups

Why? *You want to see the tile groups at the same time without scrolling.* The following steps zoom out and then zoom in to view tile groups.

1
● Stretch, or press the CTRL key and scroll backward with the mouse wheel to zoom out (Figure 3–41).

Figure 3–41

2
● Pinch, or press the CTRL key and scroll forward using the mouse wheel to zoom in (Figure 3–42).

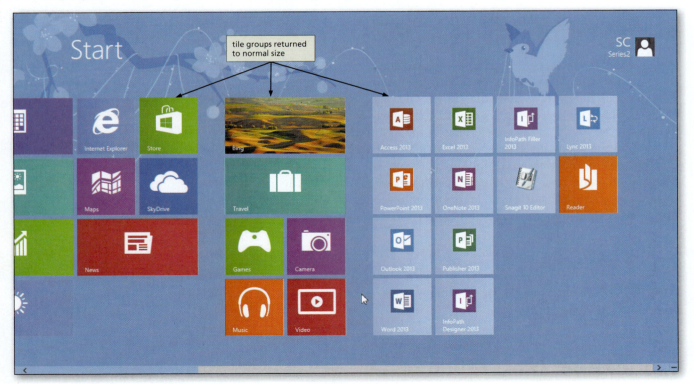

Figure 3–42

Other Ways

1. Press CTRL+PLUS SIGN (+); press CTRL+MINUS SIGN (−)

To Create a New Tile Group

The following steps create a new group using the People tile. ***Why?*** *You want to place tiles for apps you frequently use together so that they are next to each other. Organizing your tiles logically and in groups can make it much easier to locate them.*

- Drag the People tile to the left until a vertical bar appears to create a new tile group (Figure 3–43).

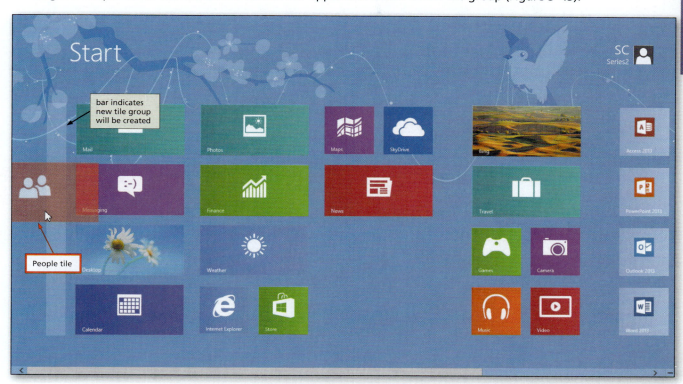

Figure 3–43

②

- Release the People tile to create the new tile group (Figure 3–44).

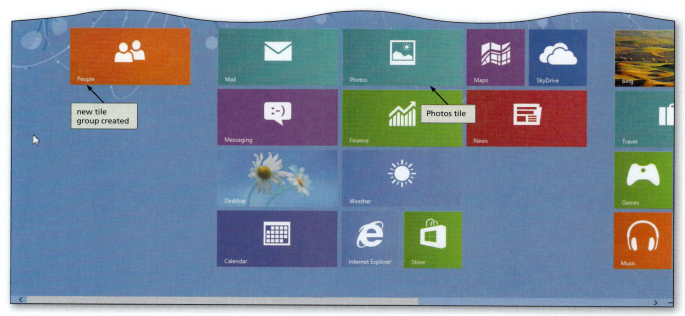

Figure 3–44

To Move a Tile to a Different Tile Group

The following step moves the Photos tile to the same tile group as the People tile. ***Why?*** *You have decided that you would also like to put the Photos tile in the new tile group because you often use that app when you use the People app.*

- Drag the Photos tile below the People tile.
- Release the Photos tile to add it to the tile group (Figure 3–45).

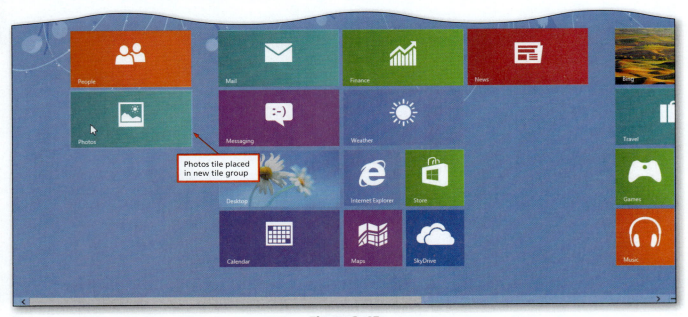

Figure 3–45

To Reorder Tile Groups

The following steps move the second group to the right. ***Why?*** *When you use a group more often, you can move it to the left to make it accessible without scrolling. Conversely, if you use a group less often, you can move it to the right.*

- Pinch, or press the CTRL key and scroll backward using the mouse wheel to zoom out (Figure 3–46).

Figure 3–46

2

- Drag the second group to the right so that it follows the third group to switch the two groups (Figure 3–47).

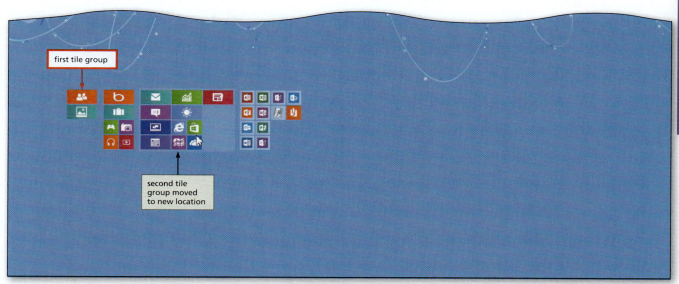

first tile group

second tile
group moved
to new location

Figure 3–47

To Name a Tile Group

Why? *You want to personalize your Start screen by naming your groups so that you know which tiles should be placed in that group.* After you name your tile group, you can remove the name by repeating these steps, but deleting the text from the 'Name this group of tiles' text box.

The following steps name a tile group.

1

- Press and hold or right-click the first tile group to display the App bar (Figure 3–48).

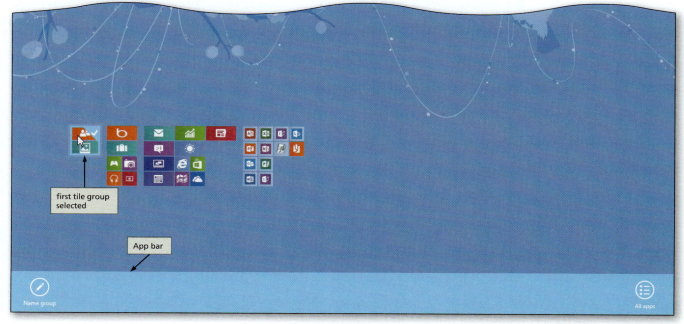

first tile group
selected

App bar

Name group
All apps

Figure 3–48

2

- Tap or click the Name group button on the App bar to display a dialog box (Figure 3–49).

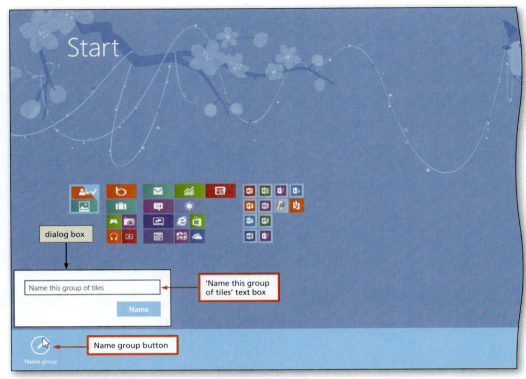

Figure 3–49

3

- Type `Favorites` in the 'Name this group of tiles' text box to enter a name for the tile group (Figure 3–50).

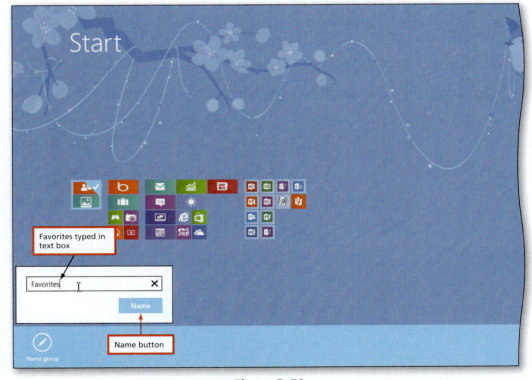

Figure 3–50

4

- Tap or click the Name button in the dialog box to name the tile group (Figure 3–51).

Q&A How can I remove the name from a tile group?

To remove the name from a tile group, repeat Steps 1 through 4. Instead of typing a name for the tile group in Step 3, delete all text from the text box.

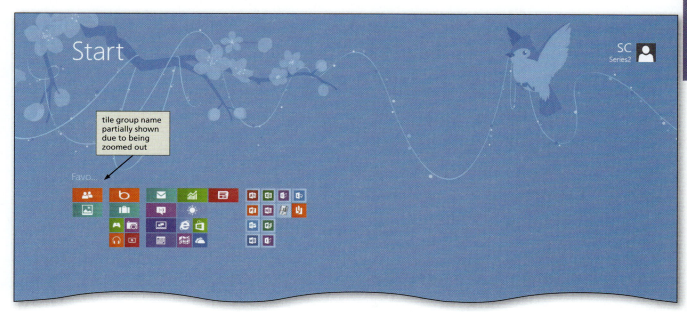

Figure 3–51

5

- Pinch, or press the CTRL key and scroll forward using the mouse wheel to zoom in (Figure 3–52).

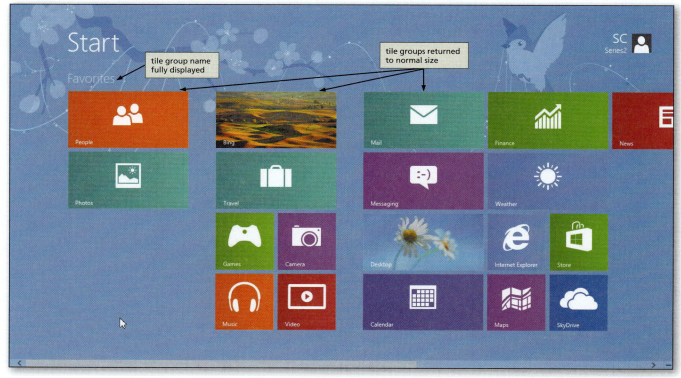

Figure 3–52

To Sign Out of an Account and Shut Down the Computer

The following steps sign out of open accounts and shut down the computer.

1 Display the Charms bar.

2 Tap or click the Start charm on the Charms bar to return to the Start screen.

3 Tap or click the user icon to display user options.

4 Tap or click Sign out to sign out of Windows.

5 Display the Charms bar.

6 Tap or click the Settings charm on the Charms bar to display the Settings menu.

7 Tap or click the Power button to display the Power menu.

8 Tap or click Shut down to sign out of your account and shut down the computer.

Chapter Summary

In this chapter, you learned how to personalize your Windows Start screen. You created user accounts, learned about cloud storage, and signed in using a Microsoft account. You customized the lock screen, changed the design of the Start screen, and created a picture password. You also learned how to arrange tiles on the Start screen by creating and naming new tile groups. Finally, you rearranged the tile groups for easier access to the tiles you use the most. The items listed below include all of the new Windows skills you have learned in this chapter.

1. Create a Microsoft Account (WIN 92)
2. Add a Local Account (WIN 94)
3. Add a Microsoft Account (WIN 98)
4. Personalize the Lock Screen (WIN 100)
5. Change the Start Screen Color Scheme (WIN 102)
6. Change the Start Screen Background Pattern (WIN 103)
7. Create a Picture Password (WIN 104)
8. Display All Apps (WIN 109)
9. Run an App from the Apps List (WIN 110)
10. Pin an App to the Start Screen (WIN 110)
11. Unpin an App from the Start Screen (WIN 113)
12. Turn Off a Live Tile (WIN 114)
13. Zoom to View Tile Groups (WIN 115)
14. Create a New Tile Group (WIN 117)
15. Move a Tile to a Different Tile Group (WIN 118)
16. Reorder Tile Groups (WIN 118)
17. Name a Tile Group (WIN 119)

Apply Your Knowledge

Changing the Start Screen

Instructions: You want to customize the look and design of the Start screen by changing theme colors and backgrounds, moving tiles, and naming tile groups.

Part 1: Changing the Start Screen Color Scheme and Background

1. Display the Charms bar and then tap or click the Settings charm to display the Settings menu.
2. Click Personalization in the PC settings pane to display the personalization options in the right pane.
3. Tap or click 'Change PC settings' to display the PC settings pane (Figure 3–53).
4. Tap or click Start screen in the right pane to display the Start screen personalization options.
5. Tap or click the fourth background option in the second row to change the Start screen background.
6. Tap or click the yellow color scheme to change the Start screen color scheme to yellow.

Part 2: Creating Tile Groups

1. Switch to the Start screen.
2. Drag the Messaging tile to the left to create a new tile group.
3. Drag the Mail tile to the newly created tile group.
4. Stretch, or press the CTRL key and scroll backward using the mouse wheel to zoom out.
5. Press and hold or right-click the newly created tile group to select it and display the App bar.
6. Tap or click the Name group button to display a dialog box.
7. Type Communication in the 'Name this group of tiles' text box.
8. Click the Name button to assign the tile group name.
9. Stretch, or press the CTRL key and scroll forward using the mouse wheel to zoom in.

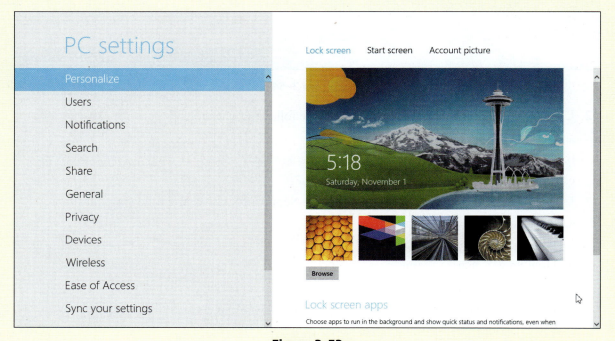

Figure 3–53

Extend Your Knowledge

Extend the skills you learned in this chapter and experiment with new skills. You might need to use Help to complete the assignment.

Using Help

Instructions: Use Windows Help and Support to perform the following tasks.

1. Find Help about customizing the Desktop by typing `themes` in the Search text box and then clicking the Search button (Figure 3–54). Tap or click the result titled 'Get started with themes' and then answer the following questions:

   a. What is a desktop background?

   b. What is a screen saver?

   c. What is a window border color?

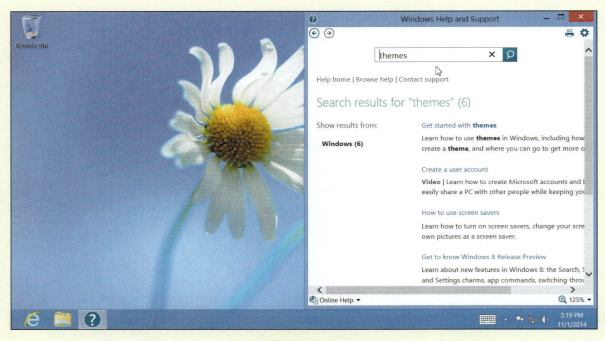

Figure 3–54

2. Use Windows Help and Support to answer the following questions:

   a. What are My Themes?

   b. What are Windows Default Themes?

   c. What are Basic and High Contrast Themes?

3. Use the Search text box in Windows Help and Support to answer the following questions:

   a. How do you create a theme?

   b. How do you save a theme?

   c. How do you share a theme?

   d. How do you delete a theme?

   e. How do you get more information about the pictures that are included in a particular theme?

4. Close the Windows Help and Support window.

In the Lab

Use the guidelines, concepts, and skills presented in this chapter to increase your knowledge of Windows 8. Labs are listed in order of increasing difficulty.

Lab 1: Customizing Settings

Problem: You would like to customize your lock screen and add a picture password for your user account.

Instructions: Use the PC settings pane to perform the following tasks.

1. Copy the img3 picture from the Windows folder to the Pictures library. You will be using this picture as a picture password later in this exercise.

2. Display the PC settings pane.

3. Click Personalize in the PC settings pane to perform the following tasks:

   a. Tap or click Lock screen in the right pane to display personalization options.

   b. If necessary, scroll to display the Lock screen apps area.

   c. Tap or click one of the add buttons to add a lock screen app.

   d. Tap or click the Weather app on the Choose an app menu to add it to the lock screen.

   e. Tap or click the Calendar icon and then click the 'Don't show quick status here' link to remove it from the lock screen.

4. Click Users in the PC settings pane and then perform the following tasks:

   a. Tap or click the 'Create picture password' button to create a picture password.

   b. After entering your password, tap or click to select the img3 picture that will be used as a picture password (Figure 3–55).

   c. Gesture or use the mouse to add a circle, line, and tap to create a picture password.

Figure 3–55

In the Lab

Lab 2: Creating and Adding an Account

Instructions: You want to add a local account for your friend, Betty Lou. Perform the following steps first to add and then to sign in to a local account.

Part 1: Creating the Local Account

1. Display the PC settings pane and then tap or click Users to display your account information.
2. Tap or click the 'Add a user' button in the right pane to add a user.
3. Tap or click the 'Sign in without a Microsoft account' link to display the account options.
4. Tap or click Local account to create a local account (Figure 3–56).
5. Enter Betty Lou's name, a password, and a hint of your choosing.
6. Follow the remaining steps on the screen to create the account.

Part 2: Switching Accounts

1. Display the Start screen.
2. Tap or click your user icon.
3. Tap or click the Betty Lou icon.
4. Enter the password for Betty Lou to switch to that account.

Part 3: Signing Out of an Account

1. Tap or click the user icon on the Start screen.
2. Tap or click Sign out to sign out of the account.

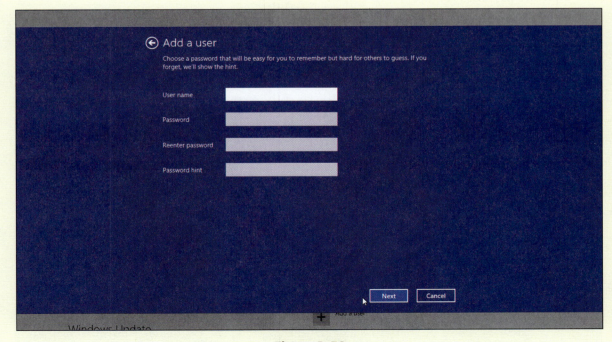

Figure 3–56

In the Lab

Lab 3: Creating a Microsoft Account

Instructions: Perform the following steps to create a Microsoft account.

Part 1: Creating a Microsoft Account

1. If necessary, connect to the Internet and display the desktop.
2. Click the Internet Explorer app button to run Internet Explorer.
3. Click the web address in the address bar to select it.
4. Type `windows.live.com` in the address bar and then press the ENTER key (Figure 3–57).
5. Tap or click the 'Sign up now' link to create a Microsoft account.
6. Enter your information to create the Microsoft account.

Part 2: Adding a Microsoft Account

1. Display the PC settings pane and then tap or click Users to display your account info in the right pane.
2. Tap or click the 'Add a user' button to add a user.
3. Enter your email address.
4. Tap or click the Next button and then tap or click the Finish button to add the account.

Part 3: Signing Out of an Account

1. Tap or click the user icon on the sign-in screen.
2. Tap or click Sign out to sign out of the account.

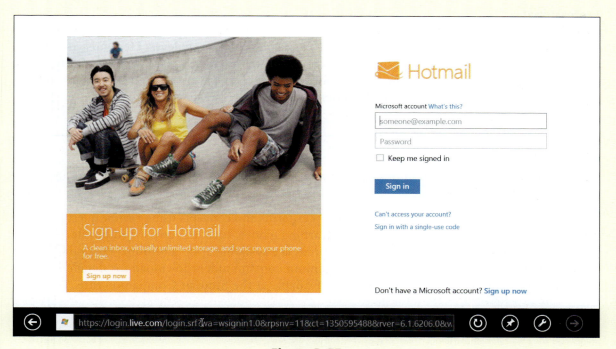

Figure 3–57

Cases and Places

Apply your creative thinking and problem-solving skills to design and implement a solution.

1: Assessing Windows 8 Compatibility

Academic

Colors, patterns, and the arrangement of the workplace can have a significant effect on worker productivity. These factors might draw attention to some objects, de-emphasize others, speed the completion of tasks, or even promote desirable moods and attitudes. Working with classmates, visit the Internet, a library, or other research facility to discover how colors, patterns, and arrangements can impact a work environment. Using what you have learned, together with the concepts and techniques presented in this chapter, create the Windows Start screen that you think would help your classmates be more efficient. Write a report describing your Start screen and explaining why you feel it would enhance productivity.

2: Creating a Picture Password

Personal

You recently bought a touch screen computer and want to use a family photo to add a picture password to your account. Download a family photo of your choice to the Pictures library. Add a picture password using the PC Settings pane. Use any three gestures to create the picture password. Write a report describing why you selected the picture you did and which gestures you decided to use. Include any thoughts on the difficulty of others to guess the password.

3: Researching Account Privileges

Professional

You are working in the technical support company for a corporation. Your boss has been wondering if he should allow users to have administrative or standard account privileges. He wants you to research this using Windows Help and Support and the Internet and create a summary for him to use in making his decision. Describe the account types and then list some of the advantages and disadvantages of each. Finally, tell which accounts you would create and explain why.

LEARN ONLINE

Reinforce what you learned in this chapter with games, exercises, training, and many other online activities and resources.

Student Companion Site: Reinforce chapter terms and concepts using review questions, flash cards, practice tests, and interactive learning games, such as a crossword puzzle. These and other online activities and resources are available at no additional cost on www.cengagebrain.com. Visit www.cengagebrain.com/ct/studentdownload for detailed instructions about accessing the resources available at the Student Companion Site.

4 | Connecting to the Internet

Objectives

You will have mastered the material in this chapter when you can:

- Understand Wi-Fi and broadband connectivity
- Understand how to connect to a wireless network
- Run the Internet Explorer app
- Display a webpage
- Search using the address bar

- Add tabs in a browser window
- Pin a website to the Start screen
- Use tabbed browsing
- Display a webpage from the desktop
- Add a website to favorites
- Subscribe to and use RSS feeds

4 | Connecting to the Internet

Introduction

One of the more popular uses of Windows today is to connect to the Internet. By connecting to the Internet, you can use any of the services available, such as email, web browsing, sharing information, and using social networking sites. Windows has built-in support to run on devices capable of connecting to networks such as the Internet. By including support for networking, Windows allows you to participate in the online environment and explore the different features of the Internet.

Overview

As you read this chapter, you will learn how to connect to the Internet by performing these general tasks:

- Connect to a wireless network
- Use Internet Explorer
- Search the web
- Manipulate tabs in the browser
- Use RSS feeds

Wi-Fi and Broadband Connectivity

Many networks today offer both broadband and Wi-Fi connectivity. **Broadband** refers to the method of transmitting data that allows for large amounts of data to be sent and received. For example, cable TV connections use broadband so that you can receive a large number of channels, including high-definition channels that require large amounts of video data. Many broadband connections are wired connections. To connect to these networks, you need a network cable or wired connection.

Wi-Fi refers to the method of transmitting data wirelessly without using a network cable. Because no cable is required, a device with Wi-Fi support can be moved from location to location while retaining the same wireless connection.

Mobility and Connectivity

When you use a mobile device, you can connect to a wireless network, such as your school's, and stay connected as long as you are in range of the network. You can use your computer in one classroom and then move to another and still use the same connection. In today's environment, people constantly are on the move and want to stay connected so that they can check up on current events, chat with friends, submit homework online, and more without having to connect their device to the network using a cable.

Connecting to a Wireless Network

Normally, when you start your computer Windows will detect any available wireless networks. If you previously have connected to a wireless network and stored the account information, Windows will connect you to the network automatically. If you have not connected to the network before, you will be prompted to connect and provide your account information. You also could use the Network and Sharing Center in the Control Panel to connect to the network if Windows does not prompt you to connect. Appendix C provides detailed steps for connecting manually to a wireless network.

Running Internet Explorer

You can run Internet Explorer from the Start screen or the desktop. The advantage of running it from the Start screen is that it is displayed in the full window and does not require displaying the desktop. You have use of the full screen and can use touch more easily to navigate within the browser. Using Internet Explorer, you can move seamlessly to the web.

To Run the Internet Explorer App

The following step runs the Internet Explorer app. *Why? You want to browse the Internet to do some research for an assignment.*

1
- If necessary, sign in to your account.
- Tap or click the Internet Explorer tile on the Windows Start screen to run the Internet Explorer app (Figure 4–1).

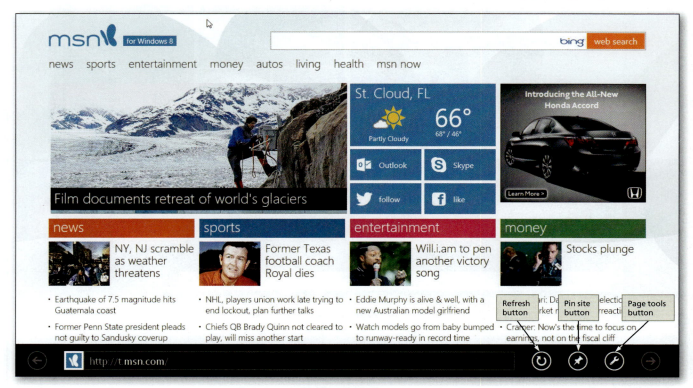

Figure 4–1

Browsing and Searching the Web

Internet Explorer initially displays the current home page for the browser, which by default is msn.com. You can use the address bar to display websites for which you know the web address; if you do not know the web address, you can search for websites using the address bar. You also can add tabs so that you can keep multiple webpages open at the same time. If you have a favorite website, you can add it to your favorites or pin it to the Start screen so that it is easily accessible.

If you want to make your browsing more secure, you can switch to an InPrivate tab. An **InPrivate** tab deletes any passwords and search and browse histories so that others will not be able to see them after you are done using the tab. You also can use Internet Options accessed via the Settings charm to delete your browsing history, as well as change other Internet Explorer settings.

To Display a Webpage

Why? *You want to find more information about mobile devices and which ones are recommended.* The following steps display the PCMAG.com webpage.

1
- Type `http://www.pcmag.com` to enter the web address (Figure 4–2).

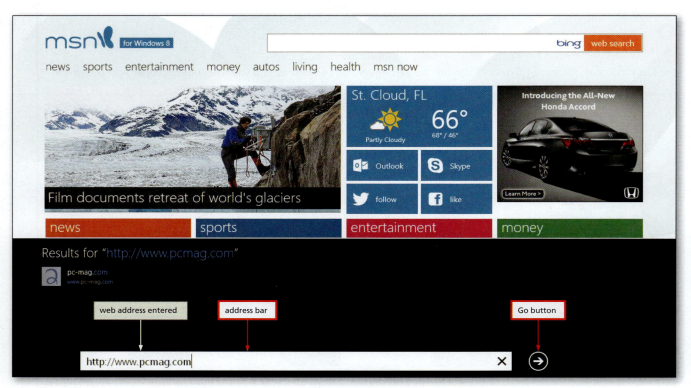

Figure 4–2

2
- Tap or click the Go button to display the PCMAG.com webpage (Figure 4–3).

Q&A Why does my webpage look different?

Webpages are updated often. The website may have been updated with information different from that shown in Figure 4–3.

Figure 4–3

To Search Using the Address Bar

Besides going directly to a webpage by typing its exact web address, you can use the address bar to find a website. ***Why?*** *You need to locate a website, but you do not know the actual web address.* The following steps use the address bar to find and then display the Facebook webpage.

1
- Tap or click the address bar and then type   facebook   to enter the search text (Figure 4–4).

Figure 4–4

● Tap or click the Facebook link in the search results to display the Facebook webpage (Figure 4–5).

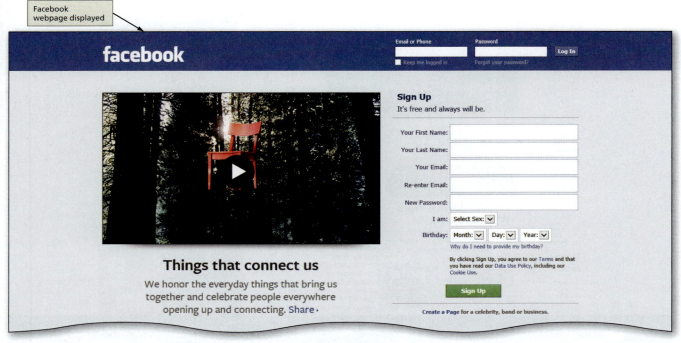

Figure 4–5

To Add a Tab in the Browser Window

When browsing, you may decide to have multiple websites displayed. ***Why?*** *You may want to review multiple websites and keep them all displayed so that you can switch between them without having to redisplay them repeatedly.* The following steps add a new tab and display the Bing webpage.

● Press and hold or right-click an open area of the webpage to display the Navigation bar (Figure 4–6).

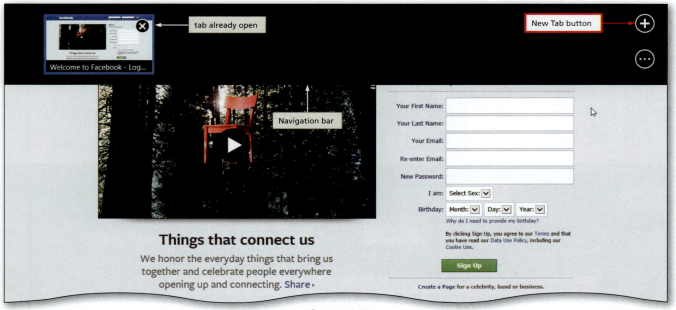

Figure 4–6

2

- Tap or click the New Tab button to add a new tab and display the address bar (Figure 4–7).

Figure 4–7

3

- Type bing in the address bar to search for the Bing website.
- Tap or click the Bing link in the search results to display the Bing webpage (Figure 4–8).

Figure 4–8

To Add an InPrivate Tab in the Browser Window

An **InPrivate tab** provides more security when browsing because when you close the tab, passwords and histories are deleted so that the next person to use the computer will not be able to see the information you submitted while browsing. *Why? You are going to be signing in to a website and do not want your password to be kept once you have finished browsing the website.* The steps on the following pages add a new InPrivate tab and display the CengageBrain website.

1

- Press and hold or right-click an open area of the webpage to display the Navigation bar.
- Tap or click the Tab tools button on the Navigation bar to display the Tab tools menu (Figure 4–9).

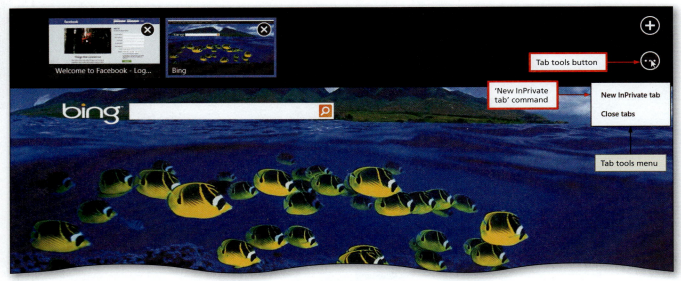

Figure 4–9

2

- Tap or click 'New InPrivate tab' on the Tab tools menu to add a new InPrivate tab (Figure 4–10).

Q&A | Why does the tab name include the text, InPrivate?

InPrivate indicates that this tab is not an ordinary tab; rather, when you close it, all password and history data will be deleted automatically.

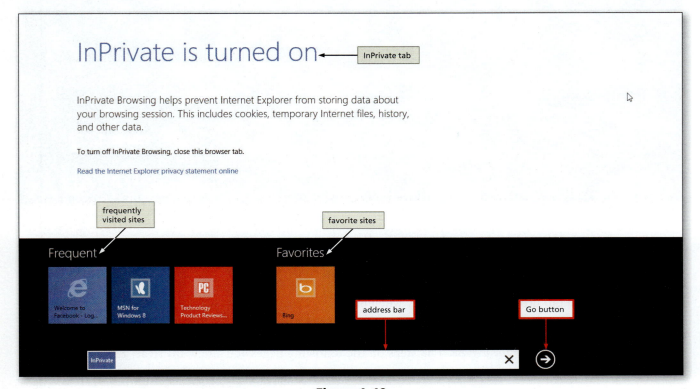

Figure 4–10

3

- Type `cengagebrain.com` in the address bar to search for the CengageBrain webpage.
- Tap or click the Go button to display the CengageBrain webpage (Figure 4–11).

CengageBrain webpage

Figure 4–11

To Switch between Tabs

Why? *You need to return to a previous tab but do not want to close the current tab at this time.* The following steps switch to the Facebook tab.

1

- Press and hold or right-click an open area of the webpage to display the Navigation bar (Figure 4–12).

Q&A
Why does the tab not just say, Facebook?

Web designers often give lengthier names to each page; what appears on the tab is the title of the page given to it by the webpage designer who built the page.

Facebook tab

Figure 4–12

2

- Tap or click the Facebook tab to return to the Facebook webpage (Figure 4–13).

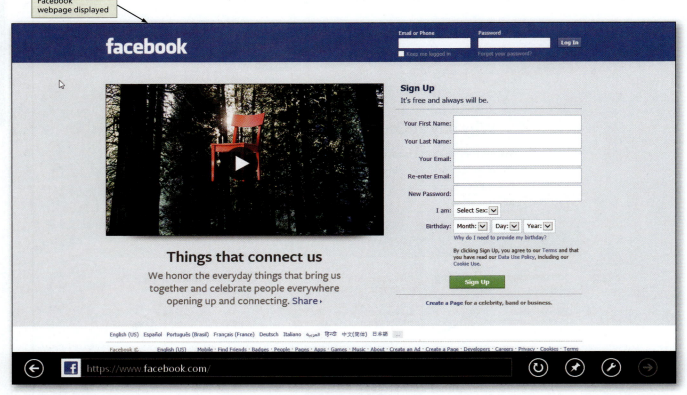

Figure 4–13

To Close a Tab

Why? *You are finished using a tab and no longer need it displayed.* The following steps close the Facebook tab.

1

- Press and hold or right-click an open area of the webpage to display the Navigation bar (Figure 4–14).

Figure 4–14

2

- Tap or click the Close Tab button on the Facebook tab to close the Facebook tab (Figure 4–15).

Q&A Why does the next tab display?

Because you closed the Facebook tab, Internet Explorer automatically moves to the next tab.

Figure 4–15

To Find Information on a Webpage

Internet Explorer also provides ways for you to search for information within a webpage. *Why? A page may contain a great deal of information, and you need to find just one part of the page or keyword(s) on the page.* Internet Explorer finds text only in the page. If the text is in an image, Internet Explorer is not able to find it. The following steps search for the word, Free, on the CengageBrain webpage.

1

- If necessary, press and hold or right-click an open area of the webpage to display the Navigation bar.

- Tap or click the CengageBrain tab to switch to the tab.

- Press and hold or right-click an open area of the webpage to display the App bar.

- Tap or click the Page tools button on the App bar to display the Page tools menu (Figure 4–16).

Figure 4–16

- Tap or click 'Find on page' on the Page tools menu to display the Find text box on the App bar.

- Type `free` in the Find text box to enter the search text (Figure 4–17).

Q&A
Why are all instances of the word, free, highlighted?

Because you chose to search for the word, free, Internet Explorer marked all occurrences of the word. Below the Find text box, you will see how many occurrences of the word were found.

Figure 4–17

To Pin a Website to the Start Screen

Why? *You visit a website often and would like to tap or click a tile on the Start screen and navigate directly to the website.* The following steps pin the CengageBrain website to the Start screen.

- Press and hold or right-click an open area of the webpage to display the App bar.

- Tap or click the Pin site button to display the Pin site menu.

- Tap or click 'Pin to Start' on the Pin site menu to display the Pin to Start dialog box (Figure 4–18).

- Tap or click the 'Pin to Start' button to pin the website to the Start screen.

Figure 4–18

2

- Display the Start screen.
- Scroll until the CengageBrain tile appears to verify that it was pinned (Figure 4–19).
- Point to the upper-left corner of the screen and move your mouse down to display the open apps.
- Tap or click the Internet Explorer app to return to the CengageBrain website.

Figure 4–19

To Add a Website to Favorites

Why? *Rather than pin a website to the Start screen, you can add it to your favorites for easy access.* The following steps pin the CengageBrain webpage to favorites.

1
- Press and hold or right-click an open area of the webpage to display the App bar.
- Tap or click the Pin site button to display the Pin site menu (Figure 4–20).

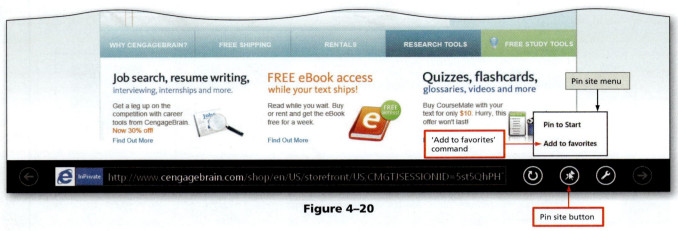

Figure 4–20

2
- Tap or click 'Add to favorites' on the Pin site menu to pin the website to favorites.
- Tap or click the address bar to display a list of frequently used websites and favorites (Figure 4–21).
- Tap or click an open space of the webpage to hide the App bar.

Q&A Why are websites appearing in the Frequent category?

As you browse the web, Internet Explorer keeps tracks of websites you view and updates the Frequent list so that you can find those sites more easily.

Figure 4–21

Running Internet Explorer in the Desktop

You can switch between running Internet Explorer in the Modern UI and running Internet Explorer in the desktop. Unlike the Internet Explorer app run from the Start screen, the desktop version cannot use the Charms bar to share websites and cannot pin websites to the Start screen; however, you easily can view your favorite locations, view RSS feeds, and work with the rest of Internet Explorer's features.

To Display a Webpage on the Desktop

The following steps display the current webpage in Internet Explorer on the desktop. *Why? You want to continue browsing, but find that you also want to use other applications that require the desktop.* For example, you may want to be able to switch quickly between Word and your browser using the taskbar.

- Press and hold or right-click an open area of the webpage to display the App bar.

- Tap or click the Page tools button on the App bar to display the Page tools menu (Figure 4–22).

Figure 4–22

- Tap or click 'View on the desktop' on the Page tools menu to display the webpage in Internet Explorer on the desktop. If necessary, maximize the window (Figure 4–23).

Figure 4–23

To Display a New Tab in Internet Explorer on the Desktop

Why? *You want to view another webpage without leaving the current webpage.* The following steps display a new tab.

- Tap or click the New Tab button to add a new tab (Figure 4–24).

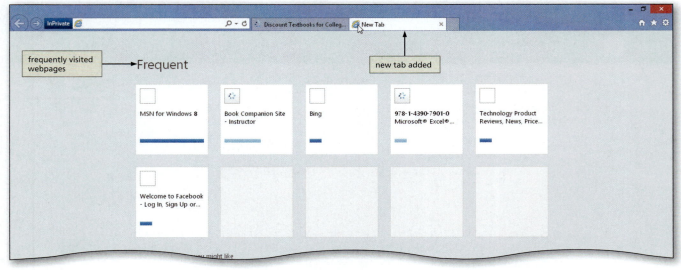

Figure 4–24

- Type `www.yahoo.com` in the address bar and then press the ENTER key to view the page (Figure 4–25).

Figure 4–25

To Search Using Keywords in the Address Bar

When you are running Internet Explorer, you can use the address bar to search for topics. *Why? You want to find information about a search topic using Internet Explorer.* The following step searches for information about Windows 8.

- Tap or click the New Tab button to add a new tab.

- Tap or click the address bar, type `Windows 8` to enter the search text, and then press the ENTER key to begin the search (Figure 4–26).

Q&A | Why does my webpage look different?

Search results change frequently; new websites are created and some websites may be removed. Also, if the person who set up Internet Explorer used another search engine, your results might appear on another search webpage, such as Google.

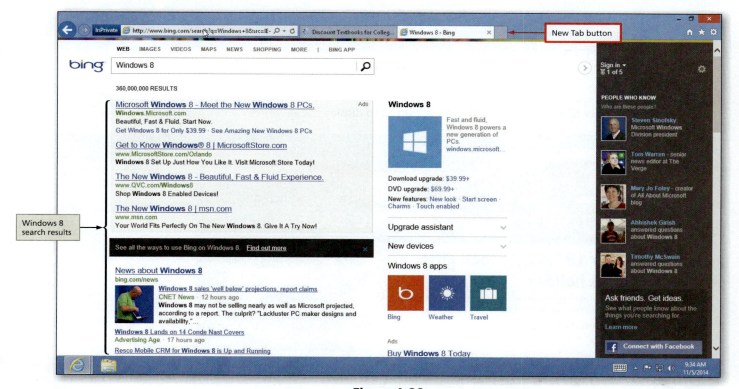

Figure 4–26

To Add a Website to Favorites from the Desktop

Why? *You would like to add a webpage to your favorites on the desktop. Anything added to favorites from the desktop will appear in your favorites if you run Internet Explorer from the Start screen.* The following steps add the CNET website to favorites from the desktop.

1

- Tap or click the New Tab button to add a new tab.

- Type `cnet.com` in the address bar and tap or click the Go button to display the CNET webpage (Figure 4–27).

Figure 4–27

2

- Tap or click the 'View favorites, feeds, and history' button to display the Favorites Center (Figure 4–28).

Figure 4–28

3

- Tap or click the 'Add to favorites' button to display the Add a Favorite dialog box (Figure 4–29).
- Tap or click the Add button (Add a Favorite dialog box) to add the webpage to favorites.

Figure 4–29

4

- Tap or click the 'View favorites, feeds, and history' button to display the Favorites Center and verify that the page was added (Figure 4–30).
- Tap or click outside the Favorites Center to close the Favorites Center.

Figure 4–30

To Add a Website to the Favorites Bar

Why? *You want to be able to just tap or click the link to the website from the browser.* The following steps add the CNET webpage to the Favorites bar.

1
- Press and hold or right-click the title bar to display a shortcut menu (Figure 4–31).

Figure 4–31

2
- Tap or click Favorites bar on the shortcut menu to display the Favorites bar (Figure 4–32).

Figure 4–32

3
- Tap or click the 'Add to Favorites bar' button on the Favorites bar to add the page to the Favorites bar (Figure 4–33).

Figure 4–33

To Display a Webpage in a New Tab

When you tap or click a link on a webpage, the new webpage is displayed, replacing the old webpage in the window. You can choose to display the webpage in a new tab instead. The tabs of the two webpages would be colored to reflect that they are part of a tab group. A **tab group** is a set of webpages displayed from the same original website. *Why? You can keep both the original webpage and new webpage displayed in the browser and switch between them as needed.* The following steps display a webpage in a new tab.

1

• Press and hold or right-click the News link to display a shortcut menu (Figure 4–34).

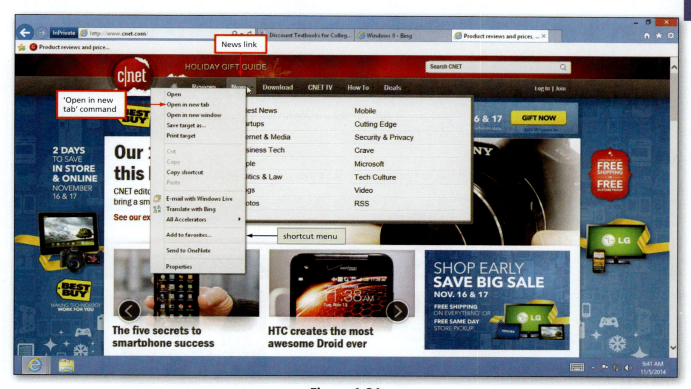

Figure 4–34

2

• Tap or click 'Open in new tab' on the shortcut menu to display the webpage in a new tab.

• Tap or click the new tab to switch to the new tab (Figure 4–35).

Figure 4–35

Using Internet Explorer to Subscribe to RSS Feeds

Internet Explorer provides access to a wealth of information on the Internet. Another technology on the Internet is **Really Simple Syndication** (**RSS**). RSS allows webpage authors to distribute, or syndicate, web content easily using **RSS feeds**. If you frequently visit multiple websites that offer RSS feeds, you can subscribe to their RSS feeds using Internet Explorer. This allows you to review quickly the feed content of all the websites in a simple list in a browser window, without first having to navigate to each individual website. For example, the CNN website contains two RSS feeds that allow visitors to view top stories and recent stories in one convenient location. RSS feeds can be found on many websites and blogs, particularly those that frequently update their content.

To Subscribe to an RSS Feed

Why? *You want to keep current about certain topics from a website without repeatedly visiting the website.* The following steps subscribe to an RSS feed.

1
- Press and hold or right-click the title bar to display a shortcut menu (Figure 4–36).

Figure 4–36

2
- Tap or click Command bar on the shortcut menu to display the Command bar (Figure 4–37).

Figure 4–37

3

- Tap or click the 'View feeds on this page' arrow on the Command bar to display a list of available RSS feeds (Figure 4–38).

Figure 4–38

4

- Tap or click 'Latest News Headlines (new)' in the list of RSS feeds to display the CNET News RSS feed (Figure 4–39).

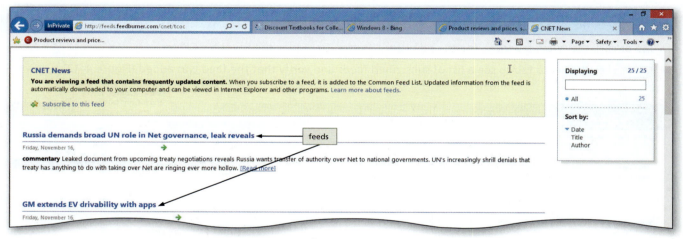

Figure 4–39

5

- Tap or click the 'Subscribe to this feed' link to display the Subscribe to this Feed dialog box (Figure 4–40).

Figure 4–40

6

- Tap or click the Subscribe button (Subscribe to this Feed dialog box) to subscribe to the RSS feed (Figure 4–41).

Figure 4–41

7

- Tap or click the 'View favorites, feeds, and history' button to display the Favorites Center.
- Tap or click the Feeds tab to see a list of subscribed feeds and verify that the feed was added (Figure 4–42).

Figure 4–42

To Modify Feed Properties

Because RSS feeds disseminate frequently updated information, Internet Explorer automatically downloads updated RSS content every day. The following steps modify the properties for the CNET News RSS feed so that the feed will update every four hours. *Why? If you want Internet Explorer to download the RSS feeds more frequently so that you are sure you are viewing the most up-to-date information, you can modify the feed properties.*

- Tap or click the 'View favorites, feeds, and history' button to close the Favorites Center.
- Tap or click the 'View feed properties' link to display the Feed Properties dialog box.
- Tap or click the 'Use custom schedule' option button in the Update Schedule area (Feed Properties dialog box) to select it.
- Tap or click the Frequency button to display the Frequency list (Figure 4–43).

2

- Tap or click 4 hours in the Frequency list to set the feed to update every 4 hours.
- Tap or click the OK button to save your changes and to close the Feed Properties dialog box.

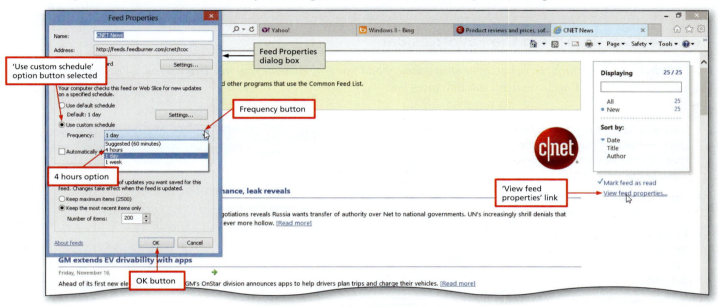

Figure 4–43

To Delete an RSS Feed

Why? When you no longer have need of an RSS feed, you can delete it. The following steps delete the RSS feed to which you have subscribed from the Favorites bar.

- Tap or click the 'View favorites, feeds, and history' button to display the Favorites Center.
- If necessary, tap or click the Feeds tab to display the available feeds.
- Press and hold or right-click the feed to display a shortcut menu (Figure 4–44).

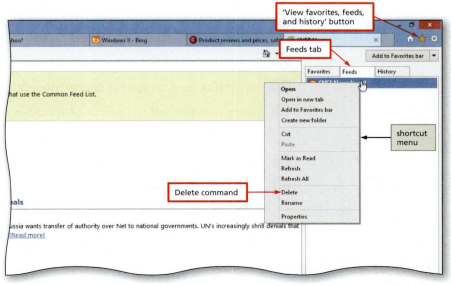

Figure 4–44

2

● Tap or click Delete on the shortcut menu to display an Internet Explorer dialog box (Figure 4–45).

● Tap or click the Yes button (Internet Explorer dialog box) to confirm the deletion.

Figure 4–45

To Delete an Item from the Favorites Bar

Why? You do not visit the website very often anymore and want to remove it from the Favorites bar. The following step deletes the CNET website from the Favorites bar.

1

● Press and hold or right-click the CNET webpage's button on the Favorites bar to display a shortcut menu (Figure 4–46).

● Tap or click Delete on the shortcut menu to delete the favorite.

● If necessary, tap or click the Yes button (Internet Explorer dialog box) to confirm the deletion.

● Exit Internet Explorer.

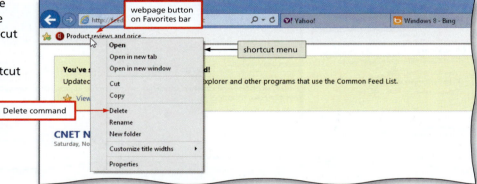

Figure 4–46

To Sign Out of an Account and Shut Down the Computer

The following steps sign out of open accounts and shut down the computer.

1 Swipe from the right or point to the upper-right corner of the screen to display the Charms bar.

2 Tap or click the Start charm on the Charms bar to return to the Start screen.

3 Tap or click the User icon to display user options.

4 Tap or click Sign out to sign out of Windows.

5 Swipe or click the Lock screen to display the sign-in screen.

6 Tap or click the Power button to display the Power menu.

7 Tap or click Shut down to shut down the computer.

Chapter Summary

In this chapter, you have learned how to connect to the Internet. You ran the Internet Explorer app on the Start screen and in the desktop. You learned how to create new tabs. You searched for webpages and added to your favorites. You learned how to subscribe to an RSS feed. You also added the Command bar and Favorites bar to the Internet Explorer window. The items listed below include the Windows skills you have learned in this chapter.

1. Run the Internet Explorer App (WIN 131)
2. Display a Webpage (WIN 132)
3. Search Using the Address Bar (WIN 133)
4. Add a Tab in the Browser Window (WIN 134)
5. Add an InPrivate Tab in the Browser Window (WIN 135)
6. Switch between Tabs (WIN 137)
7. Close a Tab (WIN 138)
8. Find Information on a Webpage (WIN 139)
9. Pin a Website to the Start Screen (WIN 140)
10. Add a Website to Favorites (WIN 142)
11. Display a Webpage on the Desktop (WIN 143)
12. Display a New Tab in Internet Explorer on the Desktop (WIN 144)
13. Search Using Keywords in the Address Bar (WIN 145)
14. Add a Website to Favorites from the Desktop (WIN 146)
15. Add a Website to the Favorites Bar (WIN 148)
16. Display a Webpage in a New Tab (WIN 149)
17. Subscribe to an RSS Feed (WIN 150)
18. Modify Feed Properties (WIN 152)
19. Delete an RSS Feed (WIN 153)
20. Delete an Item from the Favorites Bar (WIN 154)

Apply Your Knowledge

Searching Using the Address Bar

Instructions: You want to find information about degree programs for nursing, education, and computer science. Use Internet Explorer to perform the following tasks.

1. Run the Internet Explorer app.
2. Type `nursing degrees` in the address bar and then tap or click the Go button to search for websites (Figure 4–47).

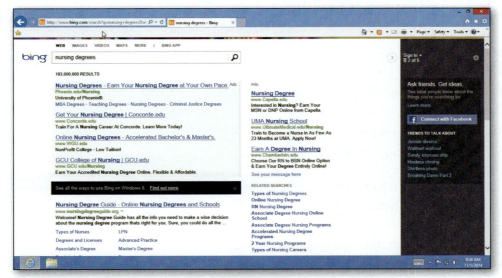

Figure 4–47

Continued >

Apply Your Knowledge *continued*

3. Note how many results were returned.

4. Tap or click one of the links and write a brief description of the degrees available.

5. Add a new tab, type `education degrees` in the address bar, and then tap or click the Go button to search for websites.

6. Note how many results were returned.

7. Tap or click one of the links and write a brief description of the degrees available.

8. Add a new tab and then type `computer science degrees` in the address bar and tap or click the Go button to search for websites.

9. Note how many results were returned.

10. Tap or click one of the links and write a brief description of the degrees available.

11. Gather your results into a brief report and submit it to your instructor.

Extend Your Knowledge

Extend the skills you learned in this chapter and experiment with new skills. You will use Help to complete the assignment.

Using Help

Instructions: Use Windows Help and Support to perform the following tasks.

1. Run Windows Help and Support.

2. Find Help about Internet Explorer Security by typing `Internet Explorer Security` in the Search box and then tapping or clicking the Search button (Figure 4–48). Then, answer the following questions:

   a. What are the security settings in Internet Explorer?

   b. How do you change the security settings?

   c. What is privacy for tabs?

3. Type `Internet Explorer Security Settings` in the Search box and then tap or click the Search button. Then, answer the following questions:

   a. How do you change Internet Explorer settings?

   b. What is a security zone?

   c. What are the different security zones?

   d. How do you add or remove sites from a security zone?

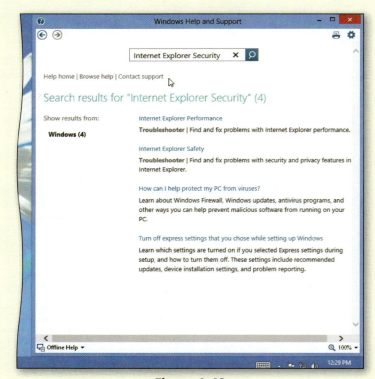

Figure 4–48

4. Type `Connect to the Internet` in the Search box and then tap or click the Search button. Then, answer the following questions:

   a. What is needed to connect to the Internet?

   b. How do you determine if a network is safe to use?

5. Type `Credential Manager` in the Search box and then tap or click the Search button. Then, answer the following questions:

   a. What is the Credential Manager?

   b. When should you trust a website?

6. Exit Windows Help and Support.

In the Lab

Use the guidelines, concepts, and skills presented in this chapter to increase your knowledge of Windows 8. Labs are listed in order of increasing difficulty.

Lab 1: Browsing the Web

Problem: You would like to browse the web to find some websites. As proof of your visit, print the first page of each website and write a brief description about the website.

Instructions: Use Internet Explorer to perform the following tasks.

1. Run the Internet Explorer app.

2. Type `youtube.com` in the address bar and then press the ENTER key (Figure 4–49).

3. Print the first page, and write a brief description about the use of the website.

4. Type `hulu.com` in the address bar and then press the ENTER key.

5. Print the first page, and write a brief description about the use of the website.

6. Type `toonuniversity.com` in the address bar and then press the ENTER key.

7. Print the first page, and write a brief description about the use of the website.

8. Type `mla.org` in the address bar and then press the ENTER key.

9. Print the first page, and write a brief description about the use of the website.

Figure 4–49

In the Lab

Lab 2: Adding, Viewing, Printing, and Removing Favorites

Instructions: Your instructor would like you to practice browsing the web and adding websites to the Favorites Center. As proof of completing this assignment, print the first page of each website you visit.

Perform the following tasks:

Part 1: Creating a Folder in the Favorites Center
1. Run the Internet Explorer app in the desktop.
2. Tap or click the 'View favorites, feeds, and history' button, tap or click the 'Add to favorites' arrow, and then tap or click Organize favorites on the 'Add to favorites' menu to display the Organize Favorites dialog box (Figure 4–50).
3. Tap or click the New Folder button (Organize Favorites dialog box) to create a new folder. Type your first and last name as the new folder name and then press the ENTER key to name the new folder.
4. Tap or click the Close button (Organize Favorites dialog box).

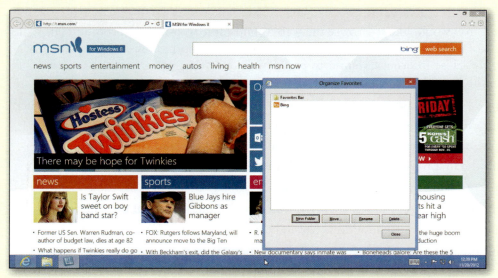

Figure 4–50

Part 2: Adding Favorites to Your Folder
1. Tap or click the address bar, type `www.whitehouse.gov` to enter the web address, and then press the ENTER key to display the White House home page.
2. Add the White House favorite to the folder identified by your name by tapping or clicking the 'View favorites, feeds, and history' button and then tapping or clicking the 'Add to favorites' button in the Favorites Center. Tap or click the Create in button, tap or click your folder in the Create in list, and then tap or click the Add button (Add a Favorite dialog box).
3. Tap or click the address bar, type `www.amazon.com` to enter the web address, and then press the ENTER key to display the Amazon.com home page.
4. Add this webpage as a favorite, change the name of the favorite to Amazon, and then create the favorite in your folder.
5. Tap or click the Home button at the top of the window to display your default home page.

Part 3: Displaying and Printing a Favorite from Your Folder
1. Tap or click the 'View favorites, feeds, and history' button to display the Favorites Center. If necessary, tap or click the Favorites tab.

STUDENT ASSIGNMENTS

2. Tap or click your folder in the Favorites Center and then tap or click The White House favorite.

3. Print the first page of the webpage.

4. If necessary, tap or click the 'View favorites, feeds, and history' button to display the Favorites Center.

5. Tap or click Amazon in the Favorites Center.

6. Print the first page of the website.

Part 4: Deleting a Folder in the Favorites Center

1. If necessary, display the Favorites Center.

2. Press and hold or right-click your folder name, tap or click Delete on the shortcut menu, and then if necessary, tap or click the Yes button (Delete Folder dialog box) to delete the folder.

3. If necessary, close the Favorites Center by tapping or clicking outside of it.

4. Verify that you have deleted your folder.

5. Submit the printed pages to your instructor.

In the Lab

Lab 3: Subscribing to RSS Feeds of News Websites

Instructions: To keep up with local and national news, you decide to subscribe to RSS feeds of two news websites. One will cover national news and the other will cover local news for the Orlando area. After subscribing to these feeds, display the feeds in Internet Explorer and print the first story for each feed.

Perform the following tasks:

Part 1: Subscribing to the FOXNews.com/News RSS Feed

1. Navigate to the FOXNews.com website (www.foxnews.com).

2. Subscribe to and display the FOXNews RSS feed.

3. Tap or click the link for the first news story.

4. Print the webpage and write your name on it.

Part 2: Subscribing to the OrlandoSentinel.com/News RSS Feed

1. Navigate to the OrlandoSentinel.com website (orlandosentinel.com) (Figure 4–51).

2. Subscribe to and display the RSS feed.

Figure 4–51

Continued >

STUDENT ASSIGNMENTS

In the Lab *continued*

3. Tap or click the link for the first news story.

4. Print the webpage and write your name on it.

5. Submit the printed webpages to your instructor.

Cases and Places

Apply your creative thinking and problem-solving skills to design and implement a solution.

1: Assessing Windows 8 Compatibility

Academic

Many websites provide their content via an RSS feed. As a student, you are interested in RSS feeds that will keep you abreast of current events while you are in school. Locate at least two news websites and at least two other websites that you are interested in that allow you to subscribe to an RSS feed. What are the advantages of subscribing to an RSS feed? Would you rather subscribe to an RSS feed or navigate directly to the website to view its content? Why or why not? Submit your answers to your instructor.

2: Social Networking

Personal

People of all ages, including children, parents, and grandparents, now are signing up for accounts on the more popular online social networks. Research four online social networks. Can anyone sign up for an account on these social networks? Do they cater to a specific audience? What steps has each social networking site taken to ensure the safety and privacy of its members? Of the four you researched, what is your preferred social network? Write a brief report containing your responses and submit it to your instructor.

3: Researching Online Safety

Professional

At work, you are tasked with writing a report about how to be safe when online to prevent identity theft and to safeguard information. Using Help, research how you can make a browser more secure. Using the browser, you should research identity theft and the measures that can be taken to prevent it. Write a brief report containing your responses and submit your report to your instructor.

LEARN ONLINE

Reinforce what you learned in this chapter with games, exercises, training, and many other online activities and resources.

Student Companion Site: Reinforce chapter terms and concepts using review questions, flash cards, practice tests, and interactive learning games, such as a crossword puzzle. These and other online activities and resources are available at no additional cost on www.cengagebrain.com. Visit www.cengagebrain.com/ct/studentdownload for detailed instructions about accessing the resources available at the Student Companion Site.

5 | Working with the Windows Desktop

Objectives

You will have mastered the material in this chapter when you can:

- Create, name, and save a document in WordPad
- Change the view and arrange objects in groups
- Create and name a folder
- Move documents into a folder
- Add and remove a shortcut on the desktop

- Open a folder using a desktop shortcut
- Open, modify, and print multiple documents in a folder
- Store files on a USB flash drive
- Delete multiple files and folders
- Work with the Recycle Bin

5 | Working with the Windows Desktop

Introduction

With thousands of hardware devices and software products available for desktops and laptops, users need to manage these resources quickly and easily. One of Windows 8's impressive features is the ease with which users can create and access documents and files. Mastering the desktop will help you to take advantage of user-interface enhancements and innovations that make computing faster, easier, and more reliable and that offer seamless integration with the Internet. Working with the Windows desktop in this chapter, you will find out how these features can save time, reduce computer clutter, and ultimately help you work more efficiently.

Overview

As you read this chapter, you will learn how to work with the desktop by performing these general tasks:

- Create and edit a WordPad document
- Move and rename a file
- Create and move a folder
- Store documents on a USB flash drive
- Delete and restore shortcuts, files, and folders using the Recycle Bin

Windows Desktop

As you have seen in previous chapters, many of the apps available in Windows run in the desktop. The desktop provides a convenient area for working with your files, folders, and apps. By default, the desktop includes the Recycle Bin shortcut. This is to allow you quick access to items you have deleted, in case you need to restore them or completely remove them from your computer. As you have seen, the taskbar contains app buttons that allow you quickly to run the File Explorer or Internet Explorer apps. In this chapter, you will see how to work with your desktop.

You can place items directly on the desktop for quick access. This includes files, folders, and even shortcuts. A **shortcut** is an icon that represents a link to a file, folder, or app. By tapping or clicking the shortcut, you can work with the item to which the shortcut is linked.

Creating a Document in WordPad

To learn how to work with the Windows desktop, you will create two course lists, one for Paulina Jones and one for Gerald Hammonds. Because they are registering for classes, you will need to update the lists with new courses as necessary. You will use WordPad, a popular word processing program available with Windows, to create the course lists. The finished documents are shown in Figure 5–1.

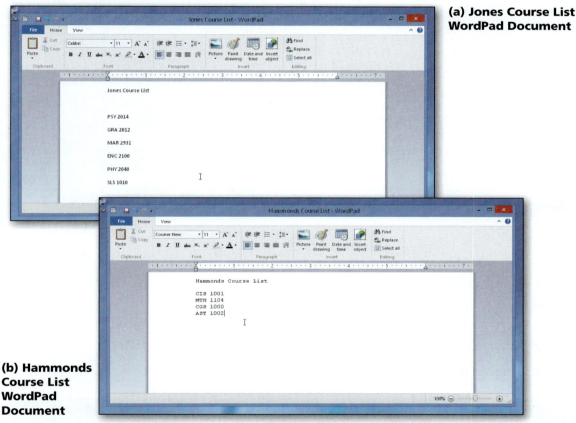

(a) Jones Course List WordPad Document

(b) Hammonds Course List WordPad Document

Figure 5–1

To Create a Document in WordPad

The steps on the following page create a document in WordPad. **Why?** *You want to create a document to hold information that you will need to reference and update in the future.*

1

- Display the Charms bar and tap or click the Search charm.
- Type `WordPad` in the Search box.
- Tap or click WordPad to run the WordPad app (Figure 5–2).

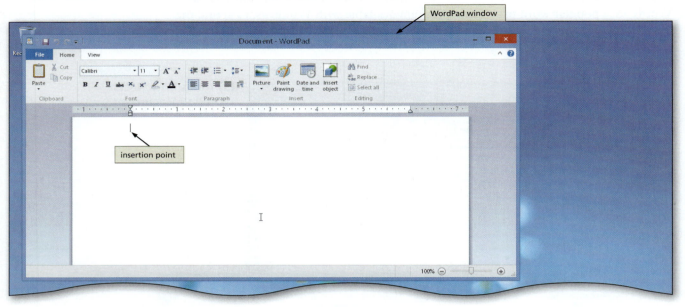

Figure 5–2

2

- Type `Jones Course List` and then press the ENTER key two times.
- Type `PSY 2014` and then press the ENTER key.
- Type `GRA 2012` and then press the ENTER key.
- Type `MAR 2931` and then press the ENTER key.
- Type `ENC 2100` and then press the ENTER key (Figure 5–3).

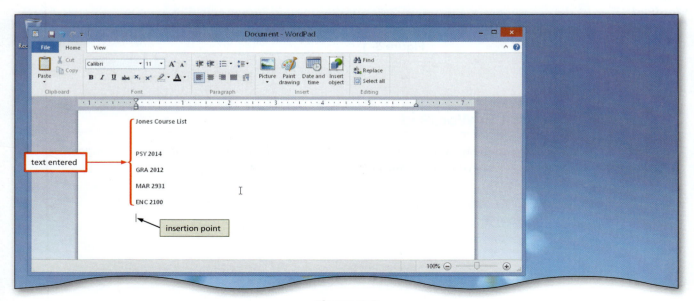

Figure 5–3

Other Ways

1. Display Start screen, display App bar, tap or click All apps button, tap or click WordPad icon

Saving Documents

When you create a document using a program such as WordPad, the document is stored in the main memory (random access memory, or RAM) of the computer. If you exit the program without saving the document or if the computer accidentally loses electrical power, the document will be lost. To protect against the accidental loss of a document and to allow you to modify the document easily in the future, you should save your document. Although you can save a file on the desktop, it is recommended that you save the document in a different location to keep the desktop free from clutter. For example, you can save files in the Documents library or on a USB flash drive.

The **Documents library** displays links to the user's documents as well as any public documents. The files and folders are not stored in the library; instead, the library links to files and folders regardless of where they are stored. You can add items to the Documents library as if you were working in the My Documents folder. The **My Documents** folder contains a particular user's documents and folders. The Documents library will show the links, although the actual folders and files will be stored in the My Documents folder. By default, the Documents library shows all files and folders in the My Documents folder.

When you save a document, you are creating a file. A **file** refers to a group of meaningful data that is identified by a name. For example, a WordPad document is a file; an Excel spreadsheet is a file; a picture made using Paint is a file; and a saved email message is a file. When you create a file, you must assign a file name to the file. All files are identified by a file name, and the file name should be descriptive of the contents of the saved file.

To associate a file with a program, Windows assigns an extension to the file name, consisting of a period followed by three or more characters. Most documents created using the WordPad program are saved as Rich Text Format documents with the .rtf extension, but they also can be saved as plain text with the .txt extension. A Rich Text Format document allows for formatting text and inserting graphics, which is not supported in plain text files.

Many computer users can tell at least one horror story of working on their computers for a long period of time and then losing all of their work because of a power failure or software problem. It is good practice to save often to protect your work.

BTW

File Names
A file name can contain up to 255 characters, including spaces. Any uppercase or lowercase character is valid when creating a file name, except a backslash (\), slash (/), colon (:), asterisk (*), question mark (?), quotation mark (' '), less-than sign (<), greater-than sign (>), or vertical bar (|) because these symbols have special meaning for the operating system. Similarly, file names cannot be CON, AUX, COM1, COM2, COM3, COM4, LPT1, LPT2, LPT3, PRN, or NUL because those are names reserved by the operating system.

To Save a Document in the Documents Library

Why? *Files should be saved so that the information they contain is not lost.* When saving files, you can use the Save button on the Quick Access Toolbar the first time to display the Save As dialog box, which allows you to choose a file name and a location in which to save your file. After the first time, when you use the Save button, you will save the file using the same file name and location. If you decide to change save locations or file names, you must use the Save as command on the File menu. The steps on the following page save the document you created using WordPad in the Documents library using the file name, Jones Course List.

1

- Tap or click the Save button on the Quick Access Toolbar to display the Save As dialog box.
- Type `Jones Course List` in the File name box (Figure 5–4).

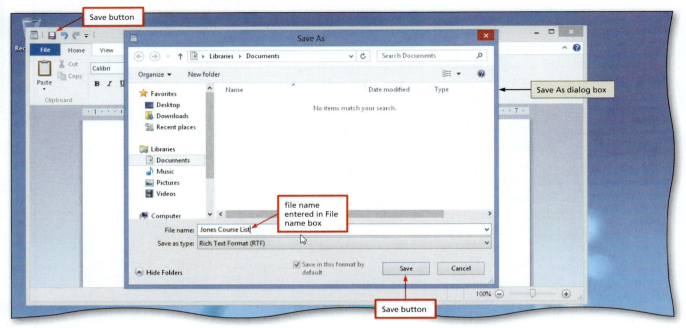

Figure 5–4

2

- Tap or click the Save button (Save As dialog box) to save the document and close the Save As dialog box (Figure 5–5).

Q&A | Why did the title bar of WordPad change?

Now that you have saved the document with a file name, the file name will be displayed on the title bar. To display a preview of the Jones Course List - WordPad window, touch or point to the WordPad app button on the taskbar.

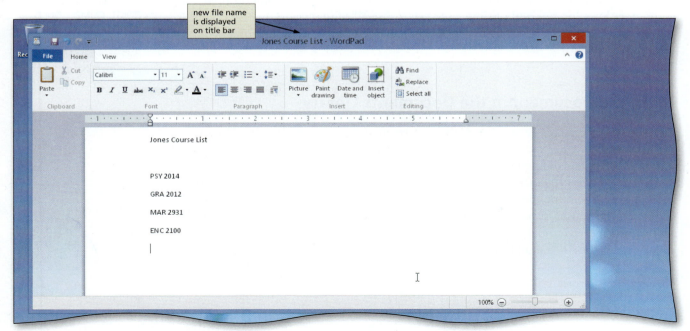

Figure 5–5

To Print a Document

Why? *Paper printouts are still an important form of output for electronic documents.* Many sophisticated programs, however, are expanding their printing capabilities to include sending email messages and posting documents to websites. One method of printing a document is to print it directly from an app. The following steps print the document.

1
- Ready the printer according to the printer's instructions.
- Tap or click File on the ribbon to display the File menu (Figure 5–6).

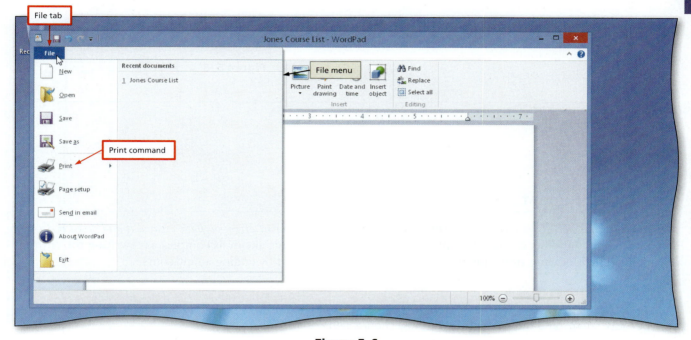

Figure 5–6

2
- Tap or click Print on the File menu to display the Print dialog box (Figure 5–7).

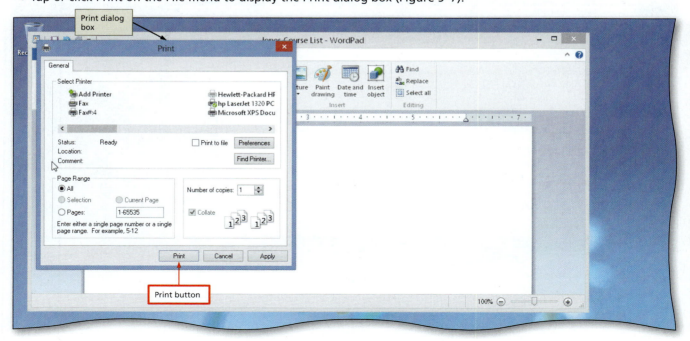

Figure 5–7

- If necessary, tap or click the appropriate printer to select your printer.
- Tap or click the Print button (Print dialog box) to print the document and return to the Jones Course List - WordPad window (Figure 5–8).

Figure 5–8

Other Ways

1. Press ALT+F, press P, tap or click appropriate printer, tap or click Print button

To Edit a Document

Why? *Undoubtedly, you often will want to make changes to a document after you have created it and saved it.* For any document, your edits can be as simple as correcting a spelling mistake or as complex as rewriting the entire document. The following step edits the Jones Course List document by adding a new course.

- If necessary, tap or click the blank line below the fourth course.
- Type PHY 2040 and then press the ENTER key (Figure 5–9).

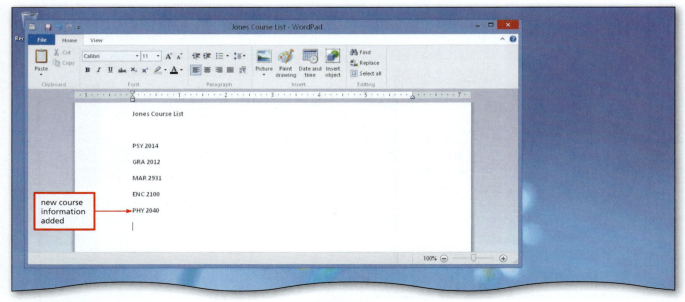

Figure 5–9

To Save and Close a Document

Why? *If you forget to save a document after you have edited it, when you attempt to close the document, a dialog box will be displayed asking if you want to save your changes.* This is how many programs help protect you from losing your work. If you choose not to save your changes, then all edits you made since the last time you saved will be lost. If you tap or click the Cancel button, your changes will not be saved, but the document will remain open and you can continue working. The following step closes and saves the Jones Course List document and then exits WordPad.

- Tap or click the Close button on the title bar to display the WordPad dialog box (Figure 5–10).

- Tap or click the Save button (WordPad dialog box) to save your changes to the document and exit WordPad.

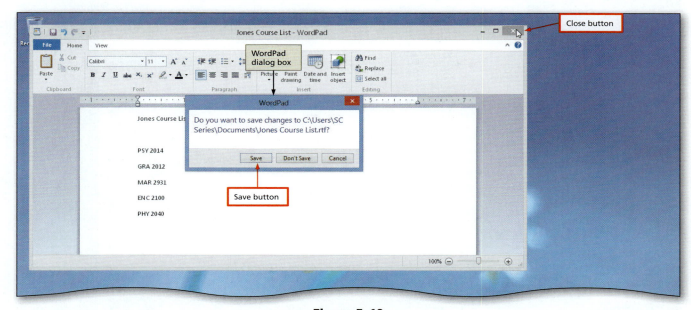

Figure 5–10

Creating a Document in the Documents Library

After completing the course list for Paulina Jones, the next step is to create a similar list for Gerald Hammonds. Running an app and then creating a document was the method used to create the first document. Although the same method could be used to create the document for Gerald Hammonds, another method is to create the new document in the Documents library without first running an app. Instead of running an app to create and modify a document, you first create a blank document directly in the Documents library and then use WordPad to enter data into the document.

To Open the Documents Library

Why? You want to work in the Documents library directly and, therefore, need to run File Explorer and switch to the Documents library. The followings step opens the Documents library.

1

- Tap or click the File Explorer app button on the taskbar to run File Explorer.

- Tap or click Documents in the navigation pane to display the Documents library (Figure 5–11).

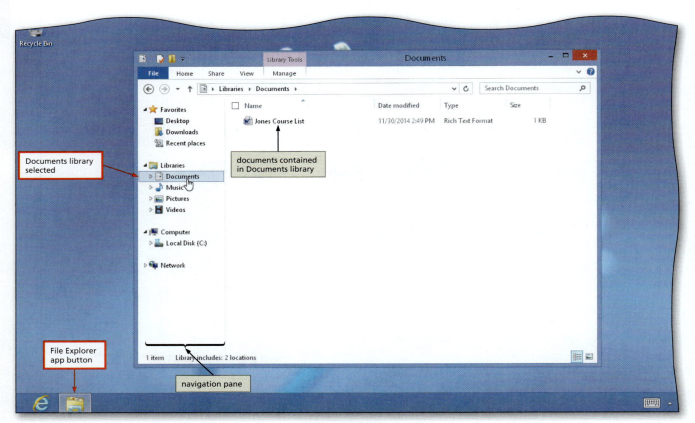

Figure 5–11

To Move a Window by Dragging

Why? You want to better manage your desktop by repositioning the window. The followings step drags the Documents library window to the upper-left corner of the screen.

1

- Drag the window (by dragging the window's title bar) upward and to the left to position the window in the upper-left corner of the screen (Figure 5–12).

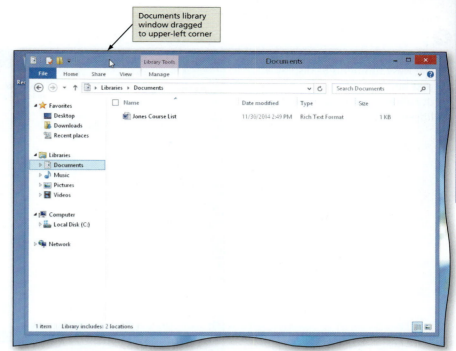

Figure 5–12

To Create a Blank Document in the Documents Library

The phrase, creating a blank document, might be confusing. The document you actually create contains no data; it is blank. You can think of it as placing a blank piece of paper with a name inside the Documents library. The document has little value until you add text or other data to it. *Why? You want to create a document but have not decided on the content yet.* The following steps create a blank document in the Documents library to contain the course list for Gerald Hammonds.

1

- Press and hold or right-click an open area of the Documents library to display the shortcut menu.

- Tap or point to the New command on the shortcut menu to display the New submenu (Figure 5–13).

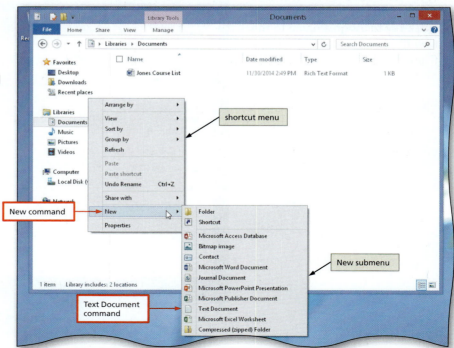

Figure 5–13

2

- Tap or click Text Document on the New submenu to display a text box and icon for a new text document in the Documents library (Figure 5–14).

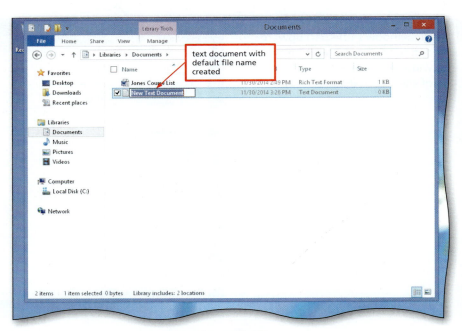

Figure 5–14

To Assign a File Name to a Document in the Documents Library

Why? *After you create a blank document, you need to assign a file name to it so that it is easily identifiable.* In Figure 5–14, the default file name (New Text Document) is highlighted and the insertion point is blinking, indicating that you can type a new file name. The following step assigns the file name, Hammonds Course List, to the blank document you just created.

1

- Type `Hammonds Course List` in the text box and then press the ENTER key to assign a name to the new file in the Documents library (Figure 5–15).

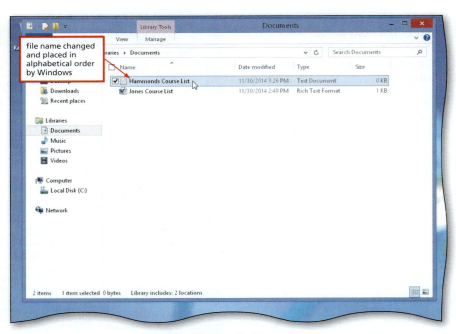

Figure 5–15

Other Ways

1. Press and hold or right-click icon, tap or click Rename on shortcut menu, type file name, press ENTER

2. Tap or click icon to select icon, press F2, type file name, press ENTER

To Open a Document in WordPad

Although you have created the Hammonds Course List document, the document contains no text. To add text to the blank document, you must open it. ***Why?*** *Because text files open in Notepad by default, you need to use the shortcut menu to open the file in WordPad.* The following steps open a document in WordPad.

1

- Press and hold or right-click the Hammonds Course List document icon to display the shortcut menu.

- Tap or point to Open with on the shortcut menu to display the Open with submenu (Figure 5–16).

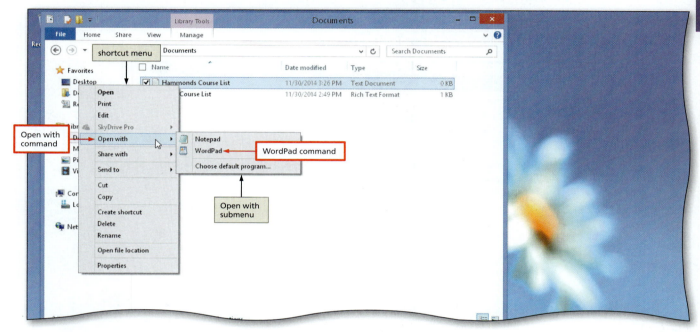

Figure 5–16

2

- Tap or click WordPad on the Open with submenu to open the Hammonds Course List document in WordPad (Figure 5–17).

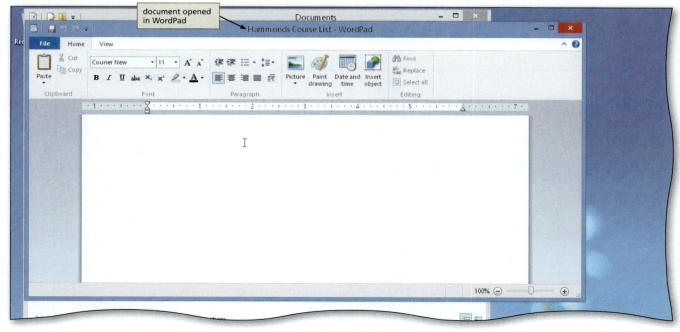

Figure 5–17

To Add Text to a Blank Document

Why? After the document is open, you can add text by typing in the document. The following steps add text to the Hammonds Course List document and then save the document.

1

- Type Hammonds Course List and then press the ENTER key twice.
- Type CIS 1001 and then press the ENTER key.
- Type MTH 1104 and then press the ENTER key.
- Type CGS 1000 and then press the ENTER key (Figure 5–18).
- Tap or click the Save button on the Quick Access Toolbar to save the file.

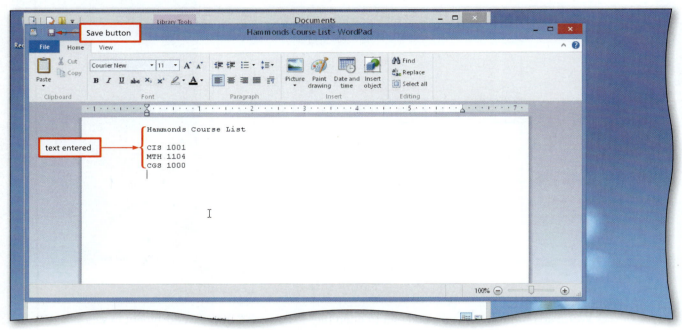

Figure 5–18

2

- If a WordPad dialog box appears, tap or click the Yes button (WordPad dialog box) to save the file as a text file (Figure 5–19).

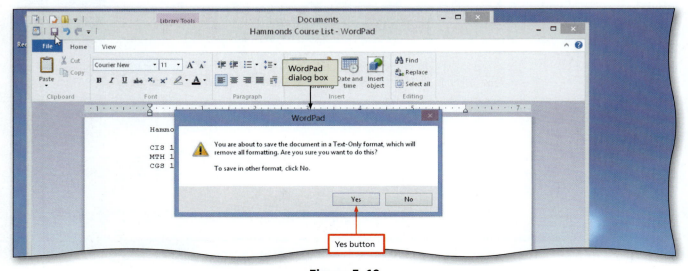

Figure 5–19

To Save a Text Document as a Rich Text Format (RTF) File

Typing text in the Hammonds Course List document modifies the document, which results in the need to save the document. If you make many changes to a document, you should save the document as you work. *Why? When you created the blank text document, Windows assigned it the .txt file name extension, so you will need to use the Save as command to save it in Rich Text Format, which is WordPad's default format.* Using the Rich Text Format allows you to use all of WordPad's features, including formatting options. The following steps save the document in Rich Text Format.

- Tap or click the File tab to display the File menu.
- Tap or click Save as on the File menu to display the Save As dialog box.
- Tap or click the 'Save as type' arrow to display the Save as type list (Figure 5–20).

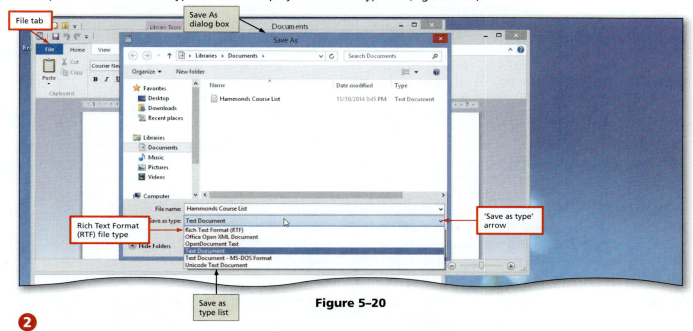

Figure 5–20

2

- Tap or click Rich Text Format (RTF) to change the file type to Rich Text Format (Figure 5–21).
- Tap or click the Save button (Save As dialog box) to save the document in Rich Text Format.

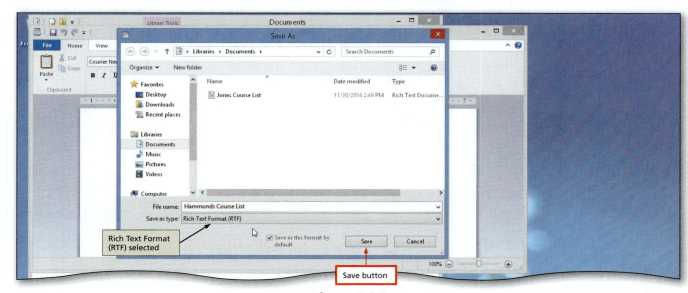

Figure 5–21

To Close the Document

You have saved your changes to Hammonds Course List, and now you can close the document. The following step closes the document and exits WordPad.

1 Tap or click the Close button on the title bar to close the document and exit WordPad.

Working with the Documents Library

Once you create documents in the Documents library using either the application-centric or document-centric approach, you can continue to modify and save the documents, print the documents, or create a folder to contain the documents and then move the documents to the folder. Having a single storage location for documents makes it easy to create a copy of the documents so that they are not accidentally lost or damaged.

To Change the View to Small Icons

Why? The default view in the Documents library is Details view. Details view shows a list of files and folders, along with common properties, such as Date Modified and Type. You can change to other views to alter the way the folder appears using the View tab on the ribbon. The Small icons, Medium icons, Large icons, and Extra large icons views display the icons in increasingly larger sizes. When Medium icons, Large icons, or Extra large icons views are selected, Windows provides a live preview option. With live preview, the icons display images that more closely reflect the actual contents of the files or folders. For example, a folder icon for a folder that contains text documents would show sample pages from those documents. List view displays the files and folders as a list of file names without any extra details. Tiles view displays the files and folders as tiles, which consist of an icon and icon description. With all of these views, the default arrangement for the icons is to be listed alphabetically by file name. The following step changes the view from Details view to Small icons view.

1

- Tap or click View on the ribbon to display the View tab (Figure 5–22).

- Tap or click the Small icons button (View tab | Layout group).

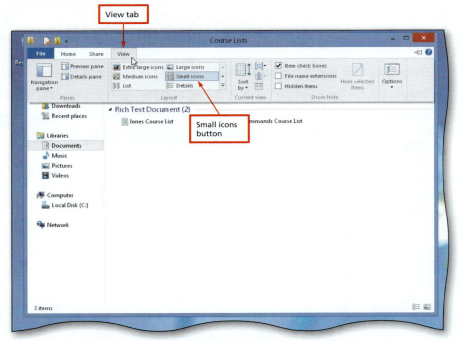

Figure 5–22

Other Ways

1. Press and hold or right-click open space in Documents library, tap or point to View on shortcut menu, tap or click Small icons on View submenu

To Arrange Items in Groups by File Type

Other methods can be used to arrange the icons in the Documents library. One practical arrangement is to display the icons in groups based upon file type. *Why? This arrangement places files of the same type (File Folder, Text Documents, Microsoft Word, Microsoft Excel, and so on) in separate groups.* When a window contains many files and folders, this layout makes it easier to find a particular file or folder quickly. The following steps group the icons in the Documents library by file type.

1

- Press and hold or right-click the open space below the list of files and folders in the Documents library to display the shortcut menu.

- Tap or point to Group by on the shortcut menu to display the Group by submenu (Figure 5–23).

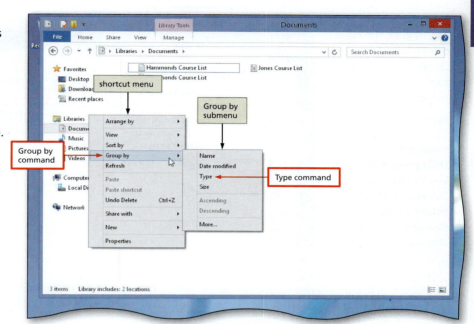

Figure 5–23

2

- Tap or click Type on the Group by submenu to display the files and folders grouped by type (Figure 5–24).

Q&A

Can I group the files and folders in other ways?

You can group the files by any of the options on the Group by submenu. This includes Name, Date modified, Type, and Size.

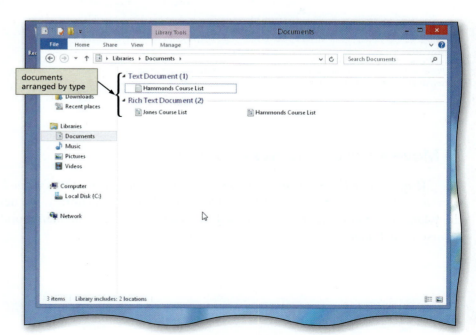

Figure 5–24

To Create and Name a Folder in the Documents Library

Why? *Windows allows you to place one or more documents into a folder in much the same manner as you might take a document written on a piece of paper and place it in a file folder.* You want to keep the Jones and Hammonds documents together so that you can find and reference them easily from other documents stored in the Documents library. To keep multiple documents together in one place, you first must create a folder in which to store them. The following step creates and names a folder titled Course Lists in the Documents library to store the Jones Course List and Hammonds Course List documents.

- Tap or click the New folder button on the Quick Access Toolbar to create a new folder.

- Type `Course Lists` in the folder's text box and then press the ENTER key to name the folder and store the folder in the Documents library (Figure 5–25).

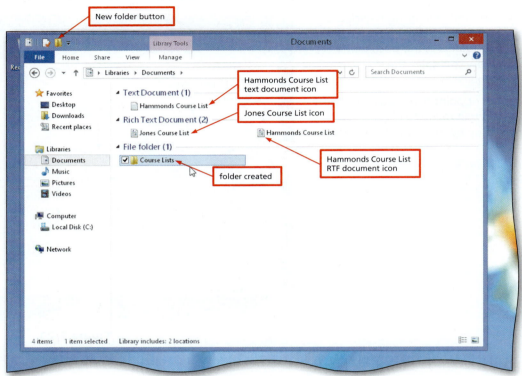

Figure 5–25

Other Ways

1. Press and hold or right-click open space in Documents library, tap or point to New on shortcut menu, tap or click Folder on New submenu, type file name, press ENTER

To Move a Document into a Folder

Why? *The ability to organize documents and files within folders allows you to keep the Documents library organized when using Windows.* After you create a folder in the Documents library, the next step is to move documents into the folder. The following step moves the Jones Course List and the Hammonds Course List documents into the Course Lists folder.

1

- Drag the Jones Course List icon (shown in Figure 5–25) to the Course Lists folder to move the Jones Course List to the Course Lists folder.

- Drag the Hammonds Course List RTF icon (shown in Figure 5–25) to the Course Lists folder to move it to the Course Lists folder.

- Drag the Hammonds Course List text icon (shown in Figure 5–25) to the Course Lists folder to move it to the Course Lists folder (Figure 5–26).

Q&A What happened to the Rich Text Document and Text Document groups?

The documents have been moved to the new folder, so the groups no longer were needed. Only if other RTF and text documents were contained in the Documents library would the groupings remain.

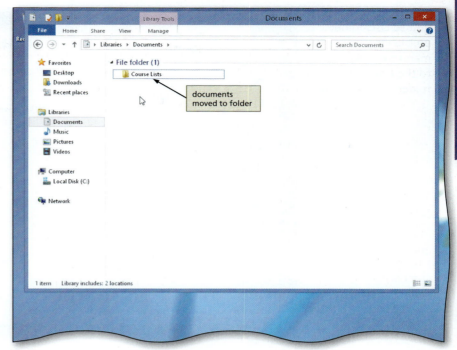

Figure 5–26

Other Ways

1. Press and hold or right-click document icon, tap or click Cut on shortcut menu, press and hold or right-click folder icon, tap or click Paste on shortcut menu

To Change Location Using the Address Bar

If you would like to navigate to the folder to see if your files are there, Windows provides several ways to do this. One way is to use the address bar. *Why? The address bar appears at the top of the Documents library window and displays your current location as a series of links separated by arrows. By clicking the arrows, you can change your location.* The Forward and Back buttons can be used to navigate through the locations you have visited just like the Forward and Back buttons in a browser. The following steps change your location to the Course Lists folder.

1

- Tap or click the Documents arrow on the address bar to display a location menu that contains a list of folders in the Documents library (Figure 5–27).

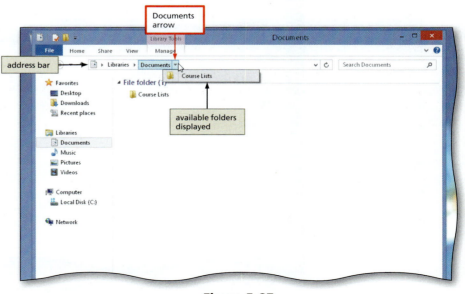

Figure 5–27

● Tap or click the Course Lists folder on the location menu to navigate to the Course Lists folder (Figure 5–28).

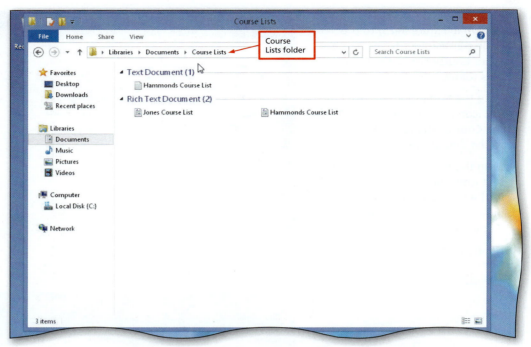

Figure 5–28

To Display and Use the Preview Pane

While you are viewing the contents of the Course Lists folder, you can add a preview pane to the layout, which provides you with an enhanced live preview of your documents. **Why?** *When you select a document, the preview pane displays a live preview of the document to the right of the list of files in the folder window.* The following steps add the preview pane to the layout of the Course Lists folder and then display a live preview of the Jones document.

● Tap or click View on the ribbon to display the View tab (Figure 5–29).

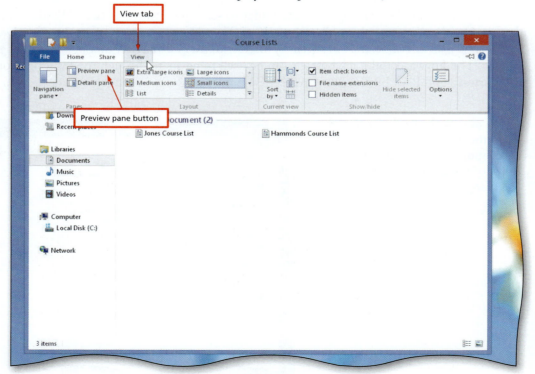

Figure 5–29

2

● Tap or click the Preview pane button (View tab | Panes group) to display the preview pane (Figure 5–30).

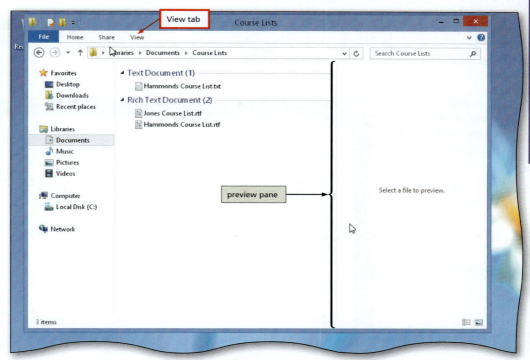

Figure 5–30

3

● Tap or click the Jones Course List document icon to display a preview of the document in the preview pane (Figure 5–31).

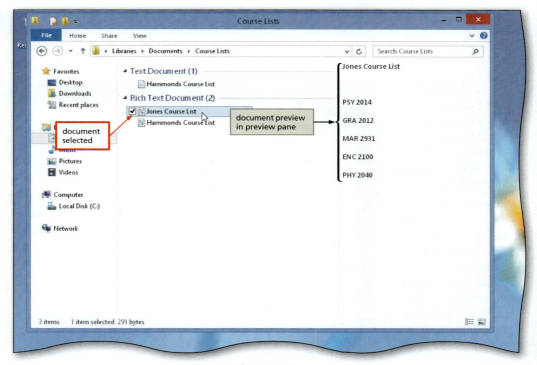

Figure 5–31

Other Ways

1. Press ALT+V+P

To View the File Name Extensions

Every file has an extension to identify the type of file. By default, Windows hides the extensions so that users do not accidentally change them. **Why?** *Sometimes, it is good to know the file types so that you can identify the apps you need.* The following steps display the file extensions.

1

• Tap or click View on the ribbon to display the View tab (Figure 5–32).

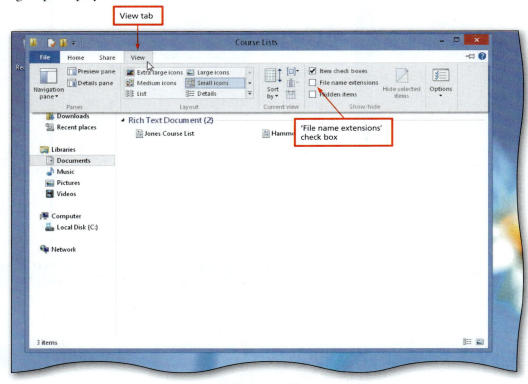

Figure 5–32

2

• Tap or click the 'File name extensions' check box (View tab | Show/hide group) to display file name extensions (Figure 5–33).

• After viewing the file name extensions, tap or click the 'File name extensions' check box (View tab | Show/hide group) to remove the check mark and hide the file name extensions.

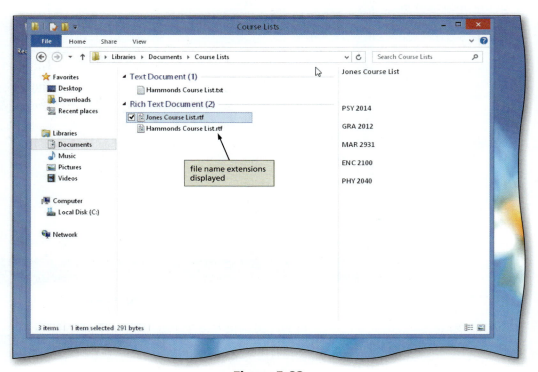

Figure 5–33

To Close the Preview Pane

Because you no longer need to preview the documents, the following step closes the preview pane.

1 Tap or click the Preview pane button (View tab | Panes group) to close the preview pane.

To Change Location Using the Back Button on the Address Bar

Why? *In addition to using the arrows on the address bar, you also can change locations with the Back and Forward buttons.* Tapping or clicking the Back button allows you to return to a location that you already have visited. The following step changes your location to the Documents library.

1

• Tap or click the Back button on the address bar one time to return to the Documents library (Figure 5–34).

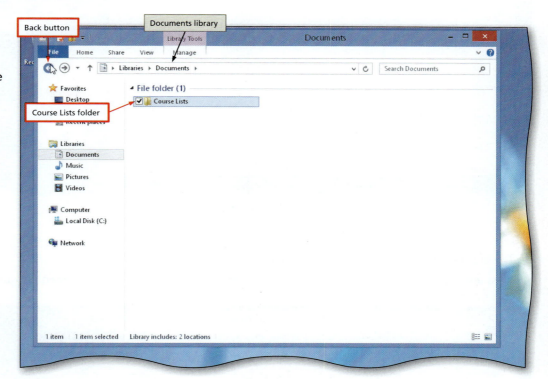

Figure 5–34

Creating Folder Shortcuts

One way to customize Windows is to use shortcuts to run apps and open files or folders. A shortcut is a link to any object on the computer or on a network, such as an app, file, folder, webpage, printer, or another computer. Placing a shortcut to a folder on the desktop can make it easier to locate and open the folder.

A shortcut icon is not the actual document or app. You do not actually place the folder on the desktop; instead, you place a shortcut icon that links to the folder on the menu. When you delete a shortcut, you delete the shortcut icon but do not delete the actual document or app; they remain on the hard disk.

To Paste a Shortcut on the Desktop

Why? When using the desktop, you can add shortcuts to frequently used files, folders, or apps. The following steps paste a shortcut for the Course Lists folder on the desktop.

1
- If necessary, select the Course Lists folder.
- Tap or click Home on the ribbon to display the Home tab (Figure 5–35).

Figure 5–35

2
- Tap or click the Copy button (Home tab | Clipboard group).
- Press and hold or right-click an open area of the desktop to display the shortcut menu (Figure 5–36).

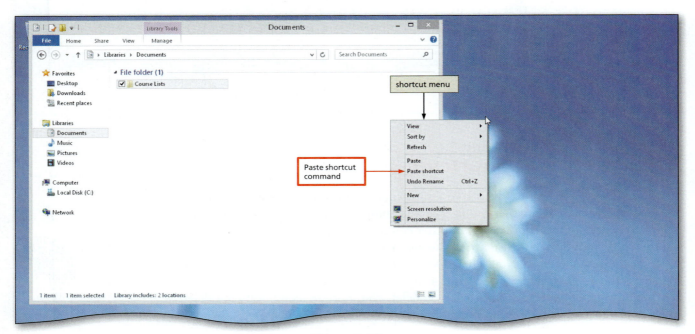

Figure 5–36

3

- Tap or click Paste shortcut on the shortcut menu to paste a shortcut on the desktop (Figure 5–37).
- Tap or click the Close button in the Documents library window to close the window.

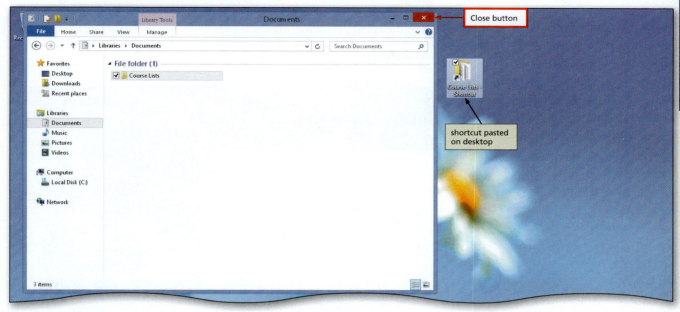

Figure 5–37

To Open a Folder Using a Shortcut

The following step opens the Course Lists folder window from the desktop. *Why? Once you create a shortcut, you can use it to open the file or folder or run the app associated with the shortcut.*

1

- Double-tap or double-click the Course Lists shortcut icon on the desktop to display the contents of the Course Lists folder (Figure 5–38).

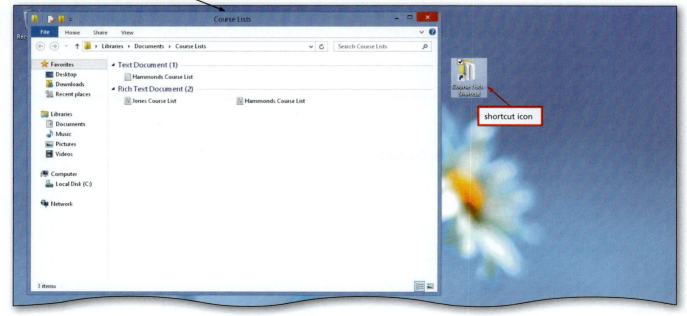

Figure 5–38

To Move a File to the Recycle Bin

Why? *When you no longer need a file, you can move it to the Recycle Bin for deletion at a later time.* The following step moves the Hammonds Course List text file to the Recycle Bin.

- If necessary, drag the Course Lists window down to make the Recycle Bin visible.
- Drag the Hammonds Course List text file to the Recycle Bin (Figure 5–39).

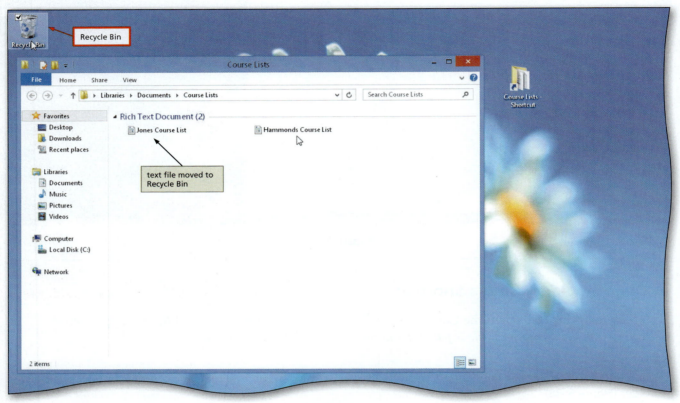

Figure 5–39

To Open and Modify a Document in a Folder

Why? *You have more text to add to the document.* The following steps open the Jones Course List document and add new text about another course.

- Use the shortcut menu to open the Jones Course List document in WordPad.

2

- Position the insertion point on the blank line below the fifth item in the list of courses.
- Type SLS 1010 and then press the ENTER key to modify the Jones Course List document (Figure 5–40).

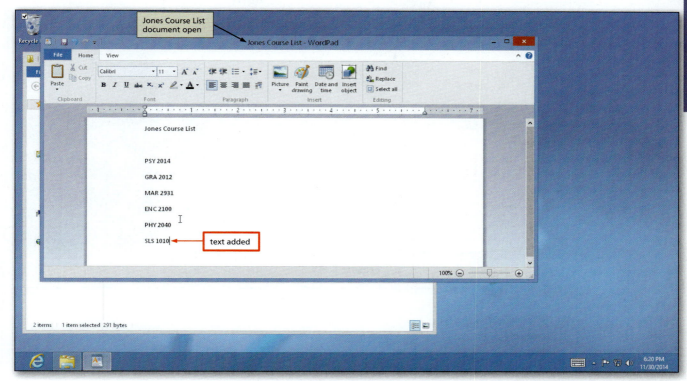

Figure 5–40

To Open and Modify Multiple Documents

Why? *Windows allows you to have more than one document open and more than one app running at the same time so that you can work on multiple documents.* The concept of multiple apps running at the same time is called **multitasking**. To illustrate how you can work with multiple windows open at the same time, you now will edit the Hammonds Course List document to include another course. You will not have to close the Jones Course List document first. The following steps open the Hammonds Course List document and add the new course.

1

- In the File Explorer window, open the Hammonds Course List document in WordPad.

Q&A

Why does the font look different in the two documents?

Because the Hammonds Course List document was created as a text file, its font will appear different from that of the Jones Course List document. Remember, Rich Text Format documents allow for more formatting than plain text files.

• Move the insertion point to the end of the document in the WordPad window.

• Type AST 1002 (Figure 5–41) and then press the ENTER key to modify the Hammonds Course List document.

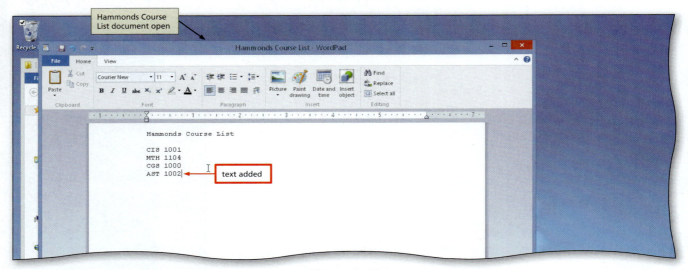

Figure 5–41

To Display an Inactive Window

Why? *While working with multiple documents, you may have to switch back and forth while editing them.* The following steps make the Jones Course List - WordPad window active.

• Tap or point to the WordPad app button on the taskbar to display a live preview of the two documents (Figure 5–42).

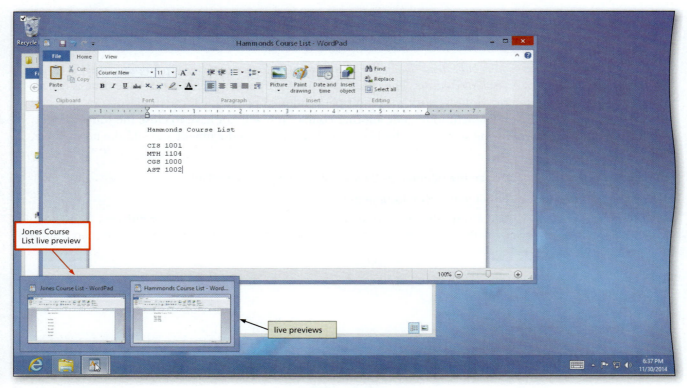

Figure 5–42

2
- Tap or click the Jones Course List live preview to make it the active window (Figure 5–43).

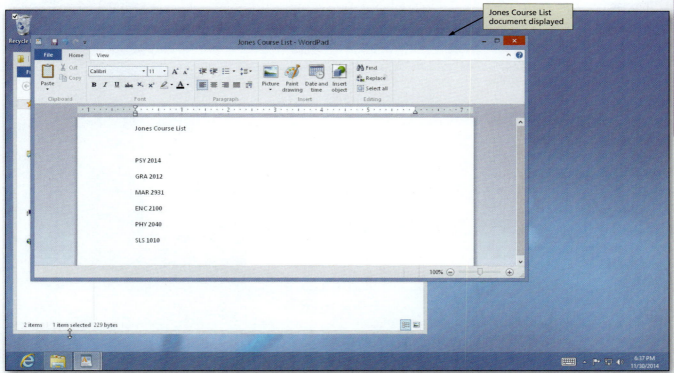

Jones Course List
document displayed

Figure 5–43

To Close Multiple Open Windows and Save Documents

Why? *When you have finished working with multiple windows, you should close them.* If the windows are open on the desktop, you can tap or click the Close button on the title bar of each open window to close them. Regardless of whether the windows are open on the desktop or are minimized using the Show desktop button, you can close the windows using the buttons on the taskbar. The following steps close the Jones Course List - WordPad and Hammonds Course List - WordPad windows using the taskbar.

1
- Press and hold or right-click the WordPad app button on the taskbar to display a shortcut menu (Figure 5–44).

Q&A
What is the Recent list?
The Recent list shows files that you have recently used WordPad to edit.

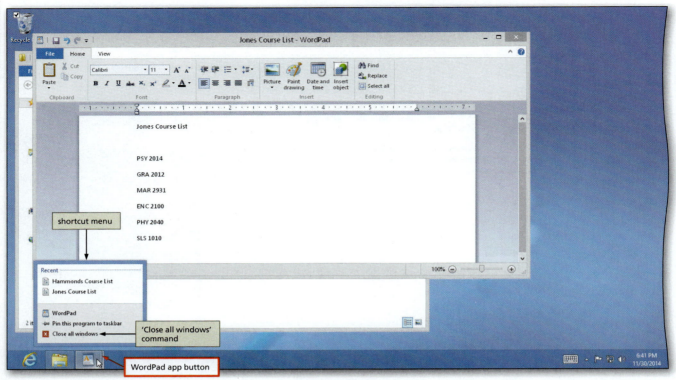

Figure 5–44

2

- Tap or click 'Close all windows' on the shortcut menu to display a WordPad dialog box (Figure 5–45).

- Tap or click the Save button (WordPad dialog box) to save the changes and close the Jones Course List document.

- Tap or click the Save button in the next WordPad dialog box that is displayed to save the changes and close the Hammonds Course List document.

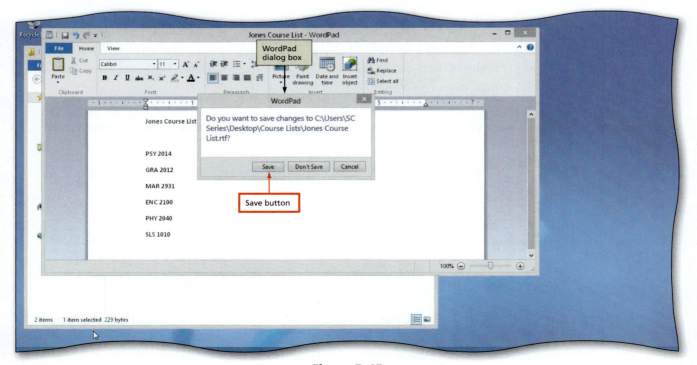

Figure 5–45

Copying a Folder on a USB Flash Drive

It is a good policy to make a copy of a folder and the documents within the folder so that if the folder or its contents are accidentally lost or damaged, you do not lose your work. This is referred to as making a backup of the files and folders. Another reason to make copies of files and folders is so that you can take the files and folders from one computer to another, for instance if you need to take a file or folder from a work computer to your home computer. A USB flash drive is a handy device for physically moving copies of files and folders between computers.

BTW

Backups

Copying a file or folder on a USB flash drive is one way to create a backup, but backing up files often is a much more elaborate process. Most backup systems use tape or portable hard disks that contain hundreds of gigabytes (billions of characters) or even terabytes (thousands of gigabytes) of storage space.

To Copy a Folder on a USB Flash Drive

Why? *You want to be able to use the files you have created on another computer. To do so, you will need to copy the files on your USB flash drive.* The following step copies the Course Lists folder on a USB flash drive.

- Insert a USB flash drive in a USB port to connect the USB flash drive.

- Navigate to the Documents library.

- Select the Course Lists folder.

- Tap or click the Copy to button (Home tab | Organize group) to display the Copy to menu (Figure 5–46).

- Tap or click command representing your USB flash drive (Removable Disk, in this case) to copy the folder to the USB flash drive.

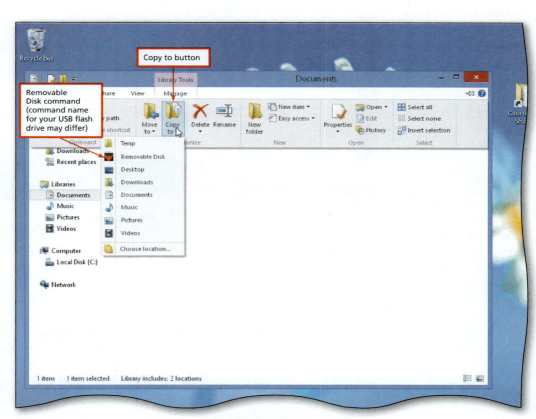

Figure 5–46

To Safely Remove a USB Flash Drive

Why? By safely removing the USB flash drive, you can be sure the information on the drive will not be accidentally lost, which can occur if you simply pull a USB flash drive from a port. The following step safely removes the USB flash drive.

- Navigate to the Computer folder.

- Press and hold or right-click the USB flash drive to display a shortcut menu (Figure 5–47).

- Tap or click Eject on the shortcut menu to eject the USB drive.

- Close the Computer window.

Q&A

Why does my USB flash drive have a different letter than what is shown in Figure 5–47?

Depending on how many devices you have connected to your computer, your USB flash drive might have been assigned a different letter, such as F or G.

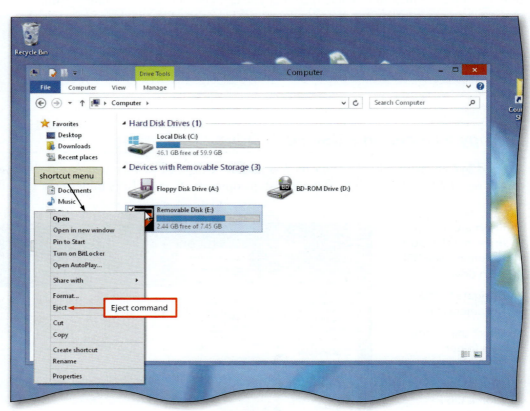

Figure 5–47

The Recycle Bin

Occasionally, you will want to delete files and folders from the Documents library. Windows offers three different techniques to perform this operation: (1) drag the object to the Recycle Bin, (2) right-drag the object to the Recycle Bin, and (3) press and hold or right-click the object and then tap or click Delete on the shortcut menu.

It is important to understand what you are doing when you delete a file or folder. When you delete a shortcut from the desktop, you delete only the shortcut icon and its reference to the file or folder. The file or folder itself is stored elsewhere on the hard disk and is not deleted. When you delete the icon for a file or folder (not a shortcut), the actual file or folder is deleted. A shortcut icon includes an arrow to indicate that it is a shortcut, whereas a file or folder does not have the arrow as part of its icon.

When you delete a file or folder, Windows places these items in the Recycle Bin, which is an area on the hard disk that contains all the items you have deleted. If you are running low on hard disk space, one way to gain additional space is to empty the Recycle Bin. Up until the time you empty the Recycle Bin, you can recover deleted files. Even though you have this safety net, you should be careful whenever you delete anything from your computer.

To Delete a Shortcut from the Desktop

The following step removes a shortcut from the desktop.

1 Drag the Course Lists shortcut icon to the Recycle Bin icon on the desktop to move the
shortcut to the Recycle Bin.

To Restore an Item from the Recycle Bin

Why? *At some point, you might discover that you accidentally deleted a shortcut, file, or folder that you did not want
to delete. As long as you have not emptied the Recycle Bin, you can restore them.* The following steps restore the Course
Lists shortcut icon to the desktop.

1
- Double-tap or
double-click the
Recycle Bin to open
it (Figure 5–48).

2
- Select the Course
Lists folder shortcut
icon.

- Tap or click the
'Restore the
selected items'
button (Recycle Bin
Tools Manage tab
| Restore group) to
restore the Course
Lists folder shortcut.

- Close the Recycle Bin
window.

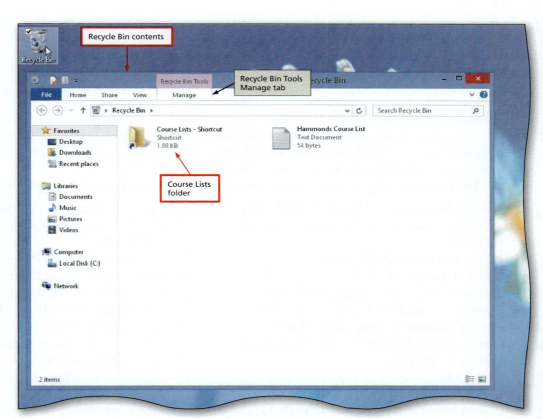

Figure 5–48

To Delete a Shortcut from the Desktop

Because you no longer need it, you now should delete the shortcut again. The
following step removes a shortcut from the desktop.

1 Drag the Course Lists shortcut icon to the Recycle Bin icon on the desktop to move the
shortcut to the Recycle Bin.

To Sign Out and Shut Down the Computer

The following steps sign out of open accounts and shut down the computer.

1 Swipe from the right or point to the upper-right corner of the screen to display the Charms bar.

2 Tap or click the Start charm on the Charms bar to return to the Start screen.

3 Tap or click the User icon to display user options.

4 Tap or click Sign out to sign out of Windows.

5 Tap or click anywhere on the screen.

6 Tap or click the Power button.

7 Tap or click Shut down on the menu.

Chapter Summary

In this chapter, you learned to create text documents using both the application-centric approach and document-centric approach. You moved these documents to the Documents library and then modified and printed them. You created a new folder in the Documents library, placed documents in the folder, and copied the new folder on a USB flash drive. You worked with multiple documents open at the same time. You placed a folder shortcut on the desktop and used the Recycle Bin.

The items listed below include the Windows skills you have learned in this chapter.

1. Create a Document in WordPad (WIN 163)
2. Save a Document in the Documents Library (WIN 165)
3. Print a Document (WIN 167)
4. Edit a Document (WIN 168)
5. Save and Close a Document (WIN 169)
6. Open the Documents Library (WIN 170)
7. Move a Window by Dragging (WIN 170)
8. Create a Blank Document in the Documents Library (WIN 171)
9. Assign a File Name to a Document in the Documents Library (WIN 172)
10. Open a Document in WordPad (WIN 173)
11. Add Text to a Blank Document (WIN 174)
12. Save a Text Document as a Rich Text Format (RTF) File (WIN 175)
13. Change the View to Small Icons (WIN 176)
14. Arrange Items in Groups by File Type (WIN 177)
15. Create and Name a Folder in the Documents Library (WIN 178)
16. Move a Document into a Folder (WIN 178)
17. Change Location Using the Address Bar (WIN 179)
18. Display and Use the Preview Pane (WIN 180)
19. View the File Name Extensions (WIN 182)
20. Change Location Using the Back Button on the Address Bar (WIN 183)
21. Paste a Shortcut on the Desktop (WIN 184)
22. Open a Folder Using a Shortcut (WIN 185)
23. Move a File to the Recycle Bin (WIN 186)
24. Open and Modify a Document in a Folder (WIN 186)
25. Open and Modify Multiple Documents (WIN 187)
26. Display an Inactive Window (WIN 188)
27. Close Multiple Open Windows and Save Documents (WIN 189)
28. Copy a Folder on a USB Flash Drive (WIN 191)
29. Safely Remove a USB Flash Drive (WIN 192)
30. Restore an Item from the Recycle Bin (WIN 193)

Apply Your Knowledge

Creating a Document with WordPad

Instructions: Use WordPad to create the shopping list shown in Figure 5–49.

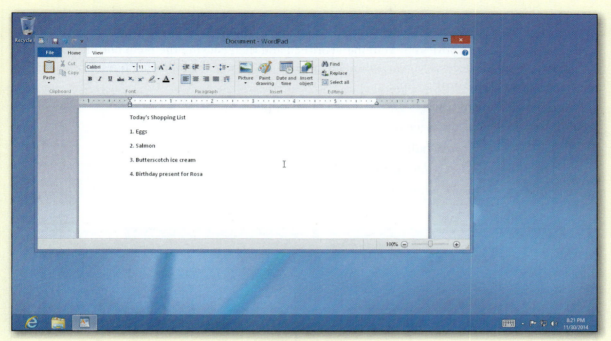

Figure 5–49

Part 1: Creating a Document Using WordPad

1. Run WordPad.

2. Type Today's Shopping List and then press the ENTER key.

3. Type 1. Eggs and then press the ENTER key.

4. Type 2. Salmon and then press the ENTER key.

5. Type 3. Butterscotch ice cream and then press the ENTER key.

6. Type 4. Birthday present for Rosa and then press the ENTER key.

Part 2: Printing the Shopping List Document

1. Tap or click the File tab and then tap or click Print to display the Print dialog box. Tap or click the Print button (Print dialog box) to print the document.

Part 3: Saving the File and Exiting WordPad

1. Insert a USB flash drive.

2. Save your document on the USB flash drive with the file name, Shopping List.

3. Exit WordPad, and close any open windows.

Extend Your Knowledge

Extend the skills you learned in this chapter and experiment with new skills. You will use Help to complete the assignment.

Using Help

Instructions: Use Windows Help and Support to perform the following tasks.

1. Find Help about WordPad by running WordPad and then clicking the Help button (Figure 5–50). If necessary, visit online Help and then answer the following questions using the How to Use WordPad link:

   a. What document features does WordPad not support?

   b. How do you change page orientation?

   c. How do you create a bulleted list?

   d. How do you insert dates, pictures, and links?

   e. How do you insert a drawing?

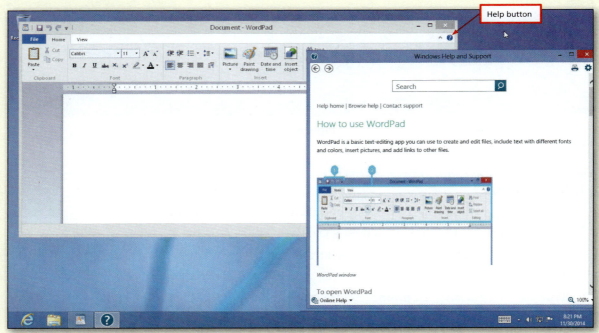

Figure 5–50

2. Exit WordPad Help and WordPad.

3. Open the Windows Help and Support window, type `files and folders` in the Search box, press the ENTER key, and browse the search results to answer the following questions:

   a. How do you sort files using column headings in File Explorer?

   b. How do you use the details pane to change file properties?

   c. How do you share a file or folder?

   d. What is a public folder?

4. Close the Windows Help and Support window.

In the Lab

Use the guidelines, concepts, and skills presented in this chapter to increase your knowledge of Windows 8. Labs are listed in order of increasing difficulty.

Lab 1: Creating a To-Do List

Problem: You have a schedule of tasks to complete today and need to create a to-do list.

Instructions: Use WordPad to perform the following tasks.

1. Open a new WordPad document. Save the document on the desktop using the file name, To-Do List. (*Hint*: When saving, save on the desktop.)

2. Type the text shown in Figure 5–51.

3. Save the document.

4. Print the document.

5. Close the document.

6. Move the document to the Documents library.

7. Create a folder in the Documents library named, Important Documents.

8. Place the To-Do List document in the Important Documents folder.

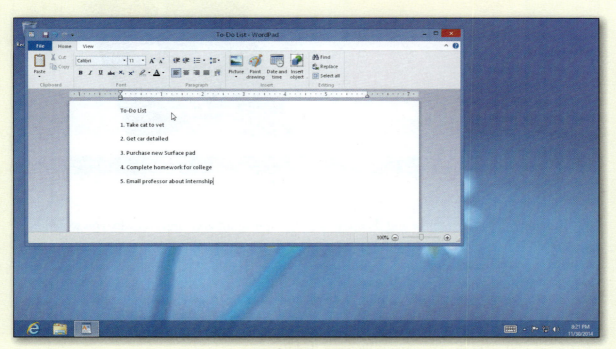

Figure 5–51

In the Lab

Lab 2: Researching Online

Instructions: You want to learn more about Windows and share the information with your friends.

Perform the following tasks:

1. Open a new WordPad document. Save the document on the desktop with the file name, Windows 8 Research. (*Hint:* When saving, save to the desktop.)

2. Run Internet Explorer and then type `http://windows.microsoft.com/en-US/windows-8/apps` in the Search box (Figure 5–52).

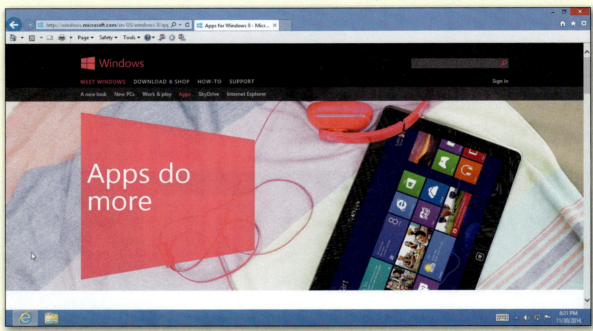

Figure 5–52

3. Find four apps that you like and then type a paragraph about each app and why you would use it in your Windows 8 Research document.

4. Save the document.

5. Print the document.

6. Close the document.

7. Move the document to the Documents library.

8. Create a folder in the Documents library called Research.

9. Place the Windows 8 Research document in the Research folder.

10. Copy the Research folder on a USB flash drive.

In the Lab

Lab 3: Selecting a Digital Camera

Instructions: You want to purchase a digital camera and decide to research them online.

Perform the following tasks:

1. Open a new WordPad document. Save the document in the Documents library with the file name, Digital Cameras.

2. Run Internet Explorer, type `digital cameras` in the Search box, and then press the ENTER key (Figure 5–53).

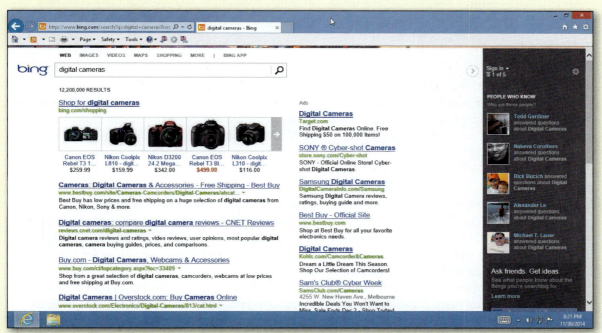

Figure 5–53

3. Find an online store that sells digital cameras, and look at the two top sellers. Enter the information about the cameras in the WordPad document. Find two more stores that sell the same digital cameras. Enter comparison information about the digital cameras in the WordPad document.

4. Save the document.

5. Print the document.

6. Close the document.

STUDENT ASSIGNMENTS

Cases and Places

Apply your creative thinking and problem-solving skills to design and implement a solution.

1: College Orientation

Academic

Managing time and resources is a challenge for incoming college freshmen. As someone who has gone through the process, prepare a guide for students who are about to begin college. Research and create your guide using information from your school. Your guide should contain two or more documents, including a schedule of key dates and times, a description of college resources, and suggestions for a smooth semester.

2: Researching Automobiles

Personal

You are looking into buying a new automobile, but want to buy only a hybrid. Use Internet Explorer to find out information about four hybrid cars. Use WordPad to create a file for each car. You plan to compare gas mileage, price, comfort, and maintenance. Save the documents in a folder in the Documents library. Back up the folder on a USB flash drive.

3: Creating a Computer Request List

Professional

Your employer is concerned that some people in the company are not thoroughly researching purchases of office computers. She has prepared a list of steps she would like everyone to follow when purchasing office computers: (1) determine your department's need for computers, (2) identify at least two websites that sell the computers you need, and (3) obtain prices for the computers from their websites.

Your employer wants you to use WordPad to prepare a copy of this list to post in every department. Save and print the document. After you have printed one copy of the document, try experimenting with different WordPad features to make the list more eye-catching. Save and print a revised copy of the document.

LEARN ONLINE

Reinforce what you learned in this chapter with games, exercises, training, and many other online activities and resources.

Student Companion Site: Reinforce chapter terms and concepts using review questions, flash cards, practice tests, and interactive learning games, such as a crossword puzzle. These and other online activities and resources are available at no additional cost on www.cengagebrain.com. Visit www.cengagebrain.com/ct/studentdownload for detailed instructions about accessing the resources available at the Student Companion Site.

Appendix A

Creating a Microsoft Account

Introduction

A **Microsoft account** is a free service that provides a personalized Windows experience across devices, apps, and services. If you previously created a Windows Live ID, this now is referred to as your Microsoft account. A Microsoft account consists of an email address and password that you can use to sign in to Windows 8 to connect to the cloud. You can sign in to any Windows 8 computer or mobile device with a Microsoft account to access your apps and customized user settings. These user settings include your lock screen picture, desktop tile layout, apps, spell check dictionaries, Internet Explorer favorites, and accessibility settings. The personalized settings associated with your Windows account are stored on the cloud. As these settings are changed or updated, they are kept in sync with each device you use.

In addition, the Microsoft account allows you to share your photos, documents, apps, and other files from places like SkyDrive, Facebook, and Flickr within Windows. For example, the People app in Windows connects to your Microsoft account to bring your contacts to one convenient location that roams across your Windows computers and phone. Using your Microsoft account credentials, you can connect to your Microsoft account by visiting outlook.com, which provides access to your documents, presentations, spreadsheets, databases, videos, and photos.

To Create a Microsoft Account

You can sign in to a Windows computer with a local user account or a Microsoft account. You can create a new Microsoft account from within Windows or on the web at outlook.com. The following steps create a Microsoft account within Windows after signing in to a user account.

1

- Swipe from the right or point to the upper-right corner of the screen to display the Charms bar (Figure A–1).

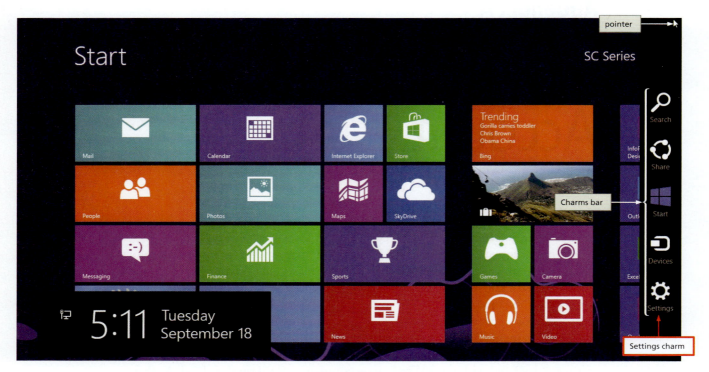

Figure A–1

2

- Tap or click the Settings charm on the Charms bar to display the Settings menu (Figure A–2).

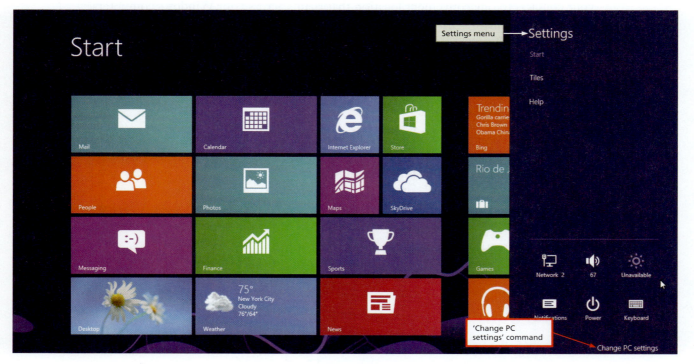

Figure A–2

3
- Tap or click the 'Change PC settings' command on the Settings menu to display the PC settings pane (Figure A–3).

Figure A–3

4
- Tap or click the Users command in the PC settings pane to display Users options in the right pane.
- If necessary, scroll down to view the 'Add a user' button (Figure A–4).

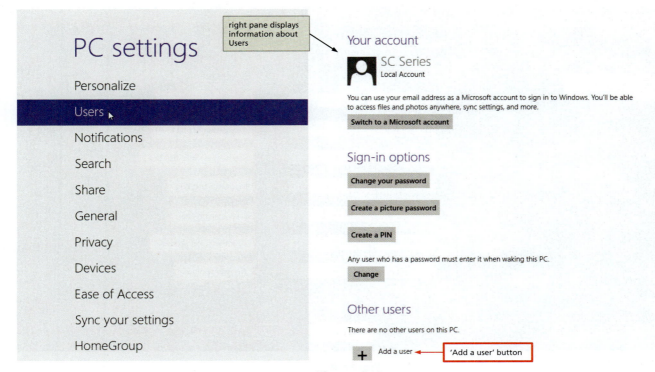

Figure A–4

5
- Tap or click the 'Add a user' button to display the 'Add a user' screen (Figure A–5).

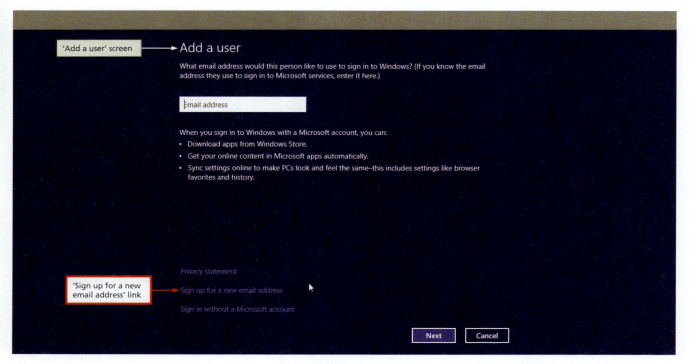

Figure A–5

6
- Tap or click the 'Sign up for a new email address' link to display the 'Sign up for a new email address' screen (Figure A–6).

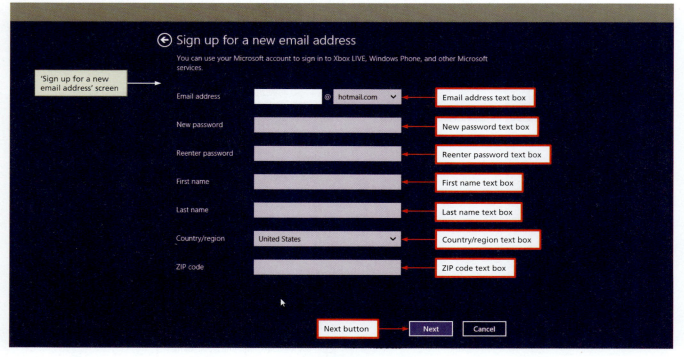

Figure A–6

7
- Tap or click the Email address text box in the 'Sign up for a new email address' screen, type your desired email address, and then tap or click the arrow to display mail options.
- Tap or click live.com or outlook.com.
- Tap or click the New password text box and type your desired password.
- Tap or click the Reenter password text box and reenter the same password as the previous step.
- Tap or click the First name text box and type your first name.
- Tap or click the Last name text box and type your last name.
- If necessary, tap or click the Country/region of your country of residence.
- Tap or click the ZIP code text box and then type your ZIP code.
- Tap or click the Next button to display the 'Add security info' screen (Figure A–7).

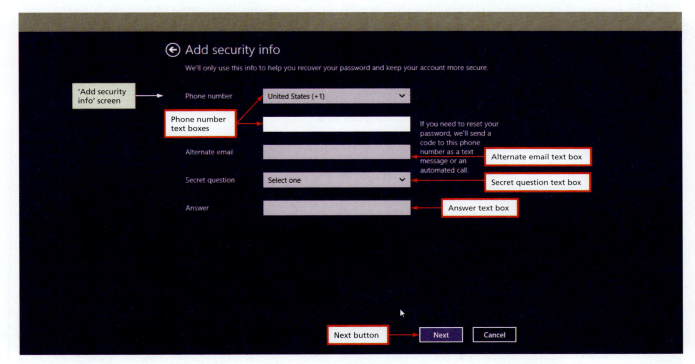

Figure A–7

8
- If necessary, select the Phone number in the 'Add security info' screen and then tap or click your country of residence.
- Tap or click the second Phone number text box and then type your phone number.
- Tap or click the Alternate email text box and then type an alternate email address.
- Tap or click the Secret question arrow and then tap or click the secret question of your choice.
- Tap or click the Answer text box and then type the answer to your secret question.
- Tap or click the Next button to display the Finish up screen (Figure A–8).

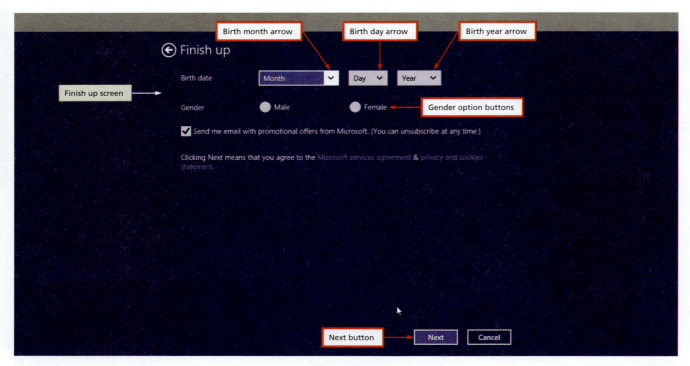

Figure A–8

9

- Tap or click the arrows to display and then select the birth date month, day, and year on the Finish up screen.
- Tap or click the appropriate Gender option button to select your gender.
- Tap or click the Next button to agree to the Microsoft services agreement & privacy and cookies statement (Figure A–9).

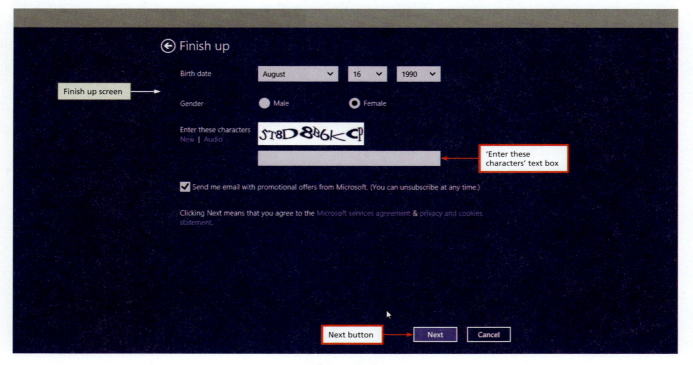

Figure A–9

- Enter the requested characters to confirm and complete your account creation process.

- Tap or click the Next button to create a user account that can sign in to this computer.

- Tap or click the Finish button to add the new user account to your computer.

Other Ways

1. Visit outlook.com, tap or click 'Sign up now' button, fill in your personal information

Appendix B

Windows 8 Security

Introduction

Windows 8 includes strong improvements in performance, security, malware protection, and system reliability. In addition, a number of updated security features help you accomplish three important goals: to enjoy a computer free from malware, including viruses, worms, spyware, and other potentially unwanted software; to have a safer online experience using Windows 8 apps and Web sites; and to understand when a computer is vulnerable and how to protect it from external threats.

Malware, short for malicious software, is a computer program that acts without a user's knowledge and deliberately alters a computer's operations. Examples of malware include viruses, worms, and spyware. A **virus** is a program that attaches itself to another program or file so that it can spread from computer to computer, infecting programs and files as it spreads. Viruses can damage computer software, computer hardware, and files. A computer **worm** copies itself from one computer to another by taking advantage of the features that transport data and information between computers. A worm is dangerous because it has the capability of traveling without being detected and to replicate itself in great volume. For example, if a worm copies itself to every contact in your email address book and then the worm copies itself to the names of all the email addresses of each of your contacts' computers, the effect could result in increased Internet traffic that slows down business networks and the Internet. **Spyware** is a program that is installed on your computer without your consent that monitors the activity that takes place to gather personal information and send it secretly to its creator. Spyware also can be designed to take control of the infected computer.

A **hacker** is an individual who uses his or her expertise to gain unauthorized access to a computer with the intention of learning more about the computer or examining the contents of the computer without the owner's permission.

To Display the Windows Action Center

The Action Center is a central location to view notifications and manage your computer's security by monitoring the status of several essential security features on your computer, including firewall settings, automatic updating, virus protection, spyware and unwanted software protection, Internet security settings, user account control settings, and network access protection. The following steps display the Action Center.

- Tap or click the Desktop tile to run the Desktop app.
- Point to the upper-right corner of the desktop to display the Charms bar (Figure B–1).

Figure B–1

2
- Tap or click the Settings charm to display the Settings menu (Figure B–2).

Figure B–2

3
- Tap or click Control Panel on the Settings menu to open the Control Panel window (Figure B–3).

Figure B–3

4
- Tap or click the 'System and Security' link to open the System and Security window (Figure B–4).

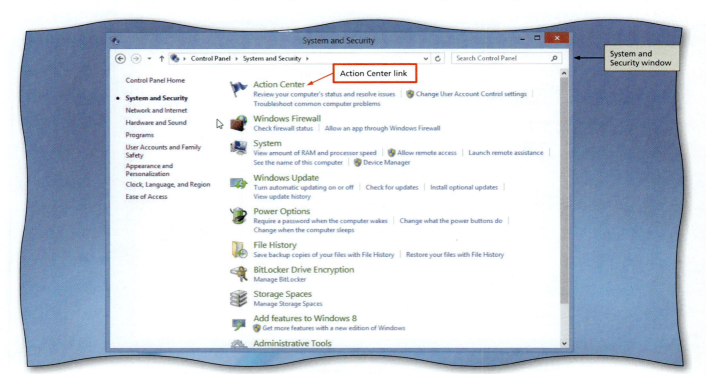

Figure B–4

5

- Tap or click the Action Center link in the System and Security window to open the Action Center window (Figure B–5).

Figure B–5

6

- Tap or click the Security section arrow to expand the Security section (Figure B–6).

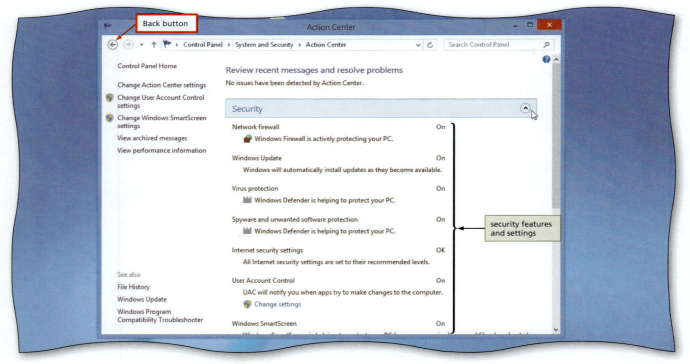

Figure B–6

Understanding the Action Center

The right pane, which has two expandable sections, displays options to let you review messages and resolve problems. The first section is the Security section. Tapping or clicking the section arrow to the right of the Security heading expands the section and displays security features. Settings labeled On and OK mean that the security feature is turned on and working properly. Settings labeled Off mean that the security feature is turned off and you should turn it on, if appropriate according to that feature. For features that have settings you can change, you will see options for adjusting them. Important messages about security and maintenance settings that need your attention are displayed in the Action Center if an issue arises. Items marked with a preceding red block indicate urgent issues that should be addressed as soon as possible, while items marked in yellow are issues that are not pressing but that you should consider addressing soon.

The second section is the Maintenance section, which allows you to view maintenance features. Similar to the Security section, settings labeled On and OK mean that the maintenance feature is turned on and working, and settings labeled Off mean that the feature is turned off and you should turn it on, if appropriate according to that particular feature. Not all maintenance features have the same options. For example, if Automatic Maintenance is turned on, you will see only the message, No action needed. For some of the features, you also can choose whether or not you want to monitor the messages that pop up when an issue arises. If you choose not to monitor a feature, the status will be listed as, Currently not monitored. As with the security features, if you can change settings, you will see options for adjusting them.

In the left pane of the Action Center window are links to Control Panel Home, Change Action Center settings, Change User Account Control settings, Change Windows SmartScreen settings, View archived messages, and View performance information. **Windows SmartScreen** helps protect your computer by warning you if a downloaded app or file is known to be malware or has an unknown reputation.

Managing Windows Firewall

Windows Firewall is a program that protects your computer from unauthorized users by monitoring and restricting data that travels between your computer and a network or the Internet. Windows Firewall also helps to block, but does not always prevent, computer viruses and worms from infecting your computer. Windows Firewall automatically is turned on when Windows 8 is started. It is recommended that Windows Firewall remain on, unless you have another firewall program actively protecting your computer. **Windows Defender** is an antivirus and malware protection program that is included in Windows 8; you also can install third-party software to protect against viruses and malware.

To Open the Windows Firewall Window

From the Windows Firewall window's right pane, you can monitor and manage the firewall settings for any network to which you are connected. Connected networks normally are classified as home, work, and public networks. Home and work networks are considered private networks and have settings that are different from public networks, which are not considered to be as secure.

From the left pane, you can allow programs or features through Windows Firewall, change notification settings, turn off Windows Firewall, restore default settings, adjust advanced settings, and troubleshoot your network. Windows Firewall is set up with the most secure settings by default, according to Microsoft. The following step opens the Windows Firewall window.

- Tap or click the Back button (shown in Figure B–6) in the Action Center window to return to the System and Security window.

- Tap or click the Windows Firewall link to open the Windows Firewall window (Figure B–7).

Q&A | Why does my window show a different network?

You can connect to different types of networks. The type of network connection you have will determine whether a home or a public network is displayed.

Figure B–7

To Allow a Feature through the Firewall

You can adjust Windows Firewall settings as needed. For example, if you have an app or feature that you want to allow to communicate through the firewall, you can allow it using the 'Allow an app or feature through Windows Firewall' link. Caution should be used because each app or feature allowed through the firewall carries the risk of making your computer less secure; that is, the computer becomes easier to access and more vulnerable to attacks by hackers. The more apps and features you allow, the more vulnerable the computer. To decrease the risk of security problems, allow only those apps or features that are necessary and recognizable, and promptly remove any app or feature that no longer is required.

One feature that sometimes is allowed for home and work private networks is File and Printer Sharing. This feature allows other computers access to files and printers that you choose to share with the network. The following steps allow File and Printer Sharing through the firewall for private networks only.

1

- Tap or click the 'Allow an app or feature through Windows Firewall' link to open the Allowed apps window (Figure B–8).

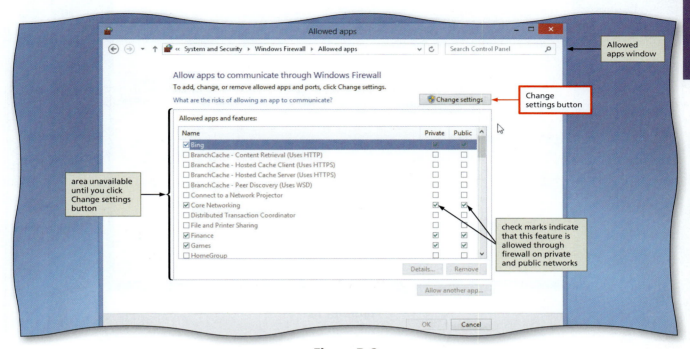

Figure B–8

2

- Tap or click the Change settings button to enable the 'Allowed apps and features' area.

- If necessary, scroll to display the 'File and Printer Sharing' feature in the 'Allowed apps and features' area (Figure B–9).

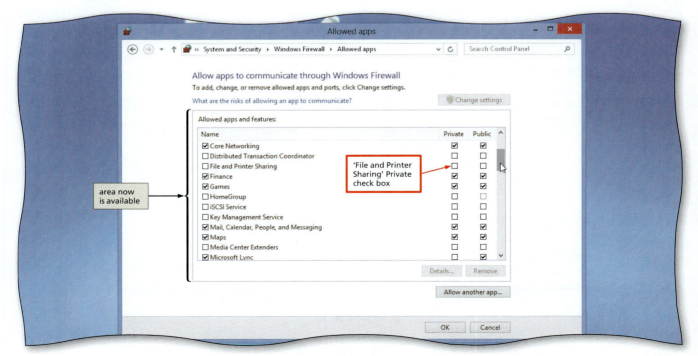

Figure B–9

3
● Tap or click to select the Private check box for 'File and Printer Sharing' (Figure B–10).

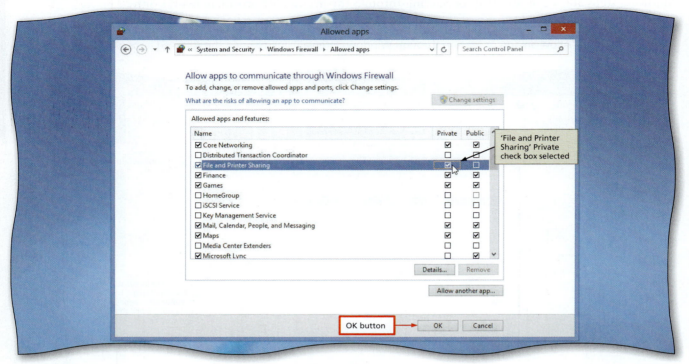

Figure B–10

4
● Tap or click the OK button to accept the changes and return to the Windows Firewall window (Figure B–11).

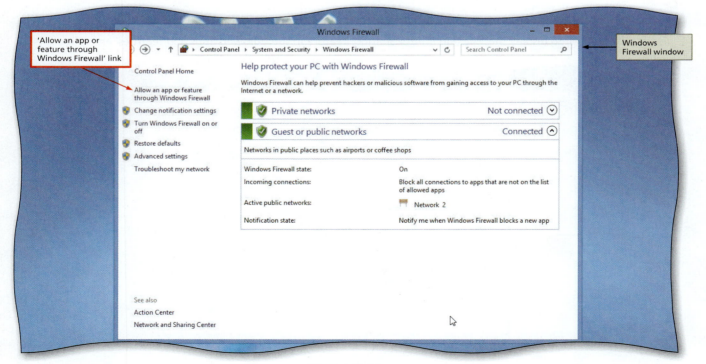

Figure B–11

To Disallow a Feature through the Firewall

If you later decide that you do not want to allow a program or feature through the Windows Firewall, you should disallow it. The following steps disallow File and Printer Sharing through the firewall for Private (home/work) networks only.

- Tap or click the 'Allow an app or feature through Windows Firewall' link to open the Allowed apps window.
- If necessary, tap or click the Change settings button to access the 'Allowed apps and features' area.
- If necessary, scroll to display the 'File and Print Sharing' feature in the 'Allowed apps and features' list (Figure B–12).

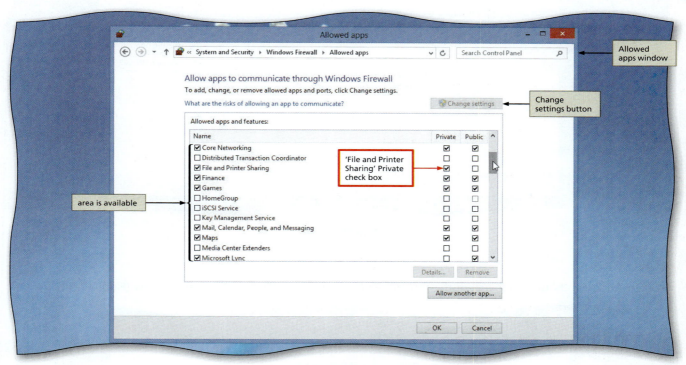

Figure B–12

2
● Tap or click the Private check box for 'File and Printer Sharing' to remove the check mark (Figure B–13).

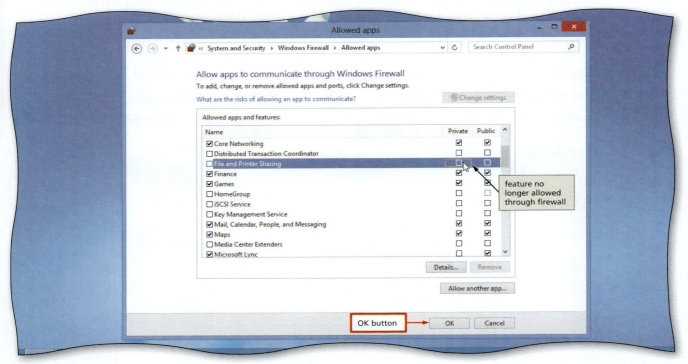

Figure B–13

3
● Tap or click the OK button to accept the changes and return to the Windows Firewall window (Figure B–14).

Figure B–14

Windows Update

Windows Update helps to protect your computer from viruses, worms, and other security risks. When Windows Update is turned on and the computer is connected to the Internet, Windows periodically checks with Microsoft to find updates for your computer and then automatically downloads them. If the Internet connection is lost while downloading an update, Windows resumes downloading when the Internet connection becomes available.

To Install Updates Automatically

You want to make sure that your computer is set to receive critical updates and install them automatically. The following steps configure an automatic update for your Windows Update settings.

- Tap or click the 'Up to System and Security' button (shown in Figure B-14) to return to the System and Security window (Figure B–15).

Figure B–15

- Tap or click the Windows Update link in the System and Security window to open the Windows Update window (Figure B–16).

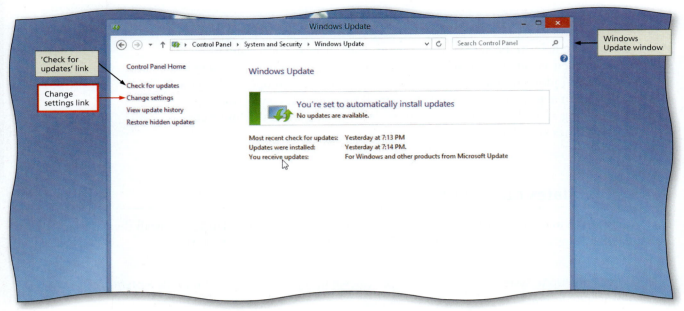

Figure B–16

❸
- Tap or click the Change settings link to open the Change settings window (Figure B–17).

❹
- If necessary, tap or click 'Install updates automatically (recommended)' in the Important updates list to install important updates to your computer automatically.

- Tap or click the OK button in the Change settings window to save the changes and return to the Windows Update window.

- Close the Windows Update window.

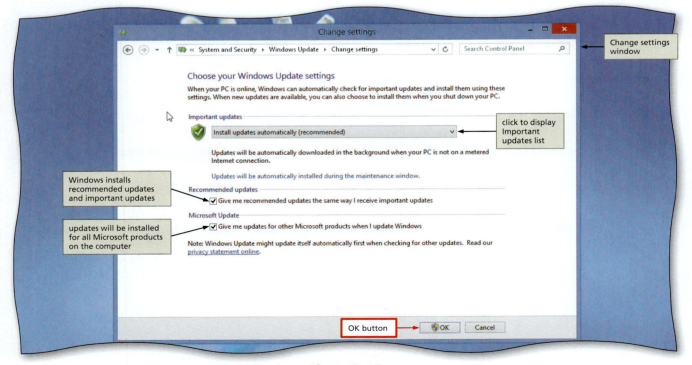

Figure B–17

Protecting against Computer Viruses and Malware

Most computer magazines, daily newspapers, and even television news channels warn of computer virus threats. Although these threats sound alarming, a little common sense and a good antivirus program can ward off even the most malicious viruses.

A computer can be protected against viruses by following these suggestions. First, educate yourself about viruses and how they spread. Downloading a program from the Internet, accessing a website, or receiving an email message can cause a virus to infect your computer. Second, learn the common signs of a virus. Observe any unusual messages that appear on the computer screen, monitor system performance, and watch for missing files and inaccessible hard disks. Third, recognize that programs on removable media might contain viruses, and scan all removable media before copying or opening files.

Windows 8 includes real-time virus detection and protection with Windows Defender. You may decide to install a third-party antivirus program for additional protection or use Windows Defender as your primary virus protection. Windows Defender helps you stay productive by protecting your computer against pop-ups, slow performance, and security threats caused by spyware and other potentially damaging software. When you scan your computer using Windows Defender, it is vital to have the most recent virus definitions. **Definitions** are the files that form a database of all the current virus signatures used by the antivirus software for malware detection. To assist in keeping the definitions up to date, automatically set your Windows Update, which installs new definitions as they are released.

To Scan Using Windows Defender

Windows Defender can notify you when malware attempts to install programs or attempts to change settings on your computer. Windows Defender can be set to scan for malware on a regular basis or at any time on demand. The following steps scan your computer using Windows Defender.

- Point to the upper-right corner of the screen to display the Charms bar (Figure B–18).

Figure B–18

2
- Tap or click the Search charm to display the Search menu (Figure B–19).

Figure B–19

3
- Type `defender` as the search text in the in the Search box, and watch the search results appear (Figure B–20).

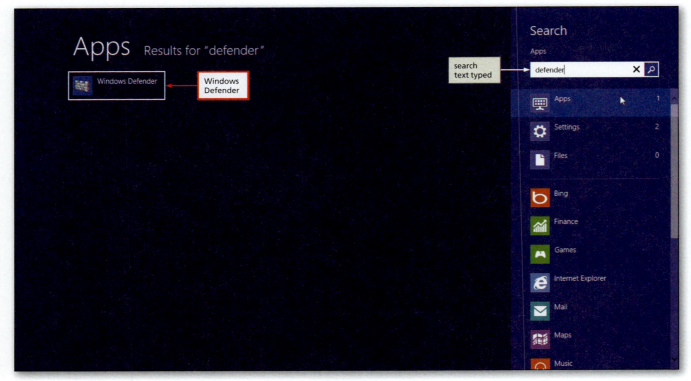

Figure B–20

4

- Tap or click Windows Defender in the search results to open the Windows Defender window (Figure B–21).

Figure B–21

5

- If necessary, tap or click the Quick option button to select it.

- Tap or click the Scan now button to scan your computer for malware (Figure B–22).

Figure B–22

To View the Windows Defender Settings for Automatic Scanning

The following steps display the automatic scanning settings in Windows Defender.

• Tap or click the Settings tab in the Windows Defender window (Figure B–23).

• If necessary, tap or click the 'Turn on real-time protection (recommended)' check box to select it.

• If necessary, tap or click the Save changes button to save the changes made to the real-time protection settings.

• Close the Windows Defender window.

Figure B–23

Summary

Security is an important issue for computer users. You need to be aware of the possible threats to your computer, as well as the security features that can be used to protect your computer. The Action Center, along with other security features in Windows, allows you to configure the security settings that will help you keep your computer safe.

Appendix C

Introduction to Networking

Introduction

A **network** is a series of computers, smartphones, and other devices connected by a communications path, which enables the devices to interact with each other. The advantages of using a network include simplified communications between users, such as email systems, text messaging, video calls, and voice conversations, as well as the capability of easily sharing resources across the network. Shared resources can include hardware (such as printers, scanners, and cameras), data and information (such as files, folders, and databases), Internet connectivity, and programs.

Setting up a Network

Computers on a network connect to each other using a communication channel. A **communication channel** is the means by which information is passed between two devices. Communication channels include wireless communication (broadcast radio, cellular radio, microwaves, communications satellites, Bluetooth, and infrared) and cable (twisted-pair, coaxial, and fiber-optic). Communication channels are measured in bandwidth. The higher the **bandwidth**, the more data and information the channel can transmit at one time. A wireless network offers the advantage of mobility.

Computer networks can be classified either as local area networks or wide area networks. A **local area network** (**LAN**) is a network that connects computers and devices in a limited geographical area, such as a home, school computer lab, office building, or closely positioned group of buildings. A LAN enables people in a small geographic area to communicate with one another and to share the computer resources connected to the network. Each device on the network, such as a computer or printer, is referred to as a **node**. Nodes can be connected to the LAN via cables; however, a **wireless LAN** (**WLAN**) is a LAN that uses no physical wires. Instead of wires or cables, WLANs use wireless media, such as radio waves. A **wide area network** (**WAN**) is a network that covers a large geographic area, such as a city or state, and uses many types of media, such as telephone lines, cables, and airwaves. A WAN can be one large network or consist of two or more LANs that are connected together. The Internet is the world's largest WAN.

If you have multiple computers in your home or small office, you can create a home or small office network using Windows 8. The advantages of a home or small office network include sharing a single Internet connection, sharing hardware devices, sharing files and folders, and communicating with others. Three types of networks that are suitable for home or small office use include wireless networks, Ethernet networks, and telephone-line networks.

Understanding Wireless Networks

A wireless network is the easiest type of network to install. Each computer uses a special network adapter that sends wireless signals through the air (Figure C–1). Any computer located within range that also has a network adapter can send and receive through floors, ceilings, and walls. The distance between devices limits this connection, and the hardware required for the system is relatively inexpensive. Most hardware devices implement the Wi-Fi (wireless fidelity) standard, which was developed by the Wi-Fi Alliance to improve the interoperability of wireless products.

Figure C–1

Several companies and industry groups have come together to create standards for wireless networking. The leader is the Wi-Fi Alliance, which certifies the interoperability of Wi-Fi (IEEE 802.11) products, offers speeds of more than 100 Mbps (megabits per second), with that speed increasing as technology advances. The two types of Wi-Fi networks are ad hoc and infrastructure. In an **ad hoc network**, every computer with a wireless network adapter communicates directly with every other device with a wireless network adapter. Although the range varies by manufacturer, ad hoc networks work best when the connecting devices are within 100 feet of one another.

An **infrastructure network** is based on an access point connected to a high-speed Internet connection. An access point functions as a bridge between two different types of networks, such as a wireless network and an Ethernet network. The access point allows for a much greater range than an ad hoc network because a computer needs to be within range of the access point and not within range of the other computers. This network is best when connecting more than two computers that are more than 100 feet apart and commonly is used in wireless networks that simultaneously share a single Internet connection.

Some infrastructure networks use a router to share an Internet connection between computers on the network. A **router** is a hardware device that can connect two networks together. Home users typically use routers to connect a cable or DSL modem to a network, allowing several computer users to use the same Internet connection simultaneously. Some network hardware manufacturers combine the access point and router in a device called a wireless router. A **wireless router** can function as a bridge between two different types of networks and allows all computers on the network to access the same Internet connection.

Understanding Wired Networks

Wired networks use cables to connect devices together (Figure C–2). Ethernet is the most popular type of network connection because it is relatively inexpensive and fast. Two types of Ethernet cables exist: **coaxial cable**, which resembles the cable used for televisions and rarely is used, and **unshielded twisted pair** (**UTP**) cable, which looks like telephone cable but with larger connectors at each end. Category 5 (CAT 5) or Category 6 (CAT 6) UTP cable typically is used for networking. A network based on CAT 5 UTP cable requires an additional piece of hardware, called a **hub**, to which all computers on the network connect.

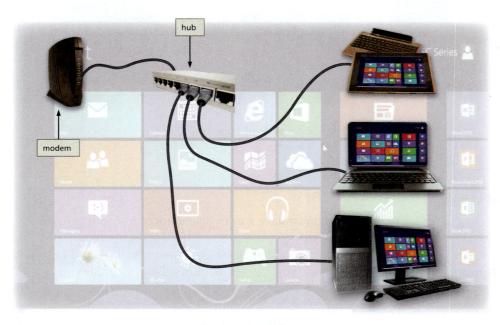

Figure C–2

Another type of wired network is a **Public Switched Telephone Network** (**PSTN**). A **telephone-line network** takes advantage of the existing telephone wiring to connect the computers on a network. This technology is supported by a group of industry experts called the Home Phoneline Networking Alliance (HomePNA). The network takes advantage of the unused bandwidth of the telephone lines, while still allowing them to be used for telephone conversations. The only equipment necessary for this type of network is a telephone-line network adapter for each computer, as well as a telephone cable long enough to connect each computer to a telephone jack.

A **modem** is used to connect to an Internet access provider. Common Internet access providers include cable service providers, phone service providers, and satellite service providers. The modem is connected to the router, which then is used to connect to the nodes on the network. A USB, CAT 5, or CAT 6 cable connects the modem to wired computers. If the network is wireless, the computers connect using wireless network adapters and an access point. Many home networks use a wireless router and support wired and wireless connections (Figure C–3).

Figure C–3

Putting It All Together

Each device on a network must have a **network adapter** to connect to the network. Both internal network adapters and external network adapters are available. Most computers are equipped with internal network adapters. An **internal network adapter** plugs into an expansion slot inside the computer. Before purchasing an internal network adapter, check to be sure that the computer has an available slot that can accept the adapter (also called an expansion card). An external network adapter plugs into a port on the system unit. In most cases, external network adapters connect to a USB port.

Wireless Security Issues

Whether you connect a single computer to the Internet or connect multiple computers on a home or small office network to the Internet, problems can develop if you do not protect computers from external threats. Hackers scan the Internet looking for unprotected computers. When an unprotected computer is found, a hacker can access and damage files on the computer and release harmful computer viruses that can render the computer unusable. A hacker with unauthorized access can steal your personal information, your identity, and company documents or can use your computer as a platform to launch malicious attacks across the Internet.

You can protect computers on a network from hackers, viruses, and other malicious attacks by using a firewall. As mentioned previously, a firewall is a security system intended to protect a network from external threats. A firewall commonly is a combination of hardware and/or software that prevents computers on the network from communicating directly with computers that are not on the network and vice versa. Many routers come with integrated firewalls. Windows 8 also contains a built-in firewall (see Appendix B).

Setting up Wireless Security

Wireless networks require careful planning, because they introduce some security concerns that wired networks do not. Because the signal travels through the air, anyone with the proper equipment can intercept the signal. As a result, a wireless network should take extra precautions to prevent unauthorized access. When you purchase a wireless router, it might include a program that allows you to set up security on your wireless network. If the wireless router does not include a program that can set up security, Windows can configure it using the 'Set up a new connection or network' link, accessible from the Network and Sharing Center window.

The key to securing a wireless network successfully is to use a multipronged defense. For best results, use more than one of the following recommended security measures. First, make sure that the wireless router's user name and password are changed from the defaults so that the hacker is unable to use the default user name and password found in the device's documentation (often kept on the manufacturer's website for public access). Second, you can turn on wireless encryption. This can include **Wired Equivalent Privacy** (**WEP**), **Wi-Fi Protected Access 2** (**WPA2**), or 802.1X authentication. Encryption protects your data by ensuring that only those with the correct encryption key will be able to understand the information being sent across the network. Third, you can set up the wireless router to not broadcast its **SSID** (**service set identifier**), the network name for the wireless router. This makes it more difficult for hackers to see your router. Next, you can change the SSID from its default setting. The most secure SSIDs are a combination of letters and numbers and do not include any part of your name or location. Finally, you can turn on MAC Address Control, so that only devices with authorized MAC (Media Access Control) addresses are allowed to connect. A **MAC address** is an address that uniquely identifies each device that is connected to a network.

Using the Network and Sharing Center

Normally when you turn on your computer, Windows automatically detects available networks and displays the available networks in the Settings menu.

To Connect to a Wireless Network

Windows allows you to connect to secured or unsecured networks. If you connect to a network that is not secure, be aware that someone with the right tools can see everything that you do, including the websites you visit, the documents you work on, and the user names and passwords that you use. The following steps connect to an open or unsecured wireless network.

1

- Display the Charms bar.

- Tap or click the Settings charm to display the Settings menu (Figure C–4).

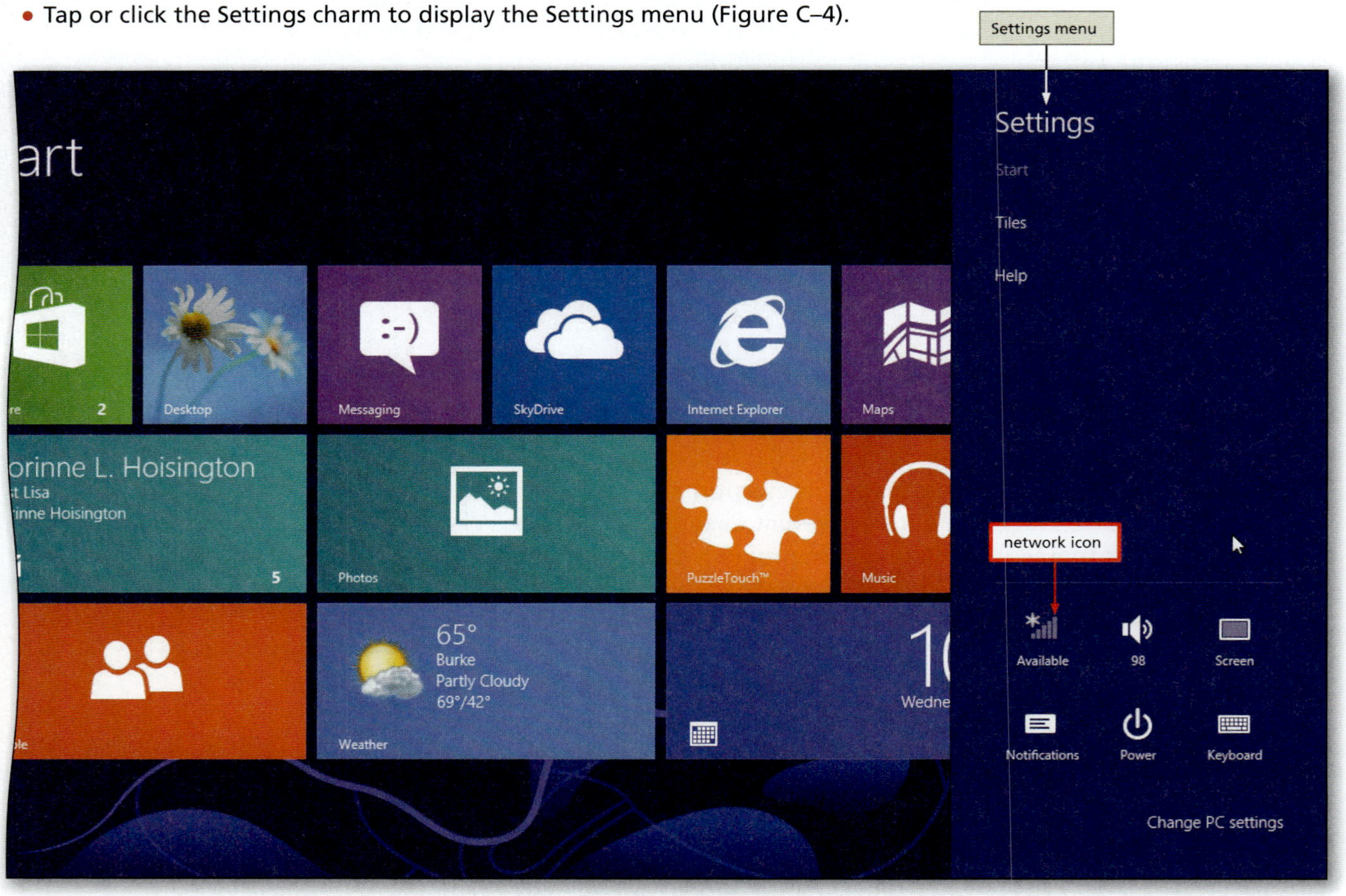

Figure C–4

2

- Tap or click the network icon (a set of bars) to display a list of available networks (Figure C–5).

Q&A Why do I have different available networks?

Your computer displays the available wireless networks that are near your physical location.

Figure C–5

3
- Tap or click the default name of your preferred router to select a wireless network (Figure C–6).

4
- Tap or click the Connect button to join the available wireless network.

Q&A
How can I locate public wireless networks?

When you view network connections, any public wireless networks should appear. Some cities and towns sponsor public Wi-Fi; many public libraries, schools, hotels, and airports offer Wi-Fi; and, occasionally, cafés and coffeehouses offer free Wi-Fi.

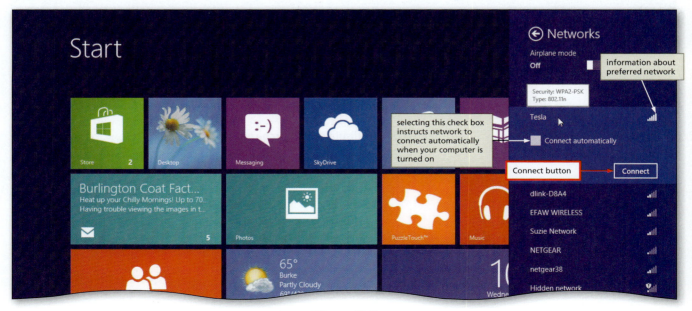

Figure C–6

To Open the Network and Sharing Center

You also can set up a connection manually by using the Network and Sharing Center. The Network and Sharing Center is designed to provide you with the tools you need to connect to a network and share information. From the Network and Sharing Center, you can view available connections, connect to a network, manage a network, set up a network, and diagnose and repair network problems. When first opened, the Network and Sharing Center window shows your current network connection and the properties for that connection. If you are not connected to a network, you are shown which networking options are available to you. The following steps open the Network and Sharing Center.

- Display the Charms bar.

- Tap or click the Search charm to display the Search menu.

- Tap or click the Settings command to display the Settings search box (Figure C–7).

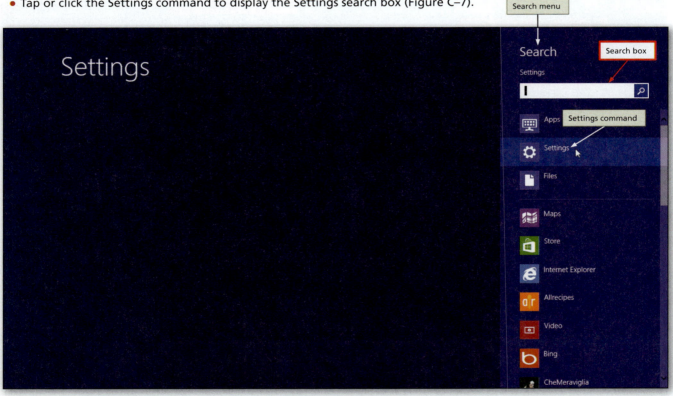

Figure C–7

- Type `network and sharing` in the Search box to display the search results (Figure C–8).

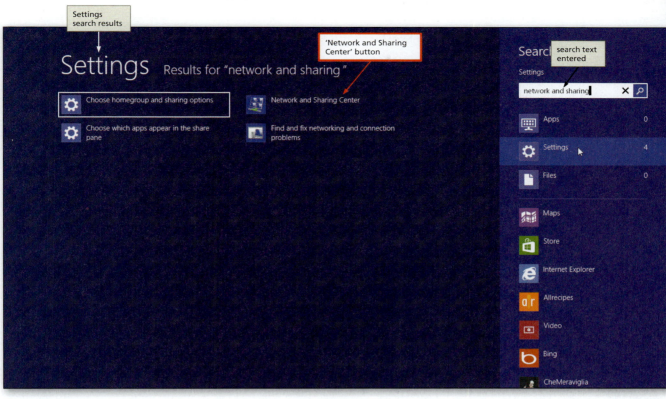

Figure C–8

3
- Tap or click the 'Network and Sharing Center' button to open the Network and Sharing Center window (Figure C–9).

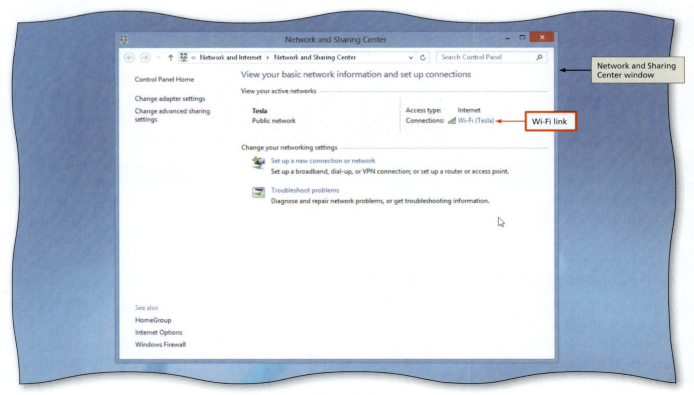

Figure C–9

To View the Status of a Connection

You can view the status of the connection from the Network and Sharing Center. The Wireless Network Connection Status window displays the properties of the connection and allows you to adjust the properties of the connection manually, disable the connection, and diagnose problems with the connection. The following steps display the connection status.

1
- Tap or click the Wi-Fi link to display the Wi-Fi Status dialog box (Figure C–10).

2
- After viewing the connection status, tap or click the Close button (Wi-Fi Status dialog box) to close it.

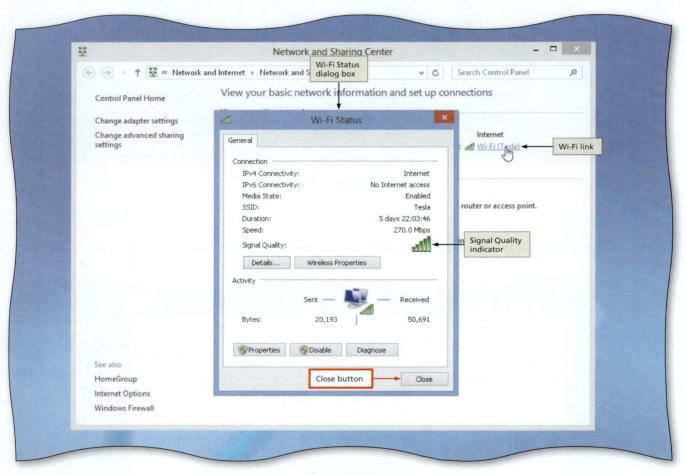

Figure C–10

To Troubleshoot a Networking Problem

If a network connection is not functioning properly, you can use the Troubleshoot problems link to allow Windows to detect problems and suggest solutions. If Windows cannot determine a solution, a message is displayed. If no problems are detected, Windows also displays an appropriate message. The following steps use the Troubleshoot problems link to acquire suggestions from Windows about how to fix an Internet connection.

1

- Tap or click the Troubleshoot problems link to open the Network and Internet window (Figure C–11).

Internet Connections link

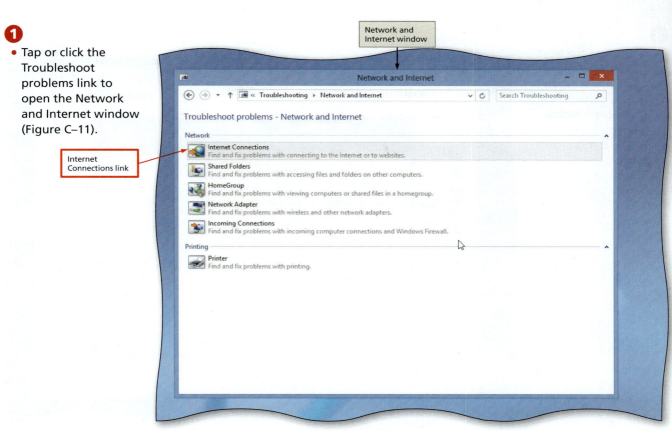

Figure C–11

2

- Tap or click the Internet Connections link to display the Internet Connections dialog box (Figure C–12).

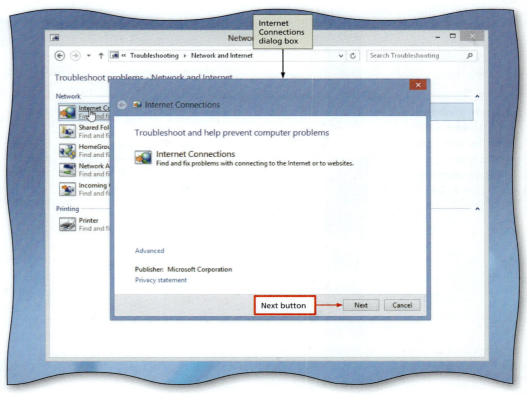

Figure C–12

● Tap or click the Next
button (Internet
Connections dialog
box) to display a list
of troubleshooting
options
(Figure C–13).

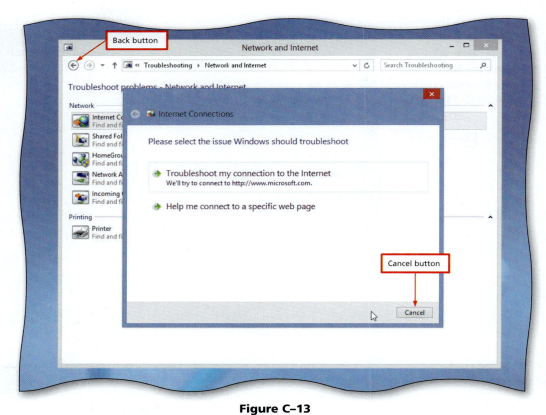

Figure C–13

❹

● Tap or click the
Cancel button after
viewing the options
to close the Internet
Connections dialog
box.

● Tap or click the Back
button to return
to the Network
and Sharing
Center window
(Figure C–14).

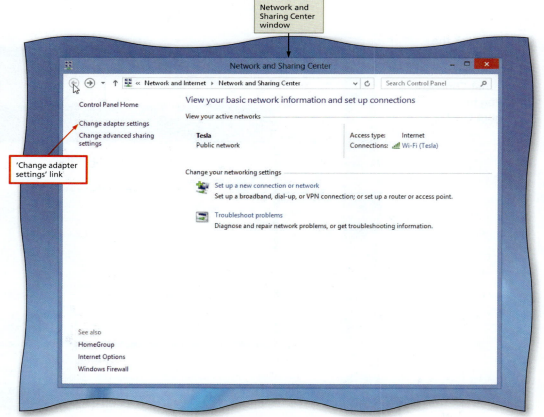

Figure C–14

To Disable a Network Connection

Windows uses a network adapter to connect a computer to a network. You can disconnect your computer from a network by disabling the wireless network adapter. Sometimes you can solve connection problems by disabling and then reenabling the wireless network adapter. The following steps disable a network connection.

1

- Tap or click the 'Change adapter settings' link to open the Network Connections window (Figure C–15).

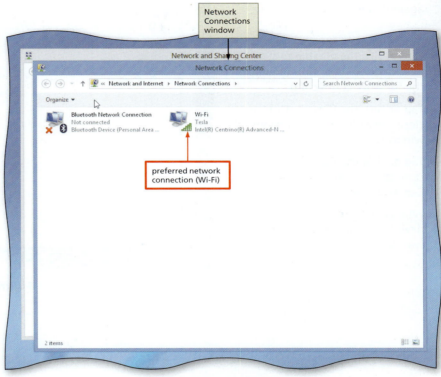

Figure C–15

2

- Tap or click your preferred network connection (Wi-Fi) to select the network and display network connections options (Figure C–16).

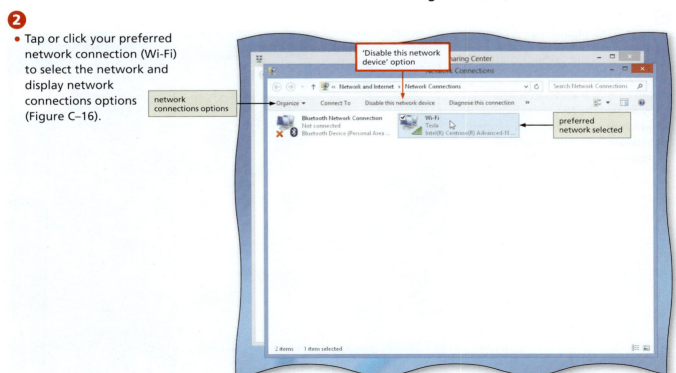

Figure C–16

• Tap or click the 'Disable this network device' option to disable the network device. The network adapter is unavailable and will appear dimmed until it is enabled again (Figure C–17).

• Tap or click the 'Enable this network device' option to enable the network connection.

• Tap or click the Close button to close the Network Connections window.

• Tap or click the Close button to close the Network and Sharing Center window.

Q&A
When I enabled the network device, my wireless connection still was disconnected. Why?

Based on your automatic settings, you may need to reconnect to the wireless connection.

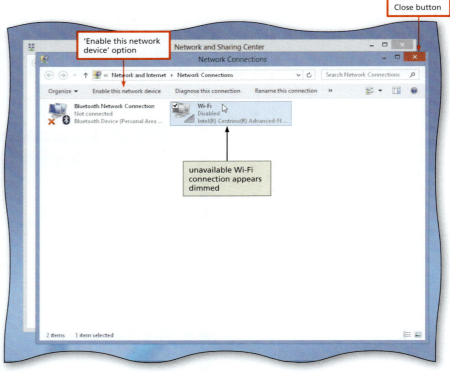

Figure C–17

To Disconnect a Computer from a Network

The following steps disconnect a computer from a wireless network.

1

• Display the Charms bar.

• Tap or click the Settings charm to display the Settings menu.

• Tap or click the network icon to display the Networks menu, which lists the connected wireless network and other available networks (Figure C–18).

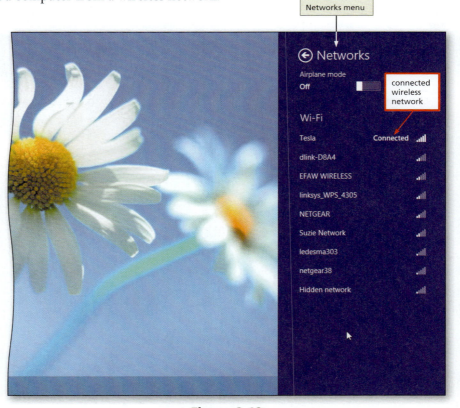

Figure C–18

2

 Tap or click the name of the
  connected wireless network
  (Figure C–19).

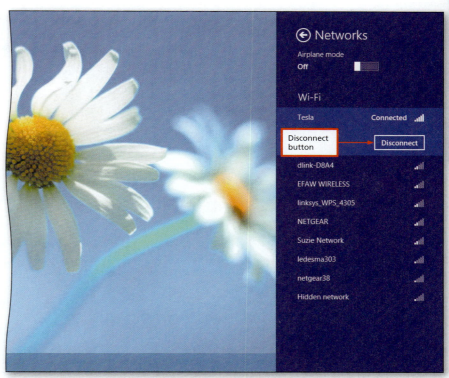

Figure C–19

3

 Tap or click the Disconnect button
  to disconnect from the wireless
  network (Figure C–20).

Figure C–20

Maintaining Your Computer

Introduction

It can be frustrating to lose data. Almost everyone has heard a story about someone who lost a file and spent hours trying to recover it. In addition, hard disks fail more often than any other component on a computer. When a hard disk fails, it is extremely difficult to recover the data without obtaining professional help, often at a hefty price.

Even if a hard disk never fails, errors made while using the computer can result in the loss of a file or group of files. If you are not careful when you save a file, you could lose the file by saving a new file with the original file's name, or by tapping or clicking the wrong button in a dialog box and wiping out the contents of the file accidentally. In either case, you most certainly are going to lose some data. If a hard disk failure occurs, all of the files you have created or saved since the last backup might be gone for good. To avoid the loss of data, you should get into the habit of backing up the data on a regular basis.

Backing up and Restoring Files

Although Windows cannot prevent you from losing data on your hard disk, taking proper steps will ensure that you can recover lost data when an accident happens. To protect data on a hard disk, you should use a backup program. A typical backup program copies and then automatically compresses the files and folders from the hard disk into a single file, called a backup file. The backup program stores the backup file on a backup medium, which can be a hard disk, optical disc, shared network folder, USB flash drive, or even another computer on the network. Instead of using a local backup medium, backup files can also be stored on SkyDrive using your Microsoft account.

File History Backup

Backing up critical files is something everyone should do. Even with everything stored on SkyDrive, you still should back up your local files. File History is a Windows backup application that protects your personal files stored in the Libraries, Desktop, Favorites, SkyDrive, and Contacts folders if you set up a network or external drive to back up your files. You can add files to your Library folder if you want a file backed up. By default, every hour, File History scans your local file system for changes and copies the changed files to your backup location. Every time any of your personal files has changed, File History stores the file on an external storage device that you select.

To Back up a File History to a Storage Device

File History keeps track of file versions to identify and restore the file version needed to its original location. The following steps keep a history of your files and back them up to an external storage device such as a USB flash drive.

1
- Insert a storage device such as a USB flash drive into your computer.
- Display the Charms bar and then tap or click the Search charm to display the Search menu.
- Tap or click Settings to display the Settings Search box (Figure D–1).

Figure D–1

2
- Type `file history` to display the search results (Figure D–2).

Figure D–2

3

- Tap or click the File History button in the search results to open the File History window (Figure D–3).

Q&A Is File History turned on by default?

No. First, you must specify where the file history will be stored.

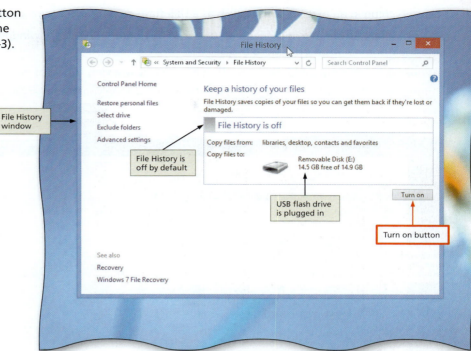

Figure D–3

4

- Tap or click the Turn on button to turn on File History, which saves copies of your files (Figure D–4).

Q&A How do I respond to a dialog box that requests if this drive should be recommended to my homegroup?

Tap or click the No button to save to your homegroup. A homegroup is a group of computers on a home network that can share files and printers.

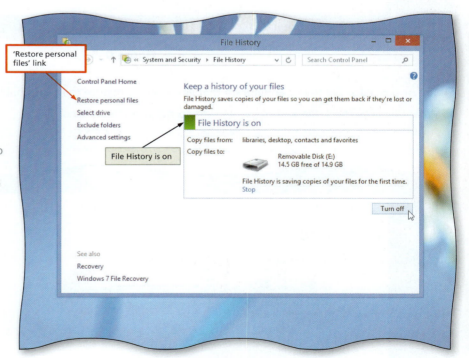

Figure D–4

To Restore Files from File History

After the files have been saved, you can restore the files created using File History if your original files are lost or deleted. The files are restored to their original location. The following steps restore the files from File History.

- If necessary, plug in an external device such as a USB flash drive that contains your File History into your computer.
- Tap or click the 'Restore personal files' link to open the Home - File History window and prepare to restore your files to their original location (Figure D–5).

Q&A What does it mean if my computer states that File History is saving copies of my files for the first time?

You must wait until your file history is completed before restoring your personal files.

Figure D–5

- Tap or click each file folder and library that you want to restore to its original location (Figure D–6).

Q&A What does the check mark in the upper-left corner of each file mean?

A check mark represents that the file or library is selected to be restored. You can select all files and libraries in a single operation by dragging from the upper-left corner downward through the files until all are selected.

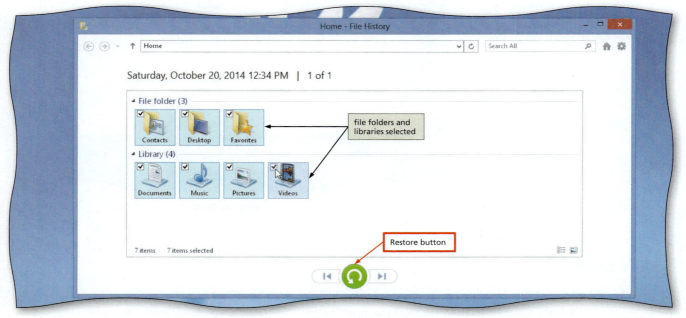

Figure D–6

3

- Tap or click the Restore button to open the Replace or Skip Files window (Figure D–7).

4

- Tap or click the Close button to close the Replace or Skip Files window.

- Tap or click the Close button to close the Home - File History window.

- Tap or click the Close button to close the File History window.

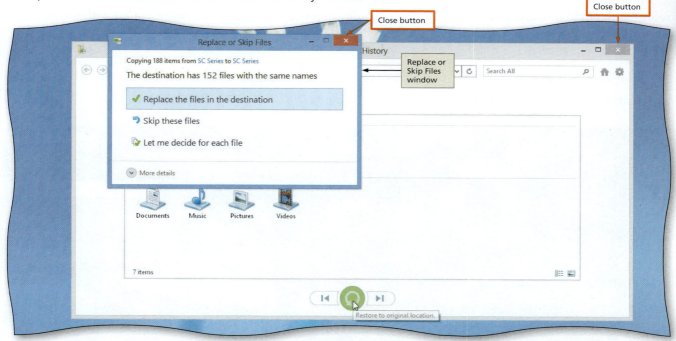

Figure D–7

Creating a Restore Point

Another safeguard for preventing damage to a computer is System Restore. **System Restore** is a tool that tracks changes to the computer and automatically creates a restore point when it detects the beginning of a change. A restore point is a representation of a stored state of the computer. System Restore automatically runs in the background and monitors changes to files, folders, and settings that are essential to the correct operation of the operating system.

System Restore creates an initial restore point when you install or upgrade to Windows 8. At regular intervals, System Restore creates a restore point to capture the current configuration of the computer and stores the configuration in the Registry. Restore points are created when you install an unsigned device driver, install a program using an installer program that is compatible with System Restore, install a Microsoft update or patch, restore a prior configuration using System Restore, or restore data from a backup set created with the backup program and store the configuration in the Registry.

Using a system image to restore your computer can help correct problems that occur when you install device drivers or programs that conflict with other device drivers or programs on the computer, when you update device drivers that cause performance or stability problems, or when the computer develops performance or stability problems for an unknown reason. System Restore cannot protect the computer from viruses, worms, and trojan horse programs. An antivirus program is your best defense against these malicious threats. System Restore does not back up personal files; use the backup features of File History for personal files.

To Manually Set a Restore Point

In addition to creating restore points automatically, Windows allows you to create and name a system restore point manually. Restore points commonly are set prior to making changes to the computer, such as when you install new hardware, install software, or install new or updated device drivers. If, after setting a restore point, you install hardware, software, or device drivers that cause your computer to function improperly, you can reset the computer to the state it was in when you set the restore point. This prevents you from losing personal files (documents, Internet favorites, email messages, and so on) that would have been lost if you needed to reformat the hard disk and reinstall Windows. The following steps manually set a restore point with the name, Restore Point – May 11, and then display the System Restore dialog box.

1
- Display the Charms bar and then tap or click the Search charm to display the Search menu.
- Tap or click Settings to display the Settings Search box (Figure D–8).

Figure D–8

2
- Type `restore` to display the search results (Figure D–9).

Figure D–9

3

- Tap or click the 'Create a restore point' button to display the System Properties dialog box (Figure D–10).

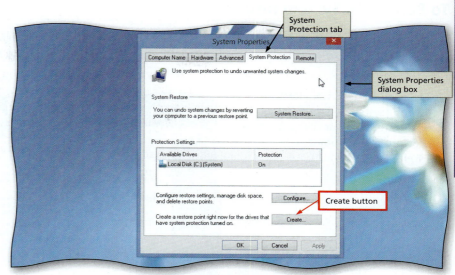

Figure D–10

4

- Tap or click the Create button (System Properties dialog box) to display the System Protection dialog box.

- Type `May 11` (System Protection dialog box) to name the restore point (Figure D–11).

Figure D–11

5

- Tap or click the Create button to create a restore point manually. The System Protection progress indicator becomes animated. When the restore point has been created, the System Protection dialog box displays a message stating that the restore point was created successfully (Figure D–12).

6

- Tap or click the Close button (System Protection dialog box) to close it.

Figure D–12

To Perform a System Restore

The following steps perform a system restore to return the computer's system files, programs, drivers, and Registry settings to an earlier point in time without affecting your personal files.

1

- Tap or click the System Restore button (System Restore dialog box) to return your computer to a previous restore point (Figure D–13).

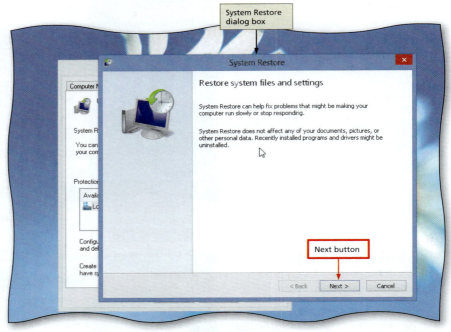

Figure D–13

2

- Tap or click the Next button (System Restore dialog box) to view a list of restore points (Figure D–14).

Q&A Why do my restore points differ from those in the figure?

Depending on the number of restore points that your system has made, the number of restore points on your computer might differ from those in the figure.

3

- After viewing the dialog box options, tap or click the Cancel button to close the dialog box without making changes.

- Tap or click the Close button (System Properties dialog box) to close it.

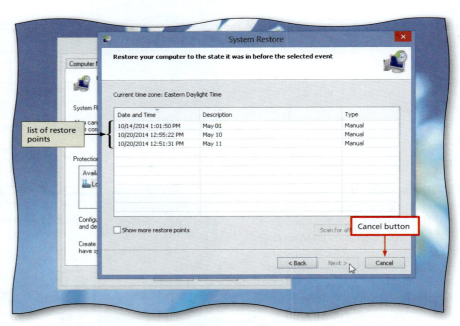

Figure D–14

Refreshing Your Computer

If your computer is having problems, you can refresh or reset it. When you **refresh** your computer, Windows keeps your personal files, settings, and any apps that you have preinstalled or that you have installed from the Windows Store. If you choose to refresh your computer, the installed apps from other websites and DVDs will be removed.

To Refresh the Computer

The following steps refresh the computer.

1

- Display the Charms bar and then tap or click the Settings charm to display the Settings menu.

- Tap or click 'Change PC settings' to display the PC settings pane (Figure D–15).

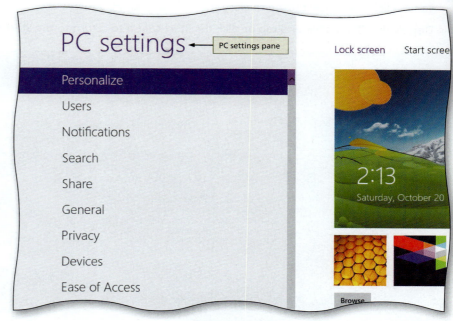

Figure D–15

2

- Tap or click General in the PC settings pane to display General options in the right pane.

- Scroll down the General options to view the 'Refresh your PC without affecting your files' option (Figure D–16).

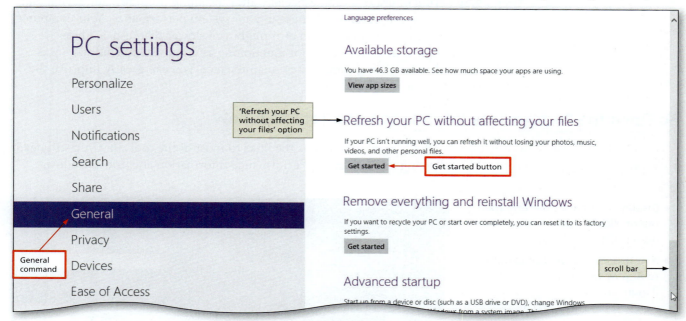

Figure D–16

3
- Tap or click the Get started button to display the Refresh your PC screen (Figure D–17).

4
- Tap or click the Cancel button to close the Refresh your PC screen.
- Display the Charms bar and tap or click the Start charm to return to the Start screen.

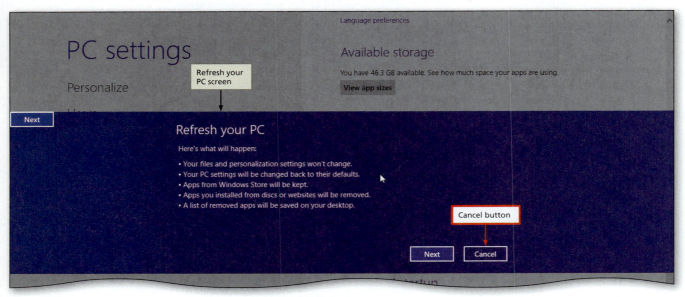

Figure D–17

Performance Information and Tools

After a long period of usage — and especially after installing programs and saving and deleting files — you might notice changes in your system performance. Your computer might not do what it is supposed to do or it might run slower than usual. These changes mean that your computer is not functioning as it did when Windows 8 was first installed. By performing some system maintenance, you can greatly improve the performance of your computer.

To Open the Performance Information and Tools Window

The Performance Information and Tools window contains the links to most of the tools that you will need to improve system performance. The following steps open the Performance Information and Tools window.

1
- Display the Charms bar and then tap or click the Search charm to display the Search menu.
- If necessary, tap or click Settings to display the Settings Search box (Figure D–18).

Figure D–18

• Type `performance` to display the search results (Figure D–19).

Figure D–19

• Tap or click the 'Performance Information and Tools' button to open the Performance Information and Tools window (Figure D–20).

Q&A What does the base score number mean?

The base number represents the Windows Experience Index, which is a measurement that tells you how well your computer works with Windows. A higher base score usually means that your computer will be faster and more responsive than a computer with a lower base score.

Recently, my computer was upgraded with new hardware, but the base score is the same. Why?

Tap or click the 'Re-run the assessment' link to assess the new base score.

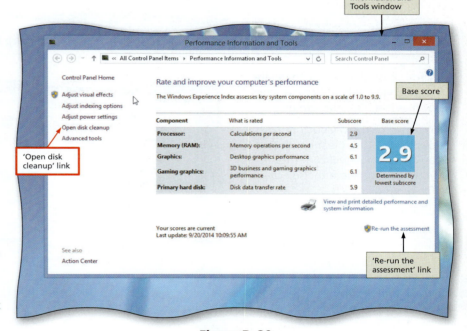

Figure D–20

To Run Disk Cleanup

Whenever you run an app, delete a file using the Recycle Bin, view a webpage, or download a file from a website, files are stored on the hard disk. As a result, the hard disk contains many unnecessary files that reduce the amount of free space. If the free space falls too low for the operating system, error messages might display when you run apps. Removing the unnecessary files and increasing the amount of free space on the hard disk will increase the performance of your computer.

The easiest method to delete unnecessary files and make more free space available is to use Disk Cleanup. **Disk Cleanup** searches the hard disk, lists the files that you can delete safely, allows you to select the type of files to delete, and then deletes those files from the hard disk. Files you can select for deletion include temporary Internet files, downloaded program files, temporary files, and files in the Recycle Bin. The following steps run Disk Cleanup.

• Tap or click the 'Open disk cleanup' link in the Performance Information and Tools window to scan the selected drive.

• When Disk Cleanup finishes scanning the computer, the Disk Cleanup for (C:) dialog box appears (Figure D–21).

Q&A Why does a Disk Cleanup: Drive Selection dialog box display on my computer?

The dialog box will appear only if you have more than one hard disk installed. If you have only one hard disk, your screen will match Figure D–21.

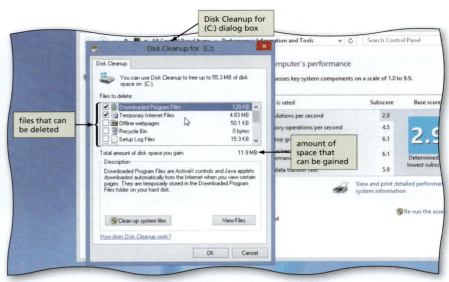

Figure D–21

• Scroll through the Files to delete area to view the additional types of files Disk Cleanup can delete.

• Tap or click the OK button to display the Disk Cleanup dialog box where you will confirm that you want to delete the selected file types (Figure D–22).

Q&A Which files should I remove?

Normally, you should delete only the downloaded program files and temporary Internet files (these are selected by default); however, you also can delete other files if you scroll and find that they are using a lot of storage space. If you are performing these steps in a computer lab, ask your instructor before deleting any files.

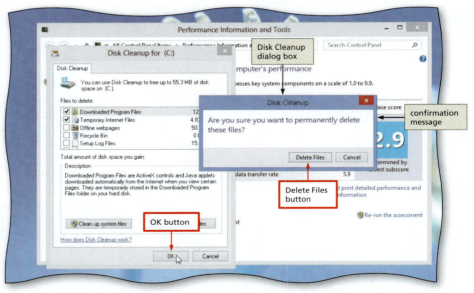

Figure D–22

• Tap or click the Delete Files button to remove the files marked for deletion (Figure D–23).

Figure D–23

To View the Performance Monitor

It often is unclear what is making your computer or program run slowly. To research this problem, you can open the Performance Monitor window. The Performance Monitor allows you to view data logs that detail the performance of your computer. The Performance Monitor displays the processor utilization over time. This can be helpful to see if the processor is being tasked too hard during a particular time period. This can help shed light on why system performance might be slow. If there are particular times when the processor is extremely busy, you then can examine which programs were running at that time. Also, if the processor always is busy, it can be a sign that a program might not be functioning properly or that you might need to add more memory to your computer. The following steps open the Performance Monitor window and display the Performance Monitor.

1
- Tap or click the Advanced tools link in the Performance Information and Tools window to open the Advanced Tools window (Figure D–24).

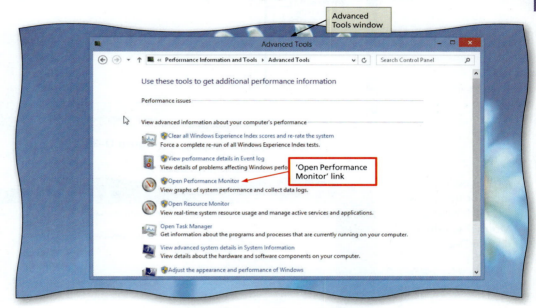

Figure D–24

2
- Tap or click the 'Open Performance Monitor' link to open the Performance Monitor window (Figure D–25).

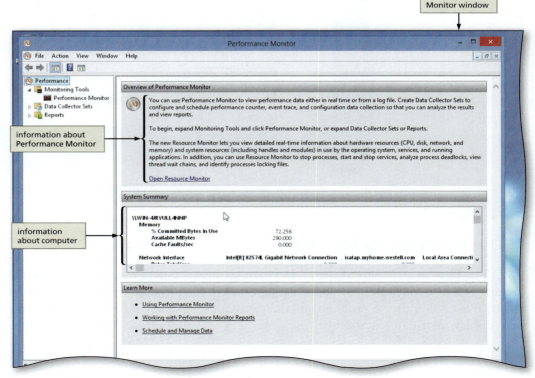

Figure D–25

● Tap or click
Performance
Monitor in the
left pane to view
Performance
Monitor data
(Figure D–26).

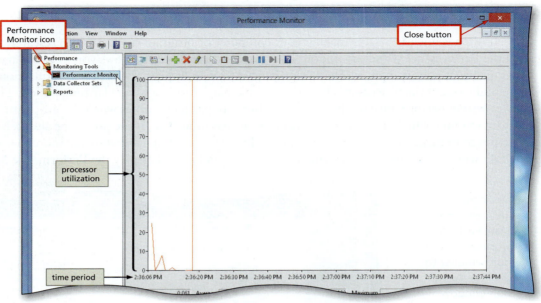

Figure D–26

● After viewing the
monitor data, close
the Performance
Monitor window
(Figure D–27).

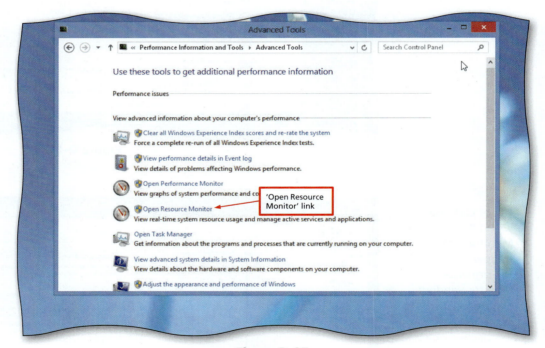

Figure D–27

To Use the Resource Monitor

The Resource Monitor displays system usage in real time. From here, you can view which programs are running and how much of the resources is being used. If a program is consuming too much of a resource, you will be able to identify the program and then attempt to reinstall, repair, or remove the program. The following steps display the Resource Monitor.

- Tap or click the 'Open Resource Monitor' link to open the Resource Monitor window (Figure D–28).

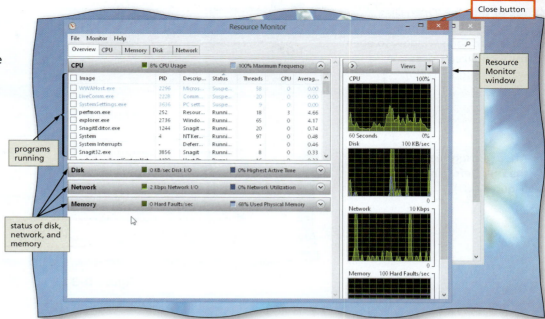

Figure D–28

2

- After viewing the resource data, close the Resource Monitor window.

- If necessary, scroll down to view the 'Open Disk Defragmenter' link (Figure D–29).

Figure D–29

To Run the Disk Defragmenter

When you delete a file from a disk, the locations on the disk used by the deleted file become free disk space on the disk, and the next file stored by the operating system might use all or part of those locations. When new files are added and deleted repeatedly, the disk locations for a single file, called clusters, are not always located together on the hard disk, which creates a **fragmented file**. For your computer to run more efficiently, these clusters need to be periodically rearranged so that each file's clusters are located together. This process is called disk defragmentation. Disk Defragmenter, an administrative tool included with Windows, rearranges the files on the hard disk in contiguous blocks with no fragmentation. In Windows 8, disk defragmentation is scheduled to occur on a regular basis. You can change the schedule, but you should leave automatic disk defragmentation enabled.

The following steps view the settings of the Disk Defragmenter.

1

- Tap or click the 'Open Disk Defragmenter' link in the Advanced Tools window to open the Optimized Drives window (Figure D–30).

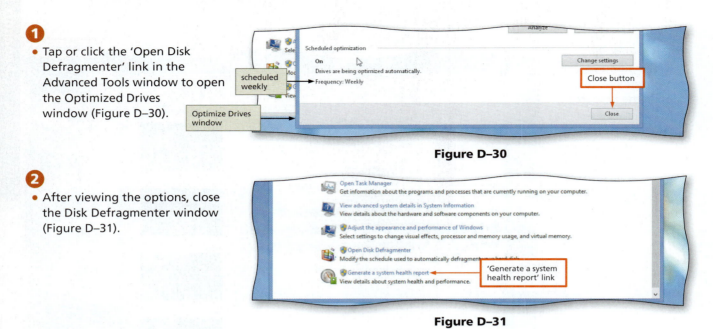

Figure D–30

2

- After viewing the options, close the Disk Defragmenter window (Figure D–31).

Figure D–31

To Generate a System Health Report

Windows allows you to generate system health reports that detail the status of your resources, response times, and processes on your computer, along with system information and configuration data. Windows analyzes the computer system for 60 seconds to generate the report. In the report, suggestions are provided to help you improve your system. The following steps generate a system health report.

1

- If necessary, scroll to and then tap or click the 'Generate a system health report' link in the Advanced Tools window to open the Resource and Performance Monitor window and generate and display a system health report after 60 seconds (Figure D–32).

2

- After viewing the system health report, close the Resource and Performance Monitor window.

- Close the Advanced Tools window.

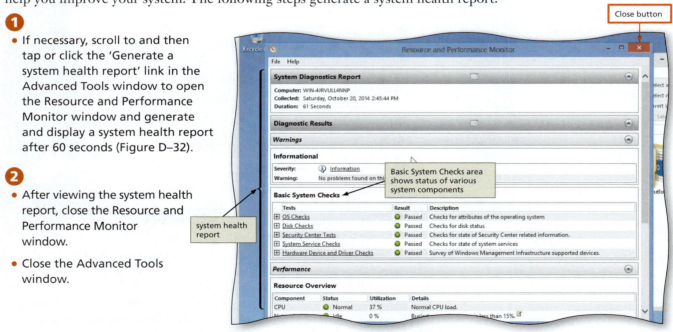

Figure D–32

Summary

Being able to maintain your computer is vitally important. An essential part of computer security is making sure that your computer functions properly. Part of the process of maintenance that people often overlook is making proper backups. By using backups, you protect yourself and your computer from valuable data loss.

Index

Note: **Bold** page numbers refer to pages where key terms are defined.

A

accounts. *See also* local accounts; Microsoft accounts; user accounts
  signing out of, WIN 37–38, WIN 54, WIN 80, WIN 154, WIN 194
Action Center
  displaying, APP 9–12
  panes, APP 13
ad hoc networks, **APP 26**
address bar
  navigating using Back button on, WIN 183
  searching the web, WIN 133–134, WIN 145
  switching folders, WIN 55–56
app(s), **WIN 2,** WIN 11–14
  displaying, WIN 109
  exiting, WIN 17
  installing, WIN 31–33
  navigating within, WIN 12–14
  pinning, WIN 110–112
  running. *See* running apps
  shortcuts. *See* shortcuts
  switching between, WIN 16–17, WIN 27
  unpinning, WIN 113–114
App bar, **WIN 11**

B

Back button, navigating using, WIN 183
background pattern, Start screen, changing, WIN 103
backing up files, APP 41–48
  File History, APP 41–45
  restoring files, APP 43–45, APP 45–48
bandwidth, **APP 25**
blank documents
  adding text, WIN 174
  creating in Documents library, WIN 171–172
broadband, **WIN 130**
browser window, adding tabs, WIN 134–137

C

charms, WIN 15–16
  returning to Start screen, WIN 15–16
  searching apps, WIN 28–29
  searching the Internet, WIN 25–27
  sharing using, WIN 30
clearing Search box, WIN 61
clicking, WIN 6
Clipboard, **WIN 67**
closing
  documents, WIN 169, WIN 176
  Local Disk (C:) dialog box, WIN 54
  multiple open windows, WIN 189–190
  tabs, WIN 138–139
cloud computing, WIN 94
coaxial cable, **APP 27**
color scheme, Start screen, changing, WIN 102–103
communication channels, **APP 25**
computer(s)
  disconnecting from networks, APP 38–39
  refreshing, **APP 48,** APP 48–50
  shutting down, WIN 39–40, WIN 154
  turning off, WIN 80
computer viruses. *See* viruses
connecting/connectivity
  broadband, WIN 130
  disabling network connections, APP 37–38
  mobility, WIN 130
  viewing status of connections, APP 34
  Wi-Fi, WIN 130
  to wireless networks, WIN 131
  wireless networks, APP 30–31
copy and paste method, **WIN 67**
copying, **WIN 67**
  files to Pictures library, WIN 67–69
  folders on USB flash drives, WIN 191
copyrights, **WIN 65,** WIN 65–66
creating documents in Documents library, WIN 169–176
customizing Windows 8, using a Microsoft account, WIN 4

D

definitions, **APP 21**
deleted items, restoring, WIN 193
deleting
  folders from Pictures library, WIN 80
  items from Favorites bar, WIN 154
  RSS feeds, WIN 153–154
  shortcuts, WIN 193
desktop, WIN 18, WIN 161–194
  adding websites to favorites, WIN 146–147
  closing documents, WIN 169
  displaying, WIN 17–18
  displaying new tabs, WIN 144–145
  displaying webpages, WIN 143–144
  editing documents, WIN 168
  printing documents, WIN 167–168
  running Internet Explorer, WIN 143–149
  saving documents, WIN 169
  shortcuts. *See* shortcuts
details pane
  displaying folder properties, WIN 57
  displaying Local Disk (C:) properties, WIN 52–53
Details view, Documents library, WIN 176
disabling network connections, APP 37–38
disconnecting computers from networks, APP 38–39
disk(s), hard, WIN 51
Disk Cleanup, **APP 51,** APP 51–52
Disk Defragmenter, APP 55–56
disk labels, **WIN 51**
displaying. *See also* viewing
  Action Center, APP 9–12
  apps, WIN 109
  folder properties in details pane, WIN 57
  folder properties in Properties dialog box, WIN 58
  inactive windows, WIN 188–189
  Local Disk (C:) dialog box, WIN 53–54
  Local Disk (C:) properties in details pane, WIN 52–53

preview pane, WIN 180–181
webpages. *See* displaying webpages
Windows desktop, WIN 17–18
displaying webpages, WIN 132–133
on desktop, WIN 143–144
in new tab, WIN 149
documents. *See also* file(s)
blank, adding text, WIN 174
closing, WIN 169, WIN 176
creating in WordPad, WIN 163–164
editing, WIN 168
in folders, modifying, WIN 187
in folders, opening, WIN 186
moving into folders, WIN 178–179
multiple. *See* multiple documents
printing, WIN 167–168
saving. *See* saving documents
Documents library, **WIN 165,** WIN 169–183
adding text to blank documents, WIN 174
arranging items in groups by file type, WIN 177
assigning file names, WIN 172
changing location using Address bar, WIN 179–180
closing documents, WIN 176
copying folders using USB flash drives, WIN 191
creating and naming folders, WIN 178
creating blank documents, WIN 171–172
Details view, WIN 176
moving documents into folders, WIN 178–179
navigating, WIN 179–180
opening, WIN 170
opening documents in WordPad, WIN 173
preview pane, WIN 180–181, WIN 183
Recycle Bin, WIN 192–193
saving documents. *See* saving documents
shortcuts. *See* shortcuts
Small icons view, WIN 176
viewing file name extensions, WIN 182
double-clicking, WIN 6
double-taps, WIN 4

dragging, WIN 5, WIN 6
moving windows, WIN 170–171
drives, viewing contents, WIN 56

E

editing documents, WIN 168
exiting apps, WIN 17

F

favorites, adding websites, WIN 142, WIN 146–147
Favorites bar
adding websites, WIN 148
deleting items, WIN 154
file(s), **WIN 165.** *See also* documents
backing up. *See* backing up files
copying to Pictures library, WIN 67–69
fragmented, **APP 55**
hidden, WIN 59
moving to Recycle Bin, WIN 186
multiple, moving into folders, WIN 71
restoring, APP 45–48
searching for, WIN 59–61
shortcuts. *See* shortcuts
zipped, **WIN 78,** WIN 78–80
File Explorer, WIN 19
File History, APP 41–45
backing up to storage devices, APP 42–43
restoring files, APP 43–45
file name(s), WIN 165
assigning to documents, WIN 172
file name extensions, WIN 165
viewing, WIN 182
finding. *See also* searching
information on webpages, WIN 139
flash drives. *See* USB flash drives
folder(s)
copying on USB flash drives, WIN 191
creating and naming in Documents library, WIN 178
creating in Pictures library, WIN 69–70
deleting from Pictures library, WIN 80
displaying properties in details pane, WIN 57

displaying properties in Properties dialog box, WIN 58
hidden, WIN 59
modifying documents, WIN 187
moving documents into, WIN 178–179
moving multiple files into, WIN 71
opening documents, WIN 186
opening using shortcuts, WIN 185
previewing properties, WIN 57
refreshing images on, WIN 72
searching for, WIN 59–61
shortcuts. *See* shortcuts
viewing contents, WIN 59
zipping, WIN 78
folder windows, **WIN 50,** WIN 50–59
details pane, WIN 52–53, WIN 57
displaying Windows folder properties, WIN 57–58
Local Disk (C:) drive Properties dialog box, WIN 53–54
maximizing, WIN 51
opening, WIN 51
previewing folder properties, WIN 57
switching folders using address bar, WIN 55–56
viewing contents of drives, WIN 56
viewing folder contents, WIN 59
fragmented files, **APP 55**
free-spinning the mouse wheel, WIN 6

G

gestures, **WIN 4,** WIN 5

H

hackers, **APP 9**
hard disks, **WIN 51**
hidden files and folders, WIN 59

I

icons
arranging by file type, WIN 177
Small icons view, WIN 176
images, refreshing on folders, WIN 72

inactive windows, displaying,
WIN 188–189
infrastructure networks, **APP 27**
InPrivate tabs, **WIN 132**
adding in browser window,
WIN 135–137
installing
apps, WIN 31–33
updates, automatically, APP 19–20
internal network adapters, **APP 28**
Internet, **WIN 2**
searching using charms,
WIN 25–27
Internet Explorer
browsing and searching the Web,
WIN 132–142
displaying new tab on desktop,
WIN 144–145
RSS feeds. *See* RSS feeds
running app, WIN 131
running on desktop, WIN 143–149
intranets, **WIN 2**
item check boxes, WIN 66

K

keyboard(s)
layouts, WIN 7
on-screen, WIN 5
keyboard shortcuts, **WIN 7**
keywords, address bar, WIN 145

L

LANs (local area networks),
APP 25
layouts, keyboards, WIN 7
live tiles, **WIN 10**
turning off, WIN 114–115
local accounts, **WIN 91**
adding to user accounts,
WIN 94–98
local area networks (LANs),
APP 25
Local Disk (C:) dialog box
closing, WIN 54
displaying, WIN 53–54
lock screen, **WIN 8**
personalizing, WIN 100–102

M

MAC addresses, **APP 29**
malware, **APP 9**
protecting against, APP 21–24

maximizing windows
folder windows, WIN 51
Snap, WIN 63
Microsoft accounts, **APP 1,**
WIN 91–93
adding to user accounts,
WIN 98–99
creating, APP 1–7, WIN 92–93
customizing Windows 8, WIN 4
signing in, WIN 99
minimizing windows
Shake, WIN 62
Show Desktop button,
WIN 63–64
mobility, connectivity, WIN 130
modems, **APP 28**
mouse, WIN 6
mouse wheel operations, WIN 6
moving
documents into folders,
WIN 178–179
files to Recycle Bin, WIN 186
multiple files into folders,
WIN 71
tiles. *See* moving tiles
windows by dragging,
WIN 170–171
moving tiles, WIN 20
between tile groups, WIN 118
multiple documents
modifying, WIN 188
opening, WIN 187
multiple windows, opening,
WIN 189–190
multitasking, **WIN 187**
My Documents folder, **WIN 165**

N

naming tile groups, WIN 119–122
navigating
within an app, WIN 12–14
Documents library, WIN 179–180
using Back button, WIN 183
network(s), **APP 25,** APP 25–39
ad hoc, **APP 26**
infrastructure, **APP 27**
LANs, **APP 25**
network adapters, APP 28
Network and Sharing Center. *See*
Network and Sharing Center
PTSNs, **APP 28**
setting up, APP 25–28
telephone-line, **APP 28**
WANs, **APP 25**

wired, APP 27–28
wireless. *See* wireless networks
WLANs, **APP 25**
network adapters, **APP 28**
Network and Sharing Center
disabling network connections,
APP 37–38
opening, APP 32–33
troubleshooting networking
problems, APP 34–36
viewing status of connections,
APP 34
nodes, **APP 25**
notification area, **WIN 18**
on-screen keyboards, WIN 5

O

opening
documents in folders, WIN 186
documents in WordPad,
WIN 173
Documents library, WIN 170
folder windows, WIN 51
folders using shortcuts, WIN 185
multiple documents, WIN 187
Network and Sharing Center,
APP 32–33
windows, WIN 61
Windows Firewall window,
APP 14
operating systems, **WIN 2**

P

passwords, **WIN 7**
picture. *See* picture passwords
pasting, **WIN 67**
shortcuts on desktop,
WIN 184–185
Performance Information and
Tools window, APP 50–56
Disk Cleanup, **APP 51,**
APP 51–52
Disk Defragmenter, APP 55–56
Performance Monitor,
APP 53–54
Resource Monitor, APP 54–55
Performance Monitor, APP 53–54
Photos app, **WIN 65, WIN 75**
viewing pictures, WIN 75–76
picture passwords, **WIN 7,**
WIN 104, WIN 104–108
creating, WIN 104–108
security, WIN 108

Pictures library, WIN 65–77
 copying files to, WIN 67–69
 creating folders in, WIN 69–70
 deleting folders, WIN 80
 moving multiple files into,
  WIN 71
 refreshing images, WIN 72
 searching for pictures, WIN 66
 viewing and changing properties
  of pictures, WIN 72–75
 viewing images, WIN 75–76
 viewing pictures as slide show,
  WIN 76–77
pinching, WIN 5
pinning apps, WIN 110–112
pointing, WIN 6
pressing
 mouse wheel, WIN 6
 thumb button, WIN 6
pressing and holding, WIN 4
preview pane
 closing, WIN 183
 displaying, WIN 180–181
 Documents library, WIN 180–181
previewing folder properties,
  WIN 57
printing documents, WIN 167–168
properties, **WIN 52**
 folders, previewing, WIN 57
 folders, displaying in details pane,
  WIN 57
 folders, displaying in Properties
  dialog box, WIN 58
 Local Disk (C:), displaying,
  WIN 52–53
 Local Disk (C:) dialog box,
  WIN 53–54
 pictures, viewing anc changing,
  WIN 72–75
 RSS feeds, modifying,
  WIN 152–153
Properties dialog box, displaying
  folder properties, WIN 58
Public Switched Telephone
  Network (PSTN), **APP 28**

R

Really Simple Syndication (RSS),
 WIN 150. *See also* RSS feeds
Recycle Bin, **WIN 18,**
  WIN 192–193
 deleting shortcuts, WIN 193
 moving files to, WIN 186
 restoring items, WIN 193

refreshing the computer, **APP 48,**
  APP 48–50
removing USB flash drives,
  WIN 192
reordering tile groups,
  WIN 118–119
resizing tiles, WIN 21–22
Resource Monitor, APP 54–55
Restart command, **WIN 8**
restore point, APP 45–48
 performing system restores,
  APP 48
 setting manually, APP 46–47
restoring
 deleted items, WIN 193
 files, APP 45–48
 windows. *See* restoring windows
restoring windows, WIN 64–75
 Shake, WIN 62
Rich Text Format (RTF) files,
  saving text documents,
  WIN 175
right-clicking, WIN 6
right-dragging, WIN 6
rotating the mouse wheel,
  WIN 6
routers, **APP 27**
RSS (Really Simple Syndication),
 WIN 150. *See also* RSS feeds
RSS feeds, **WIN 150,**
  WIN 150–154
 deleting, WIN 153–154
 modifying properties,
  WIN 152–153
 subscribing, WIN 150–152
RTF (Rich Text Format) files,
  saving text documents,
  WIN 175
running apps
 from Apps list, WIN 110
 Internet Explorer app, WIN 131
 using Search box, WIN 23–25
 using Start screen, WIN 11–12
running Internet Explorer
 app, WIN 131
 on desktop, WIN 143–149

S

saving documents, WIN 165–166,
  WIN 169, WIN 190
 Documents library,
  WIN 165–166
 as RTF files, WIN 175
ScreenTips, **WIN 57**

scroll arrows, **WIN 6,** WIN 7
scroll bar, **WIN 6,** WIN 7
scroll boxes, **WIN 6,** WIN 7
scrolling, WIN 6
Search box, **WIN 59**
 running apps using, WIN 23–25
searching. *See also* finding
 apps, using charms, WIN 28–29
 for files and folders, WIN 59–61
 Internet, using charms,
  WIN 25–27
 using address bar, WIN 133–134
 using keywords in address bar,
  WIN 145
 web using address bar,
  WIN 133–134
security, APP 9–24
 picture passwords, WIN 108
 Windows Defender. *See* Windows
  Defender
 Windows Firewall. *See* Windows
  Firewall
 Windows Update, **APP 19,**
  APP 19–20
 wireless networks, APP 29
Semantic Zoom, **WIN 108,**
  WIN 108–109
servers, **WIN 2**
service set identifier (SSID),
  APP 29
Shake, WIN 62
sharing, using charms, WIN 30
shortcuts, **WIN 162,**
  WIN 183–190
 closing multiple open windows,
  WIN 189–190
 deleting, WIN 193
 displaying inactive windows,
  WIN 188–189
 moving files to Recycle Bin,
  WIN 186
 opening and modifying documents
  in folders, WIN 186–187
 opening and modifying multiple
  documents, WIN 187–188
 opening folders, WIN 185
 pasting on desktop, WIN 184–185
 saving documents, WIN 190
Show Desktop button, minimizing
  windows, WIN 63–64
Shut down command, **WIN 8**
shutting down
 computer, WIN 39–40, WIN 154
 options, WIN 8
 Windows 8, WIN 37–40

sign-in screen, WIN 8
signing in to an account,
    WIN 8–10
  Microsoft accounts, WIN 99
signing out of an account,
    WIN 37–38, WIN 154,
    WIN 194
SkyDrive, **WIN 91**
Sleep command, **WIN 8**
slide shows, **WIN 76,**
    WIN 76–77
  ending, WIN 77
  viewing, WIN 76–77
Small icons view, Documents
    library, WIN 176
Snap, maximizing windows,
    WIN 63
spyware, **APP 9**
SSID (service set identifier),
    APP 29
Start screen, **WIN 2, WIN 10**
  changing background pattern,
    WIN 103
  changing color scheme,
    WIN 102–103
  customizing, WIN 108–115
  displaying all apps, WIN 109
  pinning apps, WIN 110–112
  pinning websites to,
    WIN 140–141
  returning to, WIN 15–16,
    WIN 19
  running apps, WIN 11–12
  running apps from Apps list,
    WIN 110
  running Internet Explorer,
    WIN 131
  turning off live tiles,
    WIN 114–115
  unpinning apps, WIN 113–114
starting
  Windows 8, WIN 7–10
  Windows Help and Support,
    WIN 33–36
stretching, WIN 5
strong passwords, WIN 7
subscribing to RSS feeds,
    WIN 150–152
swiping, WIN 5
switching
  between apps, WIN 16–17,
    WIN 27
  folders, address bar, WIN 55–56
  between tabs, WIN 137–138
System Restore, **APP 45**

T
tab(s)
  adding in browser window,
    WIN 134–137
  closing, WIN 138–139
  InPrivate, **WIN 132,**
    WIN 135–137
  new, displaying on desktop,
    WIN 144–145
  new, displaying webpages,
    WIN 149
  switching between,
    WIN 137–138
tab groups, **WIN 149**
taps, WIN 4
taskbar, **WIN 18**
telephone-line networks, **APP 28**
text, adding to blank documents,
    WIN 174
thumb button, pressing, WIN 6
tile(s)
  moving. *See* moving tiles
  resizing, WIN 21–22
tile groups, **WIN 108**
  creating, WIN 117
  moving tiles between, WIN 118
  naming, WIN 119–122
  reordering, WIN 118–119
  viewing, WIN 115–116
tile layout, WIN 115–122
tilting the mouse wheel, WIN 6
touch screens, WIN 4–5
triple-clicking, WIN 6
troubleshooting network problems,
    APP 34–36

U
unpinning apps, WIN 113–114
unshielded twisted pair (UTP)
    cable, **APP 27**
USB flash drives
  copying files on, WIN 191
  removing, WIN 192
user accounts, **WIN 7, WIN 90,**
    WIN 90–91
  adding local accounts,
    WIN 94–98
  adding Microsoft accounts,
    WIN 98–99
  setting up, WIN 94–99
  signing in to, WIN 8–10
  signing out of, WIN 37–38,
    WIN 154, WIN 194

user icons, **WIN 7**
user names, **WIN 7**
UTP (unshielded twisted pair)
    cable, **APP 27**

V
viewing. *See also* displaying
  drive contents, WIN 56
  file name extensions, WIN 182
  folder contents, WIN 59
  pictures in Photos app,
    WIN 75–76
  properties of pictures,
    WIN 72–75
  slide shows, WIN 76–77
  status of connections, APP 34
  tile groups, WIN 115–116
  zipped folder contents, WIN 79
viruses, **APP 9**
  definitions, APP 21
  protecting against, APP 21–24

W
WANs (wide area networks),
    APP 25
webpages
  displaying. *See* displaying
    webpages
  finding information, WIN 139
websites
  adding to favorites, WIN 142,
    WIN 146–147
  adding to Favorites bar, WIN 148
  pinning to Start screen,
    WIN 140–141
WEP (Wired Equivalency
    Privacy), **APP 29**
wide area networks (WANs),
    APP 25
Wi-Fi, **WIN 130**
Wi-Fi Protected Access 2 (WPA2),
    APP 29
windows. *See also specific windows*
  folder. *See* folder windows
  inactive, displaying,
    WIN 188–189
  maximizing using Snap, WIN 63
  minimizing using Show Desktop
    button, WIN 63–64
  moving by dragging,
    WIN 170–171
  multiple, opening, WIN 189–190
  opening, WIN 61

restoring, WIN 64–75
Shake to minimize and restore,
    WIN 62
Windows Defender, APP 13,
    APP 13, APP 21–24
scanning using, APP 21–23
viewing settings for automatic
    scanning, APP 24
Windows desktop. *See* desktop
Windows 8, **WIN 2**
customizing using a Microsoft
    account, WIN 4
shutting down, WIN 37–40
starting, WIN 7–10
system requirements, WIN 3
Windows 8 Enterprise,
    WIN 3
Windows 8 Pro, **WIN 3**
Windows 8 RT, **WIN 3**
Windows Firewall, **APP 13,**
    APP 13–18
allowing features through,
    APP 14–16

disallowing features through,
    APP 17–18
opening Windows Firewall
    window, APP 14
Windows folder, searching for files
    and folders, WIN 60
Windows Help and Support,
    WIN 33, WIN 33–37
browsing Help, WIN 33–36
starting, WIN 33–36
Windows SmartScreen, **APP 13**
Windows Update, **APP 19,**
    APP 19–20
installing updates automatically,
    APP 19–20
Wired Equivalency Privacy
    (WEP), **APP 29**
wired networks, APP 27–28
wireless local area networks
    (WLANs), **APP 25**
wireless networks, APP 26–27
connecting to, APP 30–31,
    WIN 131

disconnecting computers,
    APP 38–39
security, APP 29
wireless routers, **APP 27**
WLANs (wireless local area
    networks), **APP 25**
WordPad
creating documents,
    WIN 163–164
opening documents,
    WIN 173
workstations, **WIN 2**
worms, **APP 9**
WPA2 (Wi-Fi Protected Access 2),
    APP 29
wrist injury, minimizing, WIN 6

Z

zipped files, **WIN 78,**
    WIN 78–89
zooming, viewing tile groups,
    WIN 115–116